TOCQUEVILLE'S DILEMMAS,
AND OURS

Tocqueville's Dilemmas, and Ours

SOVEREIGNTY, NATIONALISM,
GLOBALIZATION

EWA ATANASSOW

PRINCETON UNIVERSITY PRESS
PRINCETON & OXFORD

Copyright © 2022 by Princeton University Press

Princeton University Press is committed to the protection of copyright and the intellectual property our authors entrust to us. Copyright promotes the progress and integrity of knowledge created by humans. Thank you for supporting free speech and the global exchange of ideas by purchasing an authorized edition of this book. If you wish to reproduce or distribute any part of it in any form, please obtain permission.

Requests for permission to reproduce material from this work should be sent to permissions@press.princeton.edu

Published by Princeton University Press
41 William Street, Princeton, New Jersey 08540
99 Banbury Road, Oxford OX2 6JX

press.princeton.edu

GPSR Authorized Representative: Easy Access System Europe - Mustamäe tee 50, 10621 Tallinn, Estonia, gpsr.requests@easproject.com

All Rights Reserved

First paperback printing, 2025
Paperback ISBN 9780691241029
Cloth ISBN 9780691191102
ISBN (e-book) 9780691228464
LCCN: 2022019154

British Library Cataloging-in-Publication Data is available

Editorial: Bridget Flannery-McCoy & Alena Chekanov
Production Editorial: Ali Parrington
Jacket/Cover Design: Heather Hansen
Production: Erin Suydam
Publicity: Kate Hensley & Charlotte Coyne
Copyeditor: Isabella Ritchie

This book has been composed in Arno

To my parents who tried to hold together an impossible world.

To my daughter hoping she might succeed.

CONTENTS

Preface ix

   Introduction   1
1 (Popular) Sovereignty and Constitutionalism   20
2 Nationalism and Democracy   62
3 Whither Globalization?   105
   Conclusion: Sustaining Liberal Democracy   149

Notes 179
Bibliography 223
Index 247

PREFACE

THIS BOOK records my long journey in the company of Alexis de Tocqueville. It began on an afternoon in the mid-1990s in Poland, at a street bookseller in downtown Kraków where I first chanced on Tocqueville's *The Old Regime and the Revolution* in the brand-new Polish edition put out by the Stefan Batory Foundation. I had recently graduated with a master's degree from Jagiellonian University's Institute of Psychology and was on a quest for new vistas. What made me look for those in *The Old Regime*, I no longer remember, but I do recall being dazzled by the bright light that Tocqueville's account of eighteenth-century France shone on the totalitarian experience that my part of the world had been through for much of the closing century.

My intellectual path, which had originated in communist Bulgaria and taken shape in Poland in the early years of the postcommunist transition, took me next to KU Leuven in Belgium where I first experienced life in Western Europe, and had a chance to grapple with Tocqueville in academic English. This paved the way for my greatest educational adventure: doctoral studies at the University of Chicago's Committee on Social Thought. Though I had spent time in the West, moving to the United States came as a shock: from the pace of daily life to its intensely participatory university culture, this country was unlike anything I had known. And amid the strangeness of America, the uncompromising spirit of the University of Chicago seemed stranger still. It was only when I reached for Tocqueville's *Democracy in America* that this unfamiliar experience began to make sense, much in the way Eastern

Europe's ancient régime had opened up while reading *The Old Regime*.

The decade I spent as a graduate student, which included a research residency at the École des hautes études de sciences sociales in Paris and a visiting lectureship at Kenyon College in Ohio, at once kindled and humbled my scholarly aspirations. My doctoral dissertation, written under the supervision of Professor Ralph Lerner, was a first attempt to think through the issues raised in this book. Yet it took another decade of helping build one of Germany's first liberal arts institutions, as well as the looming crisis of constitutional orders East and West, to show me why and how this book needed to be written. Seeing the questions that preoccupied Tocqueville are once again the urgent questions of our day, this book is an attempt to bring Tocqueville's insights to bear on the trials of the present.

In the course of my journey, I enjoyed the hospitality of many institutions and was helped by numerous benefactors: family and friends, fellow travelers, and generous mentors who shared their guidance, professional advice, inestimable friendship, and their tough love too. I would like to thank firstly my Chicago friends and teachers who induced me to imagine and pursue a life of the mind: Thomas Bartscherer, John M. Coetzee, Matthew Crawford, Joseph Cropsey, Werner Dannhauser, Lorraine Daston, Daniel Doneson, Marc Fumaroli, David Grene, Ran Halévi, Jonathan Hand, Kevin Hawthorne, Leon Kass, Edwige Katzenelenbogen, Ralph Lerner, Margaret Litvin, Heinrich Meier, Svetozar Minkov, Katia Mitova, Glenn W. Most, Emile Perreau-Saussine, Robert Pippin, James Redfield, Eric Schliesser, Laura Slatkin, Mark Strand, Nathan Tarcov, Aaron Tugendhaft, Iris Marion Young, Adam Zagajewski.

Many scholars helped me think through Tocqueville's work and its wellsprings. I am especially indebted to Barbara Allen, Fred Baumann, Richard Boyd, Nestor Capdevila, Aurelian Craiutu, François Furet, Robert T. Gannett Jr., Ran Halévi, Alan S. Kahan, Ira Katznelson, Peter Lawler, Pierre Manent, Harvey Mansfield,

Clifford Orwin, Jennifer Pitts, Rogers Smith, Tsvetan Todorov, Georgios Varouxakis, Stuart Warner, Cheryl Welch, Delba Winthrop, and Michael Zuckert.

I gratefully acknowledge my colleagues and students at Bard College Berlin (formerly European College of Liberal Arts) and especially Roger Berkowitz, Kerry Bystrom, Susan Gillespie, Peter Hajnal, David Hayes, David Kretz, Geoff Lehman, Thomas Norgaard, Jens Reich, Catherine Toal, Boris Vormann, and Michael Weinman for sharpening my understanding of liberal education and its role in sustaining a free democracy, and to Julie J. Kidd and the Christian A. Johnson Endeavor Foundation for making it all possible.

Versions of this book's arguments have previously appeared in the *American Political Science Review*, *Global Policy*, *Journal of Democracy*, *Kronos*, *Przegląd Polityczny*, the blog *Tocqueville 21*, and several scholarly volumes. I thank Helmut Anheier, Peter Baehr, Reinhard Blomert, Harald Bluhm, Steven Forde, Jacob Hamburger, Alan S. Kahan, Skadi Krause, Piotr Leszczyński, Piotr Nowak, Marc Plattner, Zbigniew Rau, Marek Tracz-Tryniecki for the opportunity to elaborate my understanding of Tocqueville, and for their informative feedback.

This book would not have gotten off the ground without the hospitality of Vienna's Institut für die Wissenschaften vom Menschen (IWM) where I had the privilege to reside as a fellow in the spring of 2019. I would like to express my deep gratitude to Shalini Randeria as well as Ira Katznelson and Ivan Krastev for their generous support and steady encouragement; and to the academic staff Clemena Antonova, Ayşe Çağlar, Ludger Hagedorn, Evangelos Karagiannis, Marcy Shore, Timothy Snyder, Miloš Vec, Ivan Vejvoda, as well as to my fellow fellows David Goodhart, Tobias Haberkorn, Geoffrey Harpham, Aishwary Kumar, Chantal Mouffe, Rabinar Samaddar, and Iliya Trojanow for many a mind-changing conversation. At the IWM, I had the opportunity to participate in a workshop on "Popular Sovereignty, Majority Rule and Electoral Politics." I thank the organizers Craig Calhoun, Dilip

Gaonkar, Charles Taylor, as well as Michael Ignatieff and Claudio Lomnitz for their critical comments and memorable exchanges.

While working on the manuscript, I took part in a scholarly initiative on popular sovereignty under the auspices of the Social Science Research Council, with the support of the Endeavor Foundation. The opportunity to teach two courses, and to coedit—with Thomas Bartscherer and David Bateman—a scholarly volume on popular sovereignty, reoriented my entire understanding of this fundamental dimension of modern society, and of Tocqueville's take on it. I am enormously indebted to Ira Katznelson and Daniella Sarnoff for including me in this project, and to all participants for their discerning engagement.

I am especially grateful to Yannis Evrigenis for hosting a manuscript workshop at Tufts University, and to Joshua Mitchell, Vicky Sullivan, and Alvin B. Tillery, Jr. whose probing criticisms helped me refine both the substance of my arguments and their rhetorical presentation. Drafts were also read by Thomas Bartscherer, Lars Behrisch, David Ciepley, Adam Davis, Gabor Egry, Dieter Grimm, Alan S. Kahan, Ira Katznelson, David Kretz, Margaret Litvin, Aaron Tugendhaft, Jerfi Uzman, Eva van Vugt, and Dominik Zahrnt. The manuscript as a whole benefitted from the meticulous attention and critical review of two dedicated research assistants: Schuyler Curriden and Alexandra Huff. Bridget Flannery-McCoy, Alena Chekanov, Eric Crahan, Ali Parrington, and Isabella Richie at Princeton University Press, as well as the three anonymous reviewers provided comprehensive comments and expert advice on how to streamline my sprawling manuscript into a book.

The intellectual trajectory that began on that afternoon in the mid-1990s would have been very different without the life-changing interventions of caring friends and guides. It is to them, last but not least, that I return in gratitude: Joseph Bartscherer, Paul Berman, Joanna Binkowski-Proulx, Lidia Cankova, Bartłomiej Dobroczyński, Georgi Gospodinov, Roger and Sophie Scruton, Iwona Zapała-Sołtysińska. To TB, my ally, who taught me how things can be made to work in English, and helped me understand myself even as I sought to understand America, I owe more than I can state.

I dedicate this book to my family all of whose Bulgarian, Polish, German, and Russian branches I deeply cherish.

TOCQUEVILLE'S DILEMMAS,
AND OURS

Introduction

IN A CULMINATING moment of the 2018 documentary film *What is Democracy?*, its director, Astra Taylor, interviews political theorist Wendy Brown at the latter's office at the University of California, Berkeley. The brief exchange, a fragment of a longer conversation, begins with Taylor asking if democracy could ever live up to its promise. As Brown's eloquent argument unfolds, the camera roams over a shelf with the collected volumes of Karl Marx and Friedrich Engels. Moving through a stack of books on latter-day revolutionaries, it lingers in front of a bright window as if to ponder the relationship between what is being said and the world outside. Democracy, Brown declares, needs clear limits: "To have democracy, there has to be a 'we.' . . . In order to govern ourselves we need to know who the "we" is who is doing the governing . . . and what our bounds or limits are." That "we," she explains, is founded on differences and exclusions, as well as on borders that delimit who is part of the democratic process and, by implication, who is not. "Democracies have almost always been premised on terrible forms of marking, stratifying, and naming who is human and who is not human . . . I am not defending those," Brown is quick to add, "but I am defending that democracy has to have bounds; it has to have a constitutive 'we.'" Only this bounded "we," she asserts, can stand up to the pernicious expansion of globalized capitalism. Brown's defense of constitutive exclusions is as striking as her insistence that these are "*almost* always . . . terrible." Could there be exclusions that are not "terrible"? She does not say, and Taylor does not ask. As if to highlight the conceptual aporia, the story moves abruptly to a contemporary Greek border where a throng of Syrian refugees armed with handmade placards demand free passage and the immediate abolition of borders. "We are human," they chant—in English.[1]

The sudden change of scenery enacts a rupture between two perspectives that reflect two meanings of democracy. On the one side is the right of a democratic people to foster and protect its collective existence and historic identity: its language, culture, territory, and distinct way of life—in short, its right to self-determination. On the other, stands an exasperated crowd of children, women, and men, young and old, diffident and hopeful, fleeing poverty and war, disenfranchised, disinherited—a makeshift gathering of what Frantz Fanon in a prophetic turn of phrase called "the wretched of the earth"—demanding their equal right to decent life and human flourishing.[2] Both sides appeal to a vision of democracy; both have a point. Between them stands a wall or a border whose meaning and validity—and with it the legitimacy of the entire system of nation-states by which the world is organized and governed—seem to be called into question. Is there a way to affirm human equality without undermining the legitimacy of particular societies and cultures, or, conversely, to mark and maintain political and cultural specificities without denying our common humanity? Can we be equal and yet legitimately different, or distinct and separate, yet, nevertheless, equal? Having forcefully visualized these questions, the film comes to a pause. Against the sunlit Greek landscape with its relentless blue sky a caption appears with Socrates's striking prophecy from book five of Plato's *Republic*: "Until philosophers become kings or those in authority begin to philosophize, there will be no rest from troubles."[3]

The irony is deeply felt. For at this point, the viewers have been encouraged to doubt that any philosopher, whether enthroned by current popularity or intellectual tradition, might have much to propose as a coherent solution to democracy's dilemma. This, the film carefully suggests, is owing to the distance between the confidence of theoretical reason and the disheartening complexity of lived human lives. And yet, if a theoretical insight may not be in a position to formulate the sought-after answer, it is, as Taylor's film eloquently testifies, uniquely fit to help us crystallize the questions and to call to our attention the gulf that separates arguments from phenomena: the logic of intellectual constructs from the conundrums with which the political and social world presents us.

The purpose of this book is not to propose a philosophical cure or defend the possibility of a conceptual solution to the challenges before us. Its aim is to help us better comprehend these challenges. In so doing it pursues two goals simultaneously. It reconstructs Alexis de Tocqueville's account of three pivotal dimensions of modern politics—popular sovereignty, nationhood, and globalization—thus putting into sharp relief neglected aspects of his thought and practice. It also seeks to shed light on contemporary trends. By bringing Tocqueville to bear on our dilemmas, this book offers a fresh analytical lens through which to view liberal democracy today and understand its travails.

I seek to show that today's crisis of liberal democracy, made palpable by the worldwide resurgence of nationalist sentiments and authoritarian movements, is not in itself a novelty. Although triggered by specific conditions that are yet to be fully understood, and catalyzed by the failures of the liberal order itself, our illiberal moment reflects and responds to dilemmas that are inherent in modern society. These dilemmas are rooted in the very tension Taylor's film points to: the tension between the universal scope of democratic principles and the particularity and limits of any social and political attempt to realize them in practice. This constitutive tension, and the dilemmas to which it gives rise, were already in plain sight in the nineteenth century, and Tocqueville's account of them is not only among the first but also among the most comprehensive and profound. Tocqueville analyzed with clarity and depth how the practical political attempts to grapple with modern society's built-in tension could lead to different democratic outcomes: liberal and illiberal. In this sense, he could be viewed as a pioneering theorist both of liberal democracy and of its illiberal others. Tocqueville's work thus offers a compelling framework for understanding the challenges of liberal democracy today and for charting a way forward.

Drawing on Tocqueville's widely celebrated analysis of American democracy and his lesser-known policy writings, my aim is to recover a broader, nondogmatic liberalism capable of weathering today's political storms.[4] If liberal democracy has a future, I suggest, it is in recognizing the enduring dimensions and deep sources of contemporary policy dilemmas and in navigating these in a moderate and nonideological way. Just as liberal democracies should refuse to choose between equality and self-determination, so too they ought to reject the false dichotomies of nationalism and democracy, and of sovereignty and globalization.

Illiberal Democracy?

The greatest challenge to liberal democracy today comes from the ascent of political movements often labeled "populist" and regimes calling themselves "illiberal" that claim the mantle of democratic sovereignty. In the name of equality and popular sovereignty, these forces seek to consolidate authority by striking at the very foundations of constitutional order. Often staying within formal electoral rules, populist parties and charismatic leaders contest embedded norms such as the rule of law, individual rights, and a constitutional system of checks and balances that have long been recognized as the bedrock of democratic freedom. By attacking liberal institutions in the name of democracy, they embrace the possibility of a democratic order that is not liberal, or is expressly anti-liberal. Behind them stand vast publics that condone or welcome this state of affairs.[5]

The popularity of illiberal models, even within established liberal democracies, reflects the deeper shifts taking place in political systems worldwide. It feeds on a growing skepticism—shared by the political Right and Left—about the capacity of liberal institutions to deliver political legitimacy, national security, and an equitable distribution of wealth. On one side, national sovereignty is reaffirmed as the only viable response to democratic deficits, economic hardship, and high waves of migration and cultural dislocation, as well as a brake on liberal globalism. From this vantage, liberal elites, driven by their own class and partisan interests, have severed ties with large parts of the electorate and failed to provide for the public good. Viewing society as a set of abstract rights or commercial transactions, the liberal crusade to emancipate individuals from the shackles of custom and tradition undermines the civic bond and the sense of belonging that any decent polity depends on. Liberalism, critics from the Right aver, lacks a coherent vision of national and economic security, and of the social glue that both constitutes individuals and holds democracy together.[6]

If the Right sees liberalism as too thin and parasitic on social and cultural conditions that it cannot reproduce, the Left views it as too thick, pointing to its structural and normative underpinnings as evidence of inegalitarian biases. From this perspective, liberal principles and the international regime they undergird have failed to guarantee genuine equality and full representation. Decrying these failures, critics on the left take to task core liberal values—such as the rule of law or human rights—unmasking them as little more than cynical instruments of political and economic exploitation. As they charge, liberalism's universalistic assumptions about reason, citizenship, and humanity are mere rhetoric covering the profit-seeking nature of corporate capitalism and the real chains of Western neocolonial domination.[7]

However different in motivation and substance, these critiques share similarities. They draw on current dissatisfactions with the political status quo in order to contest not only specific policies or orientations, but also liberalism's normative and institutional foundations. Opposed to what they see as oppressive "liberal hegemony," they appeal to democratic ideals and egalitarian aspirations, thus seeking to divorce liberalism from democracy as two distinct and separable political visions. These contestations have given rise to an impassioned debate about the meaning of democracy and its relationship to liberalism, in which questions of sovereignty, national identity, and the political and ethical dimensions of globalization stand paramount.[8]

As this book aims to show, these challenges, though newly urgent, are not new.[9] Topical and timely, they are also topoi: that is, recurring themes and, in a sense, timeless questions of modern politics. To adequately address present challenges, we need to grasp not only their immediate triggers, but also their enduring dimensions. Beyond policy proposals tailored to particular contexts, defending liberal democracy today requires that we re-examine its intellectual foundations, as well as the practices and preconditions that make it work. Such a rethinking may help us recover a richer, less ideological liberalism that can propose liberal democratic alternatives to contested policies. No modern thinker seems better placed to aid this effort of recovery than Tocqueville, one of liberal democracy's greatest champions and most incisive critics.

Why Tocqueville

Alexis de Tocqueville (1805–1859) was a liberal, yet, as he insisted, "a liberal of a new kind."[10] First among the novel facets of his liberalism was his understanding of the character of modern society and the new dilemmas it faced. Whereas his liberal predecessors—notably Baron de Montesquieu and Benjamin Constant—considered commerce and the social reorganization it involved as that which made society modern, Tocqueville proposed that not capitalism but democracy and its core value—equality—is the defining feature of the modern age. Born into an old aristocratic family decimated in the French Revolution (his parents barely escaped the guillotine), Tocqueville was preoccupied all his life with the meaning and causes of this world-historical upheaval. *Democracy in America* (1835–40), Tocqueville's most celebrated work, proclaimed the soon-to-be-global rise of democracy as the substance and motor behind revolutionary change.[11]

As early as 1835, Tocqueville announced that there were no viable alternatives to the principles of democratic equality and popular sovereignty in the modern world. The success of the Atlantic Revolutions of the eighteenth century and the resulting defeat of aristocracy as a social system relocated political struggle within the framework of democracy itself. Henceforth, the primary political question was no longer whether to have democracy, but what kind: how to embody democratic ideals in institutions and practices, and what precise shape these should take. Tocqueville expected these same questions to reach and revolutionize every corner of the world, and reshape the global order.

Tocqueville defined democracy not as a political order but above all as a "social state": a condition of society in which status is not fixed at birth but must be acquired. This democratic social condition entails a mindset characterized by the "ardent, insatiable, eternal, invincible" love of equality itself. Tocqueville credited the egalitarian mindset with driving political dynamics and transforming all aspects of social life: economic and class relations as well as the conceptual and moral horizon. Rather than a static arrangement, democracy is an ongoing process of equalization, a social revolution without visible end. Tocqueville famously called for, and pioneered, a "new political science" to instruct and guide this democratizing process.[12]

If Tocqueville proclaimed democratization "irresistible," he did not view it as following a fixed path. Inflected by historical and cultural contexts, the struggle for democracy is undetermined in crucial respects. Democracy's social base and the passion for equality that define the modern age are compatible with two radically different political scenarios: one that postulates universal rights and protects equal freedoms, the other predicated on an omnipotent state that pursues equality by demanding the equal powerlessness of all. These alternative outcomes stand as two global models, which Tocqueville identified with the United States and Russia.[13] So against the hopes of twentieth-century modernization theory, liberal democracy in Tocqueville's view is not a necessary outcome of democratization. With the demise of traditional orders and alternative regimes, the fundamental modern political choice lies between a democratic republic and egalitarian despotism. For "equality produces, in fact, two tendencies: one leads men directly to independence ... the other leads them by a longer, more secret, but surer road toward servitude." Not only does democracy's rise not necessitate a liberal outcome: the drive toward ever-greater equalization continually tempts peoples to trade their civic freedoms for another step along the egalitarian road, making liberty's prospects ever less certain.[14]

Tocqueville, then, saw from afar the danger of illiberal democracy. He was already haunted by the specter of our times. While hailing the global rise of democratic equality, his work highlights the tensions between equality and freedom that define the main challenges of modern politics. If today's anti-liberals distinguish liberalism from democracy and purport to embrace the latter while rejecting the former, Tocqueville insisted on this distinction in order to enhance liberal self-understanding and to protect democratic freedom at the same time.

Yet, unlike current and past attempts to draw a clear line between liberal and nonliberal forms of democracy, for Tocqueville the distinction is both all-embracing and ambiguous. It is not simply a matter of economic relations (free vs. regulated market) or institutional forms (representative vs. direct), of normative principles (majoritarianism vs. rule of law), or a particular definition of freedom (individual vs. collective), as recent commentators have proposed.[15] A viable and free democratic order must include all these dimensions. What is more, liberal democracy for Tocqueville depends on deeper things: intellectual and spiritual orientation, modes of relating to the past and the political community as the product of a particular historical trajectory, as well as on the place of religion in social and political life.[16] Tocqueville held these ethical and psychological aspects of democratic life as crucially important. As this book will argue, his insight into the affective foundations of liberal democracy is the moral core of his liberalism and among the most important contributions of his new political science.

Democracy's Dilemmas

While Tocqueville understood the relation between liberalism and democracy as pervasive, he traced the tension between them to two distinct, if interrelated, understandings of democracy and to the illiberal potential each of them carries. For Tocqueville, modern democratic society rests on two pillars: the universalist principle of equality, which pushes against all limits and borders, and popular sovereignty: that is, the ideals and practices of political self-rule that require both a particular community—a people—and a notion of rule or sovereignty. Democracy cannot be liberal if either of those pillars is missing. But their combination generates tensions and dilemmas that shape the stakes of modern politics. The ways in which modern societies understand and navigate the often conflicting aspirations to equality and difference, to universality and particularity, are critical for the possibility of democratic freedom.

The tensions between modern democracy's two principles—equality and self-rule—give rise to structural challenges as well as recurring policy dilemmas. Revisiting three pivotal aspects of Tocqueville's analysis, this book contends that liberal democracies face three interrelated questions: How to construe and institutionalize the principle of popular sovereignty?; How to define and mobilize the civic allegiance and social solidarity that democratic sovereignty relies on?; and finally, How to negotiate the processes of globalization that, while propelled by democracy's universalizing claims and egalitarian promise, stand in an often conflicting relation to the legitimacy of its particular instantiations? These questions yield a range of difficult choices: between sovereign power and participatory freedoms; between national cohesion and individual rights; between compliance with transnational norms and accountability to a particular people. By calling them dilemmas, I want to suggest that these are not either-or choices, where one must be opted for at the expense of the other. Like the two meanings of democracy that ground them, these dilemmas point to a set of alternatives, neither of which can fully exist on its own, nor produce a satisfactory outcome.

Drawing on Tocqueville, I argue that to remain liberal, modern societies require both horns of each of these dilemmas. They should refuse to choose, but seek to find ways to negotiate and allay the tensions between them. The language of dilemma also implies the lack of ready-to-hand ideological answers. Dilemmas complicate neat definitions and simple notions of right and wrong. They require that we weigh competing, often incommensurable, goods and corresponding dangers. While resisting definitive solutions, dilemmas structure the field of available alternatives. They call for careful consideration and balanced judgment—and for acknowledging trade-offs too. Along with being distinct and inherent—hardwired so to say—in the modern democratic project, the dilemmas that pertain to institutionalizing popular sovereignty, sustaining national identity, and deepening globalization are also imbricated. None of them can be fully understood or addressed without the others: for example, popular sovereignty and nationalism without the question of individual participation; or sovereignty and nationhood without the challenges posed to them by the processes of globalization.[17]

Proposing that we view the modern world as a matrix of interrelated conundrums, this book champions a Tocqueville-informed vision of liberalism as complex and ambivalent. While fundamentally committed to the protection of individual freedom and constitutional rights, and beholden to the universalist ethos of the Enlightenment, Tocqueville-style liberalism is not opposed to the quest for democratic sovereignty and national identity, but is premised on a certain way of understanding and institutionalizing these aspirations. Although it seeks to articulate a comprehensive approach to modern society's inherent tensions, liberalism need not—indeed ought not—strive to resolve them. I suggest that a programmatic resistance to seeing the world through a Manichean lens of stark, irreconcilable binaries distinguishes liberal democracy from illiberal variants. Whereas the latter advance clear answers or final solutions to democracy's constitutive tensions, a liberal regime strives to live with these tensions. Viewing them as persistent, and in some sense perennial, its aim is not to sap but to harness the energy of conflicts in order to enable peaceful experimentation and an ongoing search for vital compromise.

Approaching Tocqueville

This book pursues two goals simultaneously: to shed light on liberal democracy's current crisis and to enhance our understanding of Tocqueville. These two objectives, I maintain, are best pursued in tandem: approaching a classical author through a contemporary frame and, conversely, looking at the present moment through a conceptual lens drawn from the past, can deepen our understanding of the present as well as the past.

As previously suggested, putting the political dilemmas of our time in historical perspective reveals their roots and enduring dimensions, and helps us achieve greater clarity. On the other hand, approaching Tocqueville's work with our own questions in mind brings out aspects of his analysis that, while crucial, have been overlooked by generations of readers driven by different intellectual and political priorities. To give a striking example: as I show in the first chapter, Tocqueville regards the principle of popular sovereignty as the foundation of both political life and of modern republicanism. The opening chapters of *Democracy in America* call attention to the centrality of this principle for his account of the United States and modern democracy more broadly. Notwithstanding Tocqueville's emphasis, few scholars have thematized his understanding of popular sovereignty and probed its relationship to constitutionalism. The rare exceptions tend to downplay the significance of the concept, or present Tocqueville as a principled opponent to sovereignty understood as state centralization.[18] Likewise, the importance of nationalism for Tocqueville's view of democracy, though noted, is yet to receive sustained treatment.[19] Tocqueville's analysis of global politics and international relations, while heatedly debated under the rubric of empire, is often discussed in isolation from his account of democracy, or viewed as tangential to his liberalism. Considering these three dimensions—sovereignty, nationalism, and globalization—together sheds light not only on our concerns, but on Tocqueville's as well.

Tocqueville's work, moreover, is instructive for its substance as well as its approach. The tension between the universal and particular—my main object of investigation—was not only at the center of Tocqueville's analytical concerns, it also informed his methodology. Attuned, as behooves a philosopher, to the logic of ideas and to humanity's universal conundrums, Tocqueville also drew on the spirit and methods of social science (which he helped to advance) and inquired into the circumstances that would make modern society hospitable to freedom. His purpose, in short, was not merely to comprehend and describe but also to foster liberal democracy and inform political practice.[20] And he considered the study of the past as essential to this goal. This is one important reason why *Democracy in America* includes extensive descriptions of feudal society—an aspect I explore in this book. More than a foil or a straw man, premodern society is modernity's significant other, whose rethinking is as indispensable for political self-understanding as it is for imagining new ways to be modern.[21]

Yet, history also harbors dangers. While helping us recognize patterns of thought and action and unearth the sources of our political outlooks, attention to the past could buttress the view that we are who we were, or who we must become; that ensnared by habits and cultural path dependency, or propelled on an inexorable march of progress, all societies can do is embrace their role in history's predetermined narrative; that, whether as tragedy or farce, history is bound to repeat itself, or else lead us, in a Hegelian comedy, toward worldly salvation.[22] A keen observer of modern society, Tocqueville warned against the all-too democratic tendency to rush into the twin traps of excessive confidence and fatalism, and he reflected on the role historians can play in prodding or restraining these dangerous attractions.[23] In his view, the past is neither a barbarism from which, thankfully, we have been liberated, nor a destiny that we inexorably must repeat, but a mix of persisting questions and contingent possibilities. As this book aims to show, spanning different genres, disciplines, epochs, and regions, Tocqueville's writings were motivated by an antideterminist intent: one reason—perhaps the main—why they can be useful to us today.

Tocqueville, moreover, was keenly aware of the psychological dimensions of political life and the need to encourage a certain kind of mindset in order for freedom to be possible. As the penultimate paragraph of *Democracy in America* states:

> Providence has created *humanity* neither entirely independent nor completely slave. It traces around *each man*, it is true, a fatal circle out of which he cannot go; but within its vast limits, man is powerful and free; so are *peoples*.[24]

This short passage merits a closer look. Tocqueville was not a religious person in a conventional sense. As he states in an 1857 letter to a devout friend, "insatiable curiosity which found only the books of a large library to satisfy it" robbed him at the age of sixteen of his Catholic faith, which he likely never recovered. This has led scholars to suggest that the frequent invocations of Providence in Tocqueville's works were little more than rhetoric: a mode of speaking that reflects his contemporaries' sensibilities, or the audience he was addressing, rather than his own convictions.[25]

And yet, while deployed to persuade, Tocqueville's providential language is more than *mere* rhetoric. If Tocqueville himself was not a believer in Providence, he was, to borrow a phrase, a believer in belief and in the central importance of religion for democratic freedom. While estranged from the mysteries of Catholicism, he had a deep insight into the mysteries of the human psyche and the affective preconditions for a liberal order. Fleshing out this psychological dimension is a central goal of this book.[26]

Freedom, for Tocqueville, requires trust in a moral universe supportive of human endeavor. It is grounded in the faith that, to echo Martin Luther King, the arc of the human story bends toward justice. It also draws on the belief in our individual capacity to help narrow the gap between the way the world is and how it should be. Liberty, in short, requires pride: confidence that we can improve the world and achieve something important. Yet if the struggle for freedom is premised on prideful trust in one's powers and the justness of one's cause, it also needs charity and self-restraint as well as the ability to cherish what is given. Freedom, in short, necessitates aspiration *and* humility, hope *and* realism, and striving *and* acceptance. It depends on walking a fine psychological line between ambition and modesty. Here, as elsewhere, Tocqueville's appeal to Providence aims both to boost our confidence in human freedom and to reconcile us to our limited control. Although as finite beings we cannot have either complete knowledge or full command, there is always space for choice and insight whose limits, if "fatal," are also "vast."

This view of freedom and its preconditions directly informs Tocqueville's democratic vista. While calling democracy's global rise "irresistible" and "providential," he also claims that its meaning is not predetermined but must be sought out and achieved. If the movement toward equality is divinely ordained and therefore just, its outcome remains uncertain. If there is a clear arc to history—a grand narrative that can orient our judgment—there is also room for weighing practical alternatives. The possibility of human agency depends on avoiding the twin traps of complacency and disenchantment. Warning against the attraction of extremes, Tocqueville recommends a middle, a liberal course—in a word: moderation.[27]

Just as crucially, Tocquveille's passage quoted earlier indicates that the pursuit of liberty takes place on three levels simultaneously: humanity, people, individual. Illuminating the fate and freedom of peoples is as pivotal as that of individuals or humankind as a whole. Indeed, this book will argue that Tocqueville's liberalism is premised on the irreducibility of the middle term, peoplehood, either to individuals or to humanity. Stressing the political and bounded dimension of freedom, Tocqueville's is a political liberalism par excellence.[28]

Tocqueville, in other words, grapples with the stubborn fact of pluralism and the limits it puts on our political and philosophic aspirations. He cautions against forgetting that humanity, while one, is also many. Though sharing common features and similar yearnings, human beings are divided into a great multitude of different peoples, each with its own distinct vision of what it means to be human or to live a good life. As Tocqueville helps us appreciate, this necessary and often "fatal" aspect of our condition is as much a curse as it is a blessing. By pushing us to explore who we are, the differences that divide us curb our liberty and also sustain it. In that sense, human diversity and the variety of individual and collective modes of life that aspire to self-determination are both a challenge to and a precondition for the possibility of freedom.[29]

Tocqueville's appreciation for the particular, political dimensions of the human condition—and of the efforts to comprehend it—is one reason why his main analytical works prominently feature particular and, in their different ways, prototypically modern peoples: the American and the French. *Democracy in America*, which will be my main (though not exclusive) focus here, illuminates the modern situation by offering a comprehensive account of an actually existing democratic polity. Wary of abstract theorizing and its tendency to promote ideological shortcuts, Tocqueville set out to shed light on the promises and dangers of modern democracy by describing its paradigmatic liberal instantiation: the United States, then half a century old. Rather than defend liberalism in theory, Tocqueville studied it in American practice, probing its past and present, its successes and its failures, and drawing general lessons from a particular democratic experience. The result is a pioneering investigation of the conceptual understanding of liberal democracy and, at the same time, a thick sociological analysis of its specific conditions and cultural underpinnings. Stressing the need to reconcile universality and difference, Tocqueville's work models the process of ascending to general insights from a particular historical and cultural context.[30]

While I find in Tocqueville analytical and policy resources for comprehending and addressing our own times, my object is not to argue that he always got things right, or that his judgment should be adopted uncritically. By revisiting central aspects of his social and political thought, this book casts into sharp relief the tensions underlying Tocqueville's legacy: his pessimism about racial integration, his resolute (if qualified) embrace of the French colonial empire, and his preaching in theory and adopting in practice a politics of national pride that today we may well brand populist. Alongside his debatable judgments, another reason for interpretive caution is historical distance. Parallels notwithstanding, Tocqueville's situation was different from ours in important respects. To underscore the contemporary import of his work, one must grasp the historical and political span democracies have traveled over the past two centuries. For this task, too, contextualization is essential.

Tocqueville lived in a world and in a century preoccupied with its own social and political struggles and civilizational priorities. The United States, the country he pointed to as pioneering example of liberal democracy, was in fact a slaveholding republic: neither entirely liberal nor fully democratic. This young country, moreover, was yet to experience its defining historical trials: civil war and reconstruction, economic crisis, totalitarianism, and world wars—trials that would propel its development from a relatively small isolated polity to a continental and soon to be global power, from an historical outlier and a constitutional novelty to a model and defender of the free world, and from there to its current status as a self-doubting and much resented hegemon. Tocqueville saw the New World as the hopeful future of Europe, and particularly France. Though not an example to be followed blindly, American society offered empirical support for his cautious optimism about democracy's liberal prospects. Today, as liberal institutions are under pressure in the United States, and American exceptionalism, which Tocqueville helped theorize, is increasingly in doubt, such optimism does not seem readily available. Who represents whose future has become an open question.[31]

On the other hand, though Tocqueville's historical circumstances were undeniably different, there are deep continuities between his time and ours that warrant returning to the nineteenth century to seek lessons for the twenty-first. If the democratic society Tocqueville studied was a novel "spectacle for which past history had not prepared the world," in the nineteenth century, liberalism had already attained global outreach, not least thanks to its self-righteous champion and aspiring hegemon: England.[32] Extraordinarily influential and globally ascendant, nineteenth-century liberalism was also vigorously opposed. While totalitarianism was yet to appear in full stature, the ideas and sentiments that would guide liberalism's two greatest challengers in the twentieth century—scientific racism on one hand, scientific socialism on the other—were well on their way to attain persuasive formulation and popular acclaim. Liberal constitutionalism, then as today, enjoyed both fame and infamy: it was established as much as contested at home and abroad.

A participatory observer of these developments, Tocqueville was able to gauge their direction. Though the American Union he visited was still a fledgling republic without a foreign policy to speak of, his analysis anticipates the looming sectional conflict between the North and South, and points to the United States' global destiny. As a direct witness to slavery and the political construction of racialist ideology in the Americas, Tocqueville was also exposed to the doctrines of scientific racism through the work of one of its early proponents, Count de Gobineau. And while we have no evidence that he was aware of Marx, as I discuss in chapter three, the rise of socialist ideology with its statist and anti-liberal ramifications was among his greatest worries, as was religious fundamentalism in its Catholic and Islamic variety. Tocqueville's vision of the global spread of democratic civilization and his direct involvement in international politics made him a judicious interpreter of the constellation of issues and processes that shaped the following centuries, and which we today call globalization.[33]

Likewise, although Tocqueville does not use our language, and many a contemporary concept in which current trends are analyzed—including "globalization," "nationalism," "populism," "identity"—are not his own, in deploying these terms, this book aims to show that Tocqueville nevertheless had a deep apprehension of these phenomena. Because the issues Tocqueville pondered are in important respects the questions of our time, his work can be fruitfully brought to bear on our situation. And we stand to learn from his accounts, despite or perhaps even because they are set in a different context. Both the challenges before us and the avenues for addressing them might become easier to grasp when observed from afar, with the benefit of historical—and emotional—distance.

Approaching Tocqueville's writings through the prism of three modern dilemmas, the main goal of the chapters that follow is to probe and reconstruct his understanding of these dilemmas, and draw useful lessons. My primary mode in these expository chapters is a sustained analysis of important parts of Tocqueville's work, noting how these have been interpreted in the secondary literature and elaborating alternatives to established readings. To discern the precise meaning and test the internal coherence of Tocqueville's arguments, each chapter considers their historical and intellectual context. I seek to clarify Tocqueville's analytical stance by putting it in conversation with select interlocutors who deeply influenced his thinking, such as Jean-Jacques Rousseau and the authors of the *Federalist Papers* featured in chapter one, or J. S. Mill and François Guizot discussed in chapter two. In chapter three I canvas Tocqueville's vision of democracy and its global ramifications against the backdrop of its most consequential alternative: revolutionary Marxism.

To bring out the practical, rhetorical dimension of Tocqueville's analysis, each chapter features what I have called a case study examining how Tocqueville applied his ideas to political practice. Chapter one probes the view of sovereignty that informs Tocqueville's account of the United States' federal system in light of his often-ignored discussion of the politics of Andrew Jackson's presidency, and of the nullification controversy of 1831—the most significant clash over sovereignty prior to the American Civil War. In chapter two, I set Tocqueville's analysis of democratic nationhood against his position on the so-called Eastern crisis of the early 1840s and the nationalist tensions between France and England that prompted his debate with J. S. Mill on national pride. Chapter three juxtaposes Tocqueville's vision of democratic foreign policy with his involvement in France's colonization of Algeria so as to explore the mechanisms and long-term prospects of globalization.

Whereas the core of the book aims to deepen our understanding of Tocqueville and his context, the concluding chapter returns to the present in order to consider the current state of democratic "disrepair," and the prospects for liberal democracy in today's world.[34] Recapitulating the book's main findings, it seeks to imagine how Tocqueville would interpret our situation and respond to questions raised by contemporary analyses. By applying Tocqueville's analytical framework to our world, I draw lessons for sustaining liberal democracy in the twenty-first century.

1

(Popular) Sovereignty and Constitutionalism

ALEXIS DE TOCQUEVILLE was among the first to theorize the tension between liberalism and democracy, and his analysis provides a compelling framework for reconsidering their relationship today. In his account, modern democracy rests on a synthesis between the universalizing principle of equality, which pushes against all limits and borders, and popular sovereignty: the practice of political self-rule that requires a particular people and a notion of sovereignty. For Tocqueville, I will argue, the viability of liberal democracy depends on how the tensions between these distinct democratic imaginaries and the dilemmas behind them are understood and navigated. Revisiting Tocqueville's vision of democratic equality, this chapter canvasses his account of popular sovereignty as the legitimating principle of liberal democracy. It then probes the relationship between popular sovereignty and constitutionalism in the American context in order to clarify the meaning of democratic freedom and its preconditions.

Equality of Conditions

Therefore, as I studied American society, I saw more and more in *equality of conditions* the *generating fact* from which each particular fact seemed to derive, and I rediscovered it constantly before me as a central point where all of my observations came together.[1]

Among the most enduring contributions Tocqueville made to social and political thought is his conception of democracy not primarily as a set of political institutions, but as "equality of conditions" or a "social state." At once a potent cause and the effect of preexisting factors, the social state is "the generating fact," thus a key to understanding the structure and dynamics of a particular type of society. In his account, what distinguishes modern from premodern society is first and foremost the principle of equality, whose beginnings Tocqueville traces to the rise of Christianity. Premised on the notion of the moral equality of human beings, the democratic social state is one in which status is not fixed at birth but must be acquired. So understood, the "equality of conditions" need not deny that at any given point there may be extensive inequalities, say, between rich and poor, or between more or less educated, to mention Tocqueville's two chief metrics. Indeed, the universal striving for social eminence and economic success is, in a sense, what democracy is all about. Yet, if social distinctions and material disparities continue to exist, they are fluid and obey a different logic, unlike premodern inequalities. What democratic equality entails, above all, is the promise and the universal expectation that no person's status and life prospects are simply determined by the fortuitous circumstances of birth and heritage.[2]

Equality of conditions, then, connotes social mobility: the possibility of rising—and falling—on the social ladder, not the absence of such a ladder. It entails a particular way of seeing the social world that glosses over existing inequalities to insist on fundamental human similarity. It also consists in a characteristic mentality defined by the "ardent, insatiable, eternal, invincible passion for equality." Pressing against social boundaries and institutional forms, this passionate commitment ensures that the democratic social state is an ever-changing condition. Rather than a static arrangement, democracy is an ongoing process of equalization, as

Steven Smith puts it, a "perpetual work in progress." The motor of this progressive dynamic is the desire for independence and flourishing and the recognition of the individual right to shape one's own life.[3]

However, while the desire for individual independence is a central feature of democratic freedom, it can also become its foremost danger. As Tocqueville was among the first to perceive, the egalitarian social state creates the conditions for social atomization and toxic individualism. Though akin, democratic individualism is notably different from plain old selfishness. Whereas egoism is a "natural instinct," individualism is a considerate opinion that justifies civic indifference and social isolation.[4] Encouraging a fixation on private interests and goals, it tends to hide from view each person's reliance on and duty toward fellow citizens and the political world. Espoused as a creed, democratic individualism militates against social cohesion. It narrows the scope of what is held in common and facilitates making shortsighted and self-serving decisions the costs of which are externalized to invisible others: classes, generations, and, as chapter three will argue, other countries as well. This, in turn, undermines the moral preconditions of freedom: the citizens' trust in the institutions, and in their own capacity to shape their personal and collective fate. At the same time, when citizens distrust one another and each fends only for himself, the need for government to step in and take care of public business is bound to grow. The more work the government takes on for itself, the more powers it accrues, and the more it produces social isolation. Tocqueville warns that, in a kind of dialectical reversal, the obsession with individual independence is likely to augment the competences of the state and result in forms of government that are adverse to individual freedom. In his diagnosis, democracies are inherently vulnerable to a specifically democratic form of despotism: the rise of an all-powerful, ever-expanding regulatory state, whose tendencies Tocqueville saw exemplified in French history and political culture.[5]

Egalitarian societies, claims Tocqueville, face a fundamental choice between liberal democracy and democratic despotism:

> The first to be subjected to this fearful alternative, the Anglo-Americans have been fortunate enough to escape absolute power. Circumstances, origin, enlightenment, and *above all, mores* have allowed them to establish and to maintain the sovereignty of the people.[6]

Prefacing the chapter "On the Principle of the Sovereignty of the People in America," Tocqueville's statement points to popular sovereignty as a pivotal aspect of Anglo-American freedom, and to mores as crucial for sustaining it. The short chapter itself discusses the concept of popular sovereignty, which Tocqueville also dubs "dogma" or "doctrine," surveying its philosophical meaning and historic ascent in the New World. It thus sheds light both on the ideological basis of modern republicanism, and on the cultural sources of American identity.[7]

Often ignored in the secondary literature, Tocqueville's popular sovereignty chapter merits close attention. It is indispensable for fully grasping the intention of Tocqueville's analysis of American democracy and the distinctiveness of his liberal vision. As I will argue, Tocqueville considers republican institutions based on the principle of popular sovereignty as a crucial remedy for the threats posed by democratic individualism: a remedy that carries its own illiberal potential. After taking a careful look at Tocqueville's understanding of popular sovereignty and its significance for modern democracy, the rest of the chapter probes the relationship between popular sovereignty and American constitutionalism, and the meaning of democratic freedom that emerges from it. As I aim to show, for Tocqueville, an actively engaged democratic public constitutes the fullest expression of popular sovereignty. It is also a crucial precondition for a free democracy. However, along with drawing citizens into the public sphere and providing an institutional framework for their engagement, democracy must also guard against the factionalism that can ensue from popular participation. To be functional as well as liberal, democratic society needs to cultivate popular allegiance.

Having probed Tocqueville's analysis of the United States Constitution, I examine in my first case study his account of the constitutional politics of antebellum American Union and its unresolved conundrum: the identity of the American people. I contend that while for Tocqueville the proper functioning of constitutional democracy vitally depends on unwritten norms and mores, a key element of mores is the sense of belonging to "We the People" and a shared vision of what that belonging means.

The Principle of Popular Sovereignty

The principle of the sovereignty of the people, which is *more or less always* found at the base of *nearly all* human institutions, *ordinarily* remains there as if buried. It is obeyed without being recognized, or if sometimes it happens, for a moment, to be brought into broad daylight, one soon rushes to push it back *into the shadows of the sanctuary*.[8]

Chapter four, part one of the first volume of *Democracy* opens with two striking claims. The first is that "nearly all human institutions" rest on a popular foundation. To be viable, institutional arrangements need to be accepted by the people who are subject to them. And so, though often unrecognized, the people are "more or less always" the fountain of legitimacy. While there may be exceptions to this rule, Tocqueville offers no examples. His wording intimates that even regimes claiming to be based on alternative principles—divine right, say, or hereditary aristocracy—are popular at root. An aristocracy, he explains later in the book, "that has allowed the heart of the people to escape definitively from its hands, is like a tree with dead roots; the higher it is, the more easily is it toppled by the winds." If it is to endure, a political order must be grounded in a broad-based attachment and belief in its validity and, in that sense, in popular consent.[9] The second assertion is that this foundational truth usually lies "as if buried." If every regime requires a form of popular consent, more often than not this is an inconvenient fact that may easily call into question the authority of the ruling elite, regardless of whether this elite is made up of royalty, nobility, or constitutional judges. On the other hand, if acknowledging the popular foundations of political power is potentially disruptive, for a political order to function, this foundation must hide "in the shadows of the sanctuary" and behind the mysteries of faith. Political life, then, "ordinarily" rests on obfuscation.[10]

There is an implicit flipside of these two claims: if "nearly all" human institutions rest on a popular base, republican regimes that explicitly recognize this are, as a matter of principle, true to their foundation. The republican principle is what Rousseau called the "true foundation of society" that reveals to plain sight what in other political arrangements lies buried. Agreeing with Rousseau that all political orders consist of an ideological superstructure erected on a popular base, Tocqueville's discussion of popular sovereignty seems to open with a bold endorsement of republicanism.[11]

And yet, if all regimes are in some sense based on popular consent, however tacit, a government by consent is not a specifically modern phenomenon—nor is it necessarily free. As Tocqueville hurries to add, neither the republican principle nor invocations of national will based on it are in themselves conducive to liberty and flourishing. Such principles and invocations have belonged to the toolkit of "schemers of all times and despots of all ages." As if gesturing to the present moment, Tocqueville cautions that demagogic attempts to claim (or manufacture) popular legitimacy are as old as politics itself, and that they can lead to despotism as well as freedom. Likewise, pointing to popular sovereignty as the basis of all politics, he suggests that the crucial difference between political orders is not *whether* they are popular but *in what way*: how "the people" is defined and embodied in the institutional arrangement on the one hand; and how popular consent is elicited, shaped, and expressed, through institutions, political symbols, and rituals on the other.[12]

What distinguishes American democracy, then, is less the legitimating principle on which it rests, than the open recognition of this principle, as well as the way the people is construed and its sovereignty put into institutional and social practice. Though *Democracy in America* opens with the promise to illuminate the meaning and ramifications of democratic equality, the popular sovereignty chapter points to a revelation no less important: American society sheds light on the very mechanisms of political life, and "the true value" of their grounding principle.[13]

Democracy in America's opening chapters situate the inquiry by commenting on the geopolitical circumstances and colonial origins of the United States. Tocqueville's historical overview shows that, implicit in the practice of self-government, the principle of popular sovereignty was widespread in colonial America. Lodged deeply into English habits, it was brought to the New World with the first immigrants, and played a key part in shaping the colonial system of "township government, this fertile seed of free institutions." However, if in Tocqueville's view "the sovereignty of the people had been the generative principle of most of the English colonies of America," as a political and legal norm it was far from being dominant. "Two obstacles, one external, one internal, slowed its invasive march," and the American Revolution was critical to overcoming both.[14]

As Tocqueville's chapter "On the Principle of the Sovereignty of the People in America" intimates, the two obstacles—social hierarchy and subordination to Britain—amounted to a single roadblock: the absence of a coherent self-understanding that would motivate the desire for political sovereignty and unite the different classes in each colony, and the people across the thirteen colonies, into a joint struggle for independence. In Tocqueville's brief retelling, social equalization and political sovereignty went hand in hand in America. They were two sides of the same revolutionary struggle. Both were propelled by what

Edmund Morgan has referred to as "inventing the people." Once the existence of a distinct American people was declared and appealed to—both as a "common sense" justification for seeking independence and as a means for rallying broad-based support for the revolutionary war—popular sovereignty was quickly recognized as the foundation of government and established as "the law of laws" of the American republics.[15] In the wake of independence, Tocqueville claims, democratization and constitutional change proceeded apace. The colonies turned states revised their fundamental charters, not merely by invoking popular sovereignty in principle, but by effecting it in practice: amending property laws, extending suffrage, and experimenting with new democratic forms. This, in turn, proved to be a vital preparation for the constitutional founding. So irresistible was the popular élan that the classes that stood to lose most hastened the triumph of the new democratic order.[16]

Readers of Tocqueville have long been puzzled by his silence on the Declaration of Independence (1776), which inaugurated the American Revolution and, by spelling out its universal creed, critically shaped American self-understanding. Some have gone so far as to suggest that, by omitting to acknowledge this momentous document, Tocqueville misunderstood the American founding and the political identity of the new republic. While this allegation is not without grounds, there may well be a reason for Tocqueville's omission. His account, I suggest, advances an implicit counterclaim that is worth spelling out.[17]

Reading the Declaration closely, Danielle Allen observes that, while universal in scope, the Declaration's principles were wielded as an instrument of people building. They were invoked in order to produce the very people declared to be already in existence: the "one people" announced in the opening line that is distinct both from its "British brethren" and from the fractious and diverse colonies the Declaration sought to unite. The act of the Declaration, then, is both a proclamation of unity as well as separation, an assertion of national distinctiveness as much as of universality. These two dimensions—universal and particular—appear as two sides of the same declarative purpose.[18]

Yet, for the Declaration to be able to achieve its rhetorical intent, the principles and aspirations it announced must have been broadly recognizable to the "one people" in whose name it spoke. If the act of declaring independence was to effectively galvanize popular action, the truths it declared could not be entirely new or appear strange to its primary audience. Even if never before so clearly stated, "these truths" must have been heard and received precisely as "self-evident." Put differently, for "one people" to be able to strive for social unity and political existence, it must already exist in some form.[19]

It is this prior form of peoplehood that *Democracy in America*'s opening chapters set out to explore. Tocqueville's return to Puritanism and the colonial "point of departure" highlights popular sovereignty as "the generative principle of most of the English colonies of America." Tocqueville's account suggests that if equality of conditions is the "generating fact" of modern society, and of the rising democratic civilization, Anglo-American societies had an originating principle of their own that marked their specificity within the wider democratic current.[20] Above and beyond revolutionary rhetoric, Tocqueville probes the deep sources—historical, sociological, psychological, and moral—of American peoplehood. Rather than declarations of abstract principles (a genre in which his countrymen much excelled), he examines the practices and mindsets that undergirded political doctrines and translated rhetorical speech into a lived reality. And so, while Americans first announced to the world the creed of human rights and declared republican principles as the basis of their society, what shaped the American way, in Tocqueville's view, is not only (or mainly) the act of declaring the "self-evident truths" of republicanism and universal equality, but the social and cultural conditions that allowed the embodiment of these truths into particular institutions and practices.[21]

Tocqueville's chapter on popular sovereignty states its main point in the final paragraphs:

> Today in the United States the principle of the sovereignty of the people has attained all the practical developments that imagination can conceive. It has been *freed from all the fictions* that have been carefully placed around it elsewhere; it is seen successively clothed in all forms according to the necessity of the case. Sometimes the people as a body make the laws as at Athens; sometimes the deputies created by universal suffrage represent the people and act in their name under their almost immediate supervision.[22]

The great novelty of American democracy is less its legitimating principle or the annunciation of a new political dogma than the astonishing degree to which this dogma has been embodied in actual practice. Against fictional invocations and political mystiques, Tocqueville highlights the reality of popular rule in the United States and the variety of political forms it has produced.[23] The bulk of volume one of *Democracy in America* is a detailed description of these forms. Stating that "the principle of sovereignty of the people hovers over the entire political system of the Anglo-Americans," Tocqueville announces that "each page" of his book will "show some new applications of this doctrine" and explore the wide variety of institutional arrangements that allow the people to exercise political power.[24]

Popular Sovereignty and Constitutionalism

Tocqueville depicts the full range of American institutions—from the local township, in which he glimpses an image of ancient Athens, through the state governments to the grand design of the federal Union—as different modes of popular self-rule. In his view, the difference between spontaneous and established associations, or between direct and representative institutions—could be understood as functional. They are various applications of the same popular principle "according to the necessity of the case." This is why, as one chapter heading has it, "It Can Be Strictly Said that In the United States It Is the People Who Govern."[25]

In the American context, this claim about the continuity between participatory and representative institutions, or between abstract popular legitimation and people's actual rule, is striking. The *Federalist Papers*, the classic exposition of the United States Constitution, maintain that the novelty of the American polity consists in its departure from ancient models of direct democracy and the invention of the modern representative republic. In the terse formulation of the *Federalist* no. 63, "The true distinction between [ancient republics] and the American governments, lies *in the total exclusion of the people, in their collective capacity*, from any share in the *latter*."[26] To be sure, the preamble to the Constitution, with its invocation of "We the People" anchors the institutional arrangement in the will of the people, and expressly draws its authority from this popular source. And yet, as David Ciepley has argued, the idea that the people as a body would wield inalienable sovereignty "seemed not the constitutional solution, but the very constitutional problem," which the American framers set out to address. Such a monolithic sovereignty was in their view no less antithetical to limited government than the sovereignty of an absolute monarch. Any direct intervention of the people "in their collective capacity," which is to say "in their sovereign capacity," in the task of ruling would be a threat to the constitutional order.[27]

In expounding and defending the project for the Constitution, the *Federalist* articulates the paradox that underpins all modern constitutional regimes.[28] Possessed of an inalienable right to sovereignty, and of the power to collectively determine their fate, the people are viewed as the ultimate source of governmental authority and legitimacy. And yet, to be liberal, the exercise of this authority must be constrained by legal principles and channeled into separate constitutional forms. This tension between unbounded sovereignty and limited power lies at the heart of theoretical attempts, dating back to the seventeenth century, to distinguish sovereignty from government: what Rousseau called the "general will" of society from particular implementations or acts of enforcement of that will.[29] To address this conundrum, the framers designed institutions whose republican form ensured that the people, while authorizing the governing power, do not exercise it. According to the *Federalist* and its later interpreters, modern representative government effectively replaced direct popular rule (or governmental sovereignty) with "constituent" or "indirect" sovereignty. Unlimited in theory, this constituent power is confined to the moment of ratification. By contrast, the actual power of the government is constrained by the solemn agreement to constitute and delegate it, and by the clear terms of that agreement: the Constitution. So construed, the "indirect" sovereignty of the people helps to counter any claims, whether monarchical or majoritarian, to unlimited power thus guarantee a liberal order. For its part, the popular sovereign is reduced to an imaginary body and a constitutional fiction. Invoked for the purpose of creating a certain kind of political and legal reality, the sovereign people is not, beyond the moment of creation, supposed to partake in that reality.[30]

Although deeply indebted to the political vision of the *Federalist*, in *Democracy in America* Tocqueville advances a different view.[31] Like Rousseau, he remains unconvinced that modern liberty and its signature—representative institutions—can be sustained without ancient elements; or that the people once summoned to the sovereign task of constituting a new order can be easily dispensed with—put to sleep, as it were—through a legal fiction.[32] Following Rousseau, in both volumes of *Democracy in America* Tocqueville insists on the indispensability of popular participation.

In *The Social Contract* (1762), Rousseau famously rejects the proposition that the sovereign authority can be represented. His conceptual distinction between sovereignty and government underscores the irreducibility of the one to the other, thus resisting the claim that the representatives of the people could ever fully speak for the people themselves. This resistance, Bryan Garsten has proposed, is motivated by fear of two kinds of usurpation that might ensue either when governors can claim the people's sovereign authority for themselves, or, conversely, when the people, imbued with the power of its sovereignty, would take to governing. Waxing poetic about direct democracy, Rousseau points out that, precisely because it collapses sovereignty into government, this "perfect government" is made for "a people of Gods." Where humans are concerned,

> It is not good that he who makes the laws execute them, nor that the body of the people turn its attention away from general considerations, to devote it to particular objects....
>
> A people which would never misuse the Government, would not misuse independence either; a people which would always govern well would not need to be governed.[33]

For Rousseau, in other words, republican freedom faces two kinds of danger: when the government claims to be sovereign; and when the sovereign people presume to govern. Whereas the American-style representative government and the idea of "indirect sovereignty" guard against popular usurpation, they seem less well-suited—or so Rousseau's followers have charged—to protect against reducing the people's sovereignty to mere fiction, or to resist the domination of the many by the few.[34] Neither does the conceptual distinction between sovereignty and government by itself suffice to guarantee a liberal order.[35] An attentive reader of Rousseau as well as of French revolutionary history, Tocqueville contends that what sustains such an order are institutions, practices, and not least mindsets that ensure popular accountability and enable the people's active and orderly participation in the task of government.[36]

In volume one of *Democracy in America*, Tocqueville labored to show that the explicit invocation of the popular principle commits the American polity to a standard of legitimacy that makes it inescapably beholden to public opinion and popular approval. More than that, he passionately argued for the necessity of ongoing popular participation, and celebrated the institutional arrangements, informal practices, and widespread understandings that make such an engagement possible and salutary. Tocqueville credited popular rule and the participatory spirit of public life in America with the "real advantages" of America's democratic government; advantages that notably include economic dynamism, public spiritedness, commitment to rights, and respect for law. Meddling in politics and the habits of engagement resulting from it instill civic virtue and advance the people's grasp of institutional rules and forms. It is the people's widespread perception—and, to a significant degree, the reality—of being in charge that sustain their commitment to democratic institutions and constitutional norms. Without this popular commitment, Tocqueville claimed, the balanced government mandated by the Constitution would be a mere theory, and the Constitution itself would be reduced to a "dead letter."[37]

The second volume of *Democracy in America* generalizes the American experience to develop a comprehensive argument for the crucial importance of civic associations for liberal democracy. It insists on the indispensability of a pluralistic public sphere through which citizens can directly partake in and shape civic life. Tocqueville's emphatic defense of participatory institutions and broad-based popular involvement—what we have come to call civil society—is based on the claim that actual involvement in public life is a crucial element of civic education, and a precondition for sustaining the habits of freedom and the constitutional allegiance of the citizens. Alongside the legal enshrining of constitutional rights, democratic liberty requires the active exercise of those rights: the opportunity to partake, individually and collectively, in determining one's present and future. Important as the Bill of Rights is for setting judicial standards and legal guarantees, it is only by ongoing practice and sustained exposure to the practical exigencies of governing that these rights can be securely enshrined in the mind and hearts of the citizens.[38]

Freedom, in short, implies sovereignty, and the meaning of sovereignty is participation in ruling: a government, in Abraham Lincoln's words, not only *of* the people and *for* the people, but in decisive ways *by* the people as well.[39] So understood, self-government defies a clear-cut distinction between direct and representative forms, between constitutional mechanisms and popular power. Both are indispensable for a free democracy. Both require the support of public opinion and of a vibrant and broadly shared political culture. From Tocqueville's perspective, then, the claim of the *Federalist* no. 63 is at once accurate and false. True, there is no political forum in which the whole of the American people, or any modern people, could exercise collective sovereignty or partake in the government directly. And yet, to be viable, a representative system based on *the total exclusion of the people in their collective capacity* nonetheless requires broad-based political capacity and popular allegiance. Such a system is thus in need of institutions and practices, associations and rituals that foster allegiance and sustain this capacity.[40]

For Tocqueville, then, the various institutions—direct and representative, local, state and national, formal and informal—through which popular sovereignty is expressed and enacted are diverse instances of a single principle. Despite the variety of ways in which they articulate and embody this principle, all institutional arrangements answer to the same legitimating source, the people, and to a single court, public opinion.[41] These forms, moreover, are interdependent. Crucial for sustaining the people's grasp on and trust in institutions and norms, participatory practices are a bulwark of the constitutional order. Representative institutions, in turn, provide the conditions and the expertise on which local and participatory forms rely.[42]

Institutions and Mores

Let us return to modern democracy's original dilemma: the choice between liberal democracy and democratic despotism. What makes American democracy *liberal*, on Tocqueville's account, is its being robustly *republican*: the many ways in which the people actually participate in governing, as opposed to merely being said to do so. Beyond a legitimating fiction or political slogan, Tocqueville stresses the reality of popular rule in the United States, and extrapolates from it a general prescription for liberal democracy, or rather a method of keeping democracy liberal: namely, by multiplying the centers of popular power rather than curtailing that power.[43]

This line of argument, often branded 'republican' in contradistinction to 'liberal,' has been met with considerable skepticism both in Tocqueville's century and in ours. The gist of the critique can be found in Benjamin Constant's 1819 lecture on "The Liberty of the Ancients Compared with that of the Moderns." Constant contends that ancient liberty, which he defined as active participation in sovereignty, was conditioned by small-scale societies based on slavery and warfare. Modern commercial polities, whose citizenry is engaged in productive activity, can afford little leisure or have little desire for the robust political participation that classical authors extolled as true freedom. Modern liberty means above all the right to private enjoyment in a sphere of life uncontrolled by the state. Thus redefined, liberty requires representation: delegating political activity and concern for the public good to professionalized politicians and periodically reviewing their work through elections.[44]

As chapter two will argue, Tocqueville is fully alert to the differences between ancient and modern society and makes these differences both an explicit concern and a framing distinction. Nevertheless, *Democracy in America* calls into question and considerably modifies the historicization of liberty advanced by Constant. Recuperating Rousseau's critique of representation, Tocqueville argues that without opportunities for citizens' intervention in public affairs, the conditions for nondomination and private enjoyment cannot be maintained—a point Constant acknowledges.[45] What is more, against nineteenth-century and latter-day critiques of direct participation as impracticable in large-scale commercial societies, Tocqueville offers an argument that is as intellectually astute as it is institutionally nuanced.

Participation, in his view, need not mean that all citizens take part in the same forums, at the same time, with the same degree of commitment. Just as the economy is a network of many different modes, practices and projects, with the result that general employment does not require that all labor on the same job, or work the same hours with a similar level of productivity, so too the polity is an ensemble of institutional settings and a myriad of civic efforts, formal and informal, that afford diverse opportunities for acquiring skills and eliciting civic contributions of different kinds. Moreover, while needed to defend individual rights from the overreach of the state, citizens' engagement is also necessary to guard against the other major threat to democratic freedom: individual self-isolation. Protecting citizens' privacy from the encroachment of state power, broad-based civic participation is indispensable to counter the corrosive effects of individualism that Tocqueville diagnoses as an inherent democratic ill.

To be free, then, a democratic people must find practical institutional ways to determine its own will rather than acquiesce in elite fabrications of that will. Not the sleeping sovereign of the Constitution, but an alert and active democratic public is what defines a free democracy and constitutes the fullest expression of popular sovereignty. And yet, as Tocqueville knew from ancient history as much as from the violent upheavals of the French Revolution, actualizing such a free democracy meets with considerable challenges.[46] Popular participation and the mobilization of the civic passions that propel it are as much a danger for a free society as they may be said to be its prerequisite. While pointing to the young American republic as empirical evidence of its possibility under modern conditions, Tocqueville's *Democracy in America* is a lengthy rumination on the circumstances that make broad-based popular engagement possible and render it supportive rather than destructive of the public weal. Carefully sifting through the various factors—"circumstances, origin, enlightenment, and above all, mores"—that enable popular sovereignty in America, Tocqueville underscores the crucial importance of mores, which he defines as "the whole moral and intellectual state of a people." And he points to that demonstration as a key objective of his work.[47]

In the final chapter of volume one, Tocqueville reflects on the durability of republican institutions. As he argues, what crucially sustains the democratic republic in America is the degree to which the popular principle penetrates all of society and has come to define it.

> In the United States, the dogma of the sovereignty of the people is not an isolated doctrine that is attached neither to the habits nor to the ensemble of dominant ideas; you can on the contrary envisage it as the last link in a chain of opinions that envelops the entire Anglo-American world.[48]

Referring back to the social state, Tocqueville argues that popular sovereignty is a pervasive principle that informs every aspect of social organization and political life: from the individual to the family and the neighborhood, through the local township and the state, all the way up to the great body of the Union. "Recognized by mores; proclaimed by the laws," popular sovereignty is constitutive not simply of political institutions, but of social relations, ideas, and practices, as well as religious beliefs.[49]

Throughout volume one, Tocqueville highlights the critical role of republican mores in upholding the institutional edifice and sustaining an orderly republic. Having thus penetrated the political culture, popular sovereignty is the backbone both of the institutional arrangement and of American self-understanding. The federal Union, Tocqueville asserts, is "only a modification of the republic, a summary of political principles spread throughout the entire society before the federal government existed, and subsisting there independently of it." Far from deflating the United States Constitution, or downplaying the institutional imagination of its framers, this statement points to what Tocqueville considers the key factor that conditioned its extraordinary success: the widespread diffusion and internalization of republican norms and practices across broad sections of the people.[50]

"Thus in the United States the generative principle of the republic is the same one that regulates most human actions." Constituting the vital core of the citizens' self-understanding, republicanism in Tocqueville's view is the substance of the American civic and national identity. It "penetrates the ideas, the opinions and all the habits of the Americans at the same time that it is established in their laws."[51] So pervasive is the hold of this principle on the social organization and the collective self-image of American society that to abolish it and change the political order would require nothing less than founding a new people:

> If the republican principles must perish in America, they will succumb only after a long social effort, frequently interrupted, often resumed; several times they will seem to arise again, and will disappear never to return only when an entirely new people will have taken the place of those who exist today.[52]

Tocqueville, to repeat, argues that the durability of republican institutions crucially depends on mores. And he points to peoplehood—to collective identity and self-understanding—as the repository of these mores. Democracy, in his view, is not simply a system of government but a comprehensive political culture, whose foundations are lodged in the moral character and disposition of the people and run deep into the past. This, however, does not mean that democracy is unchanging, forged once and for all at the dawn of society. Should societies be entirely determined by their origins, there would be little Tocqueville could say beyond observing the fact, and hardly a useful lesson he could teach his French readers. This illiberal lesson, moreover, would be difficult to reconcile with his insistence on the inherent dynamism of the democratic social state and its American instantiation.[53] Likewise, although Tocqueville's account highlights the English ancestry of the first colonists, and stresses the role of Puritanism in shaping American political culture—so much so that he "seem[ed] to see the whole destiny of America in the first Puritan who reached its shores, like the whole human race in the first man"—he does not thereby suggest either that these factors can fully explain the

American experience; or that to perpetuate republican culture, future generations must be imbued with Puritan radicalism.[54] If religious fervor was the point of departure and a critical factor that enabled bold experimentation and the innovative institutions of Britain's North American colonies, a different spirit was necessary to develop and capitalize on these institutions. As Harvey Mansfield quips, the "point of departure needed to be departed from."[55]

Arguably, it is to underscore this point that Tocqueville recapitulates toward the end of volume one the causes that sustain free institutions in America. Reiterating the importance of the point of departure for shaping American political life, he places it under "accidental and providential causes," alongside geopolitical circumstances and natural resources. Originally standing as "generative fact," and a "first cause," the colonial beginnings become part of a larger set, which Tocqueville expressly evaluates as less important than laws and mores.[56]

On the other hand, whereas the "reflection and choice" epitomized by the constitutional framing serve more than heritage to maintain the democratic republic in the United States, these factors in turn are secondary to mores, which, like the social state, are only partly chosen, and though changeable and changing over time, are not easily addressed by legal means and policy efforts. In short, if societies are not fully determined by their origins any more than individuals are, they are not entirely free to develop at will. In both cases, as discussed in the introductory chapter, the sphere of choice is circumscribed by a "fatal circle" drawn by a combination of many different factors. And the preservation of democratic freedom crucially depends on the sober recognition of its limits.[57]

Peoplehood

Having probed the ramifications of popular sovereignty and the conditions that have allowed Americans "to establish and maintain" republican government, Tocqueville concludes his survey of American institutions by analyzing the dilemmas faced by the

American Union of his day, and of its future prospects. Volume one's final chapter on "The Three Races that Inhabit the Territory of the United States," the longest in the book, refocuses the inquiry from the political system to the issue of race: a term that for Tocqueville marked cultural rather than natural differences, including social, economic, and political dimensions. The so-called "race chapter" makes it clear that the people whose institutions Tocqueville has examined—"the Anglo-Americans"—make up only a fraction of the population of the United States; and that even this dominant fraction did not at the time of his writing share a self-definition. Tocqueville's assessment of the prospects for the United States, the liberal democratic society par excellence, gestures at the construction of comprehensive peoplehood and the integration of differences—racial, institutional, material, and moral—as both decisive for and the most momentous challenge to the Union's existence. If the principle of popular sovereignty had become "the law of laws" and inextricable core of American democracy, the meaning of peoplehood or who can belong to the people was the great question on which hung the destiny and future of the American Union.[58]

Tocqueville's poignant ruminations on America society's demographic and cultural diversity evince his concerns about overcoming racial inequality and the limits of democratic inclusion. Presciently, they point out the three deep-seated prejudices—"the prejudice of the master, the prejudice of race, and finally the prejudice of the white"—that would need to be overcome for full integration to be possible.[59] Along with the deeply ingrained prejudices of the European population, the crucial obstacles Tocqueville identifies are the very republican mores the bulk of his work has celebrated. This prompts him to contemplate the vexing conundrums of liberty.

> If a man happens to stand outside of the prejudices of religion, of country, of race, and this man is king, he can work surprising revolutions in society. An entire people cannot so to speak rise above itself in this way.[60]

Tocqueville claims that an absolute king or benevolent despotism—of the kind the British Empire exercised over its colonies—would be better placed to combat the deep-seated prejudices that stand in the way of racial inclusion. Situated above and beyond the social body, such a despot represents a superior principle that could "work surprising revolutions" in political institutions and moral opinion. A republic, which Tocqueville defines as "the slow and tranquil action of society on itself," cannot easily or suddenly effect such a revolution.[61]

If in 1835, Tocqueville could not foresee the possibility of racial equality working itself out, he was no less pessimistic about overcoming the fault lines within the group that at the time enjoyed exclusive membership in the American people: the whites. Calling attention to the challenges posed by racial diversity as decisive for democracy's future, he spotlighted intra-white difference as the most immediate danger to the Union's existence. Long before Lincoln's fateful speech, Tocqueville pointed to the divided house—half free and half slave—of the American Union as unlikely to long endure, notwithstanding the shared political culture and ethno-religious identity between the North and the South.[62] Differences in mores and way of life within what may otherwise appear as a homogenous group posed a formidable threat to the Union's future.

Scholars have uncovered numerous shortcomings in Tocqueville's account of Jacksonian America. Critics charge that Tocqueville paid insufficient attention to material conditions and the political economy of the United States. His exposure to American society was largely shaped by and limited to elite opinions. The account he gave of the South was superficial or not sufficiently nuanced. And he seems to have misjudged the strength and capacity of the federal Union as well as its potential for addressing racial difference. To explain Tocqueville's blindness, some cite his own racial prejudice and allege sympathies with Southern secessionism. Others urge the need to get beyond Tocqueville altogether.[63]

These critiques are not without merit. Although the longest in the book, the race chapter does not match the depth of consideration, or the empirical standards set in the rest of Tocqueville's work. Intensely rhetorical, it is, as Jennifer Pits puts it, "a tableau more than an argument." More problematic still, though observing the depravities of removal, slavery, and segregation, Tocqueville did not in the end withdraw his overall endorsement of American democratic practices. Perhaps he did see potential after all.[64]

For all its limitations, however, Tocqueville's analysis was remarkably prescient. As the following case study illustrates, it grasped the fundamental alternatives the American Union was facing, the overall dynamic of the federal bond, and where it was likely headed at that particular moment in American history. More pertinently for my purpose, Tocqueville's critical consideration of the constitutional politics of the antebellum American Union contains a broader analytical argument for why a modern constitutional democracy based on the principle of popular sovereignty requires a strong sovereign power, and its preconditions: a coherent political identity and a shared vision of "We the People."[65]

Case Study I: Constitutional Politics in the Antebellum American Union

Tocqueville visited the United States from 1831 to 1832. During his nine month sojourn he witnessed some of the events and policy conundrums that marked Andrew Jackson's presidency, including the forced migration of Indian tribes, the debates about extending slavery and statehood to new territories, the outcry surrounding the national bank, and last but not least the nullification controversy: the most significant clash over sovereignty before the American Civil War. Drawing on this experience, in the final pages of the first volume of *Democracy in America*, originally published in 1835, Tocqueville anticipated Southern secession. He also predicted that, were the Union to break down, it would disintegrate into regional units rather than revert to the original states. Both of these predictions turned out to be correct. Yet, if Tocqueville was tragically prophetic, he also missed the mark in important ways. In 1835, he doubted the Union's capacity and will to fight in defense of its integrity. He also failed to see how such a military effort could be galvanized and legitimated in a constitutional polity based on popular consent. Last but not least, he was pessimistic about the Union's long-term capacity to integrate racial minorities. Tocqueville's analysis of American federalism should be assessed in this light.[66]

Throughout the first volume of *Democracy in America*, Tocqueville refers to the United States alternately as one people and as a confederation of sovereign nations. Far from cavalier, this ambiguity in usage pinpoints what he considered the central dilemma of the federal constitution: the indeterminate character of the American people. Tocqueville devotes the penultimate section of volume one's final chapter to clarifying this dilemma. Following Tocqueville's considerations of the plight of Indians and the Blacks, the section on the whites is an extended rumination on the meaning—and politics—of peoplehood.[67]

Democracy in America contains two accounts of the federal system. The first, appearing in part one of the first volume, is a comprehensive survey of the federal constitution and its most important provisions. Closely following the arguments of the *Federalist*, this initial assessment enumerates the successes of the constitutional founding. It celebrates the charter as "the most perfect of all known federal constitutions" based on "an entirely new theory that will be marked as a great discovery in the political science of our day."[68] Among its innovations, Tocqueville highlights that the United States Constitution vests the federal authority with the power to not only dictate the law but also execute it. Further, it addresses itself not merely to member states as is typical for federations but directly to individual citizens, as is the case with unitary governments. At the same time, since the powers of the central government are enumerated, its sovereignty remains "hindered and incomplete" and its use "is not dangerous for freedom." Hence the Union's authority is neither strictly national nor strictly federal. By integrating elements of both, the framers devised an unprecedented political form that, for lack of a "new word that ought to express the new thing," Tocqueville calls an "incomplete national government."[69]

Echoing Montesquieu's discussion of federations, Tocqueville depicts American federalism as a unique arrangement combining advantages that are otherwise in tension: the freedom and civic virtue characteristic of small republics with the dynamism, capacity, and resources of large monarchical states.[70] Emphasizing the Union's benefits, he affirms its stated end—to preserve the self-government of localities, while unifying their commercial and political strength—as well as the means to achieve it: institutional innovation. Among the factors that made this innovation possible, Tocqueville foregrounds the geopolitical location and relative "homogeneity in civilization" of the American republics.[71]

If Tocqueville's first assessment of American federalism is for the most part laudatory, the second is skeptical.[72] Prefaced by a searching account of the conditions of the Indians and the Blacks, it paints a dimmer picture. If the Constitution's political goal was to combine local diversity with security and strength, and reconcile freedom and civic virtue with governing capacity, on a second look Tocqueville judges the Union's actual ability to deliver on its foundational promise as structurally limited. Running through the final chapter of the first volume of *Democracy* is an indictment of the United States government's failure to protect the Black and native populations residing on its territory and under its jurisdiction. This failure was due in great part to the weakness of the federal authority, which lacked essential prerogatives or the real power to assert them.[73] Yet, if racial minorities were the main victims of these limits in governing capacity, they were not the only ones. The very striving for "a more perfect union" was threatened by the federal government's weakness.

The Trouble with the Union

In revisiting the question of federalism, Tocqueville draws on his firsthand experience of the policy debates that convulsed Jackson's presidency. Zooming in on contested policies and their immediate outcomes, he seeks to show why the federal Union, despite all its constitutional prerogatives, is "by its very nature a weak government" whose ability to get things done, even within the limited sphere of its enumerated powers, is hamstrung by the conflict between powerful interests. Among the most momentous of these Jacksonian debates was the so-called nullification controversy. Begun as a disagreement over an 1828 federal law raising import tariffs, the controversy escalated into a constitutional crisis and the most significant contest over sovereignty in antebellum America.[74]

At the center of this crisis was Senator John C. Calhoun of South Carolina, Jackson's former vice president, whose key contribution to the political debate was to propose a theory—the so-called "compact view"—of the federal Union. The Constitution, Calhoun argued, was not, as the *Federalist* had alleged, a unitary government authorized by a single national people, but a voluntary agreement between sovereign states and their separate peoples. In uniting, the states had never given up their original sovereignty. This included the duty to interpret federal law and, if need be, to suspend or nullify its execution. As a consequence of this original compact, the states have retained what in German constitutional jargon is called the *Kompetenz-Kompetenz*: the competence to decide who has the right to decide.[75]

Tocqueville zooms in on Calhoun's constitutional theory and the politics of South Carolina in order to consider the challenges they posed to the federal system. While expressly rejecting Calhoun's thesis as de jure untenable and synonymous with anarchy, Tocqueville's analysis corroborates it as a matter of fact. Even though Calhoun's "compact view" neither held water as constitutional interpretation, nor carried the day in the Senate, it was borne out in practice by South Carolina's power to assert her position.[76] Tocqueville thus suggests that the relationship between the Union and the states is not simply or primarily juridical—that is fixed once and for all by the Constitution, and its provisions—but *political*. It is liable to negotiation and renegotiation in light of the changing power balance. As Chief Justice Marshall put the point, the Constitution was "incomplete." Both as a jurisprudential doctrine and as a political and social reality, the American Union, and its complex matrix of powers and interests, was a work in progress.[77]

Whereas Tocqueville's initial account stresses the advantages of the federal constitution and the factors that conditioned its adoption, the concluding chapter of volume one highlights the fragility of the federal Union. Having praised its ingenious theory and unprecedented political form, Tocqueville shows that in practice the Union's "incomplete national government" is an unstable equilibrium that can evolve in one of two directions: greater integration or dismemberment. To clarify the dilemma faced by the American Union of his day, he sketches a theory of sovereignty.

Tocqueville distinguishes between three objects of sovereignty. At one extreme are national interests like "war and diplomacy" that affect the entire polity and are "by their nature" the prerogative of the general government. At the other end stand objects like local budgets that are "provincial in their nature" and "can only be conveniently treated in the locality itself." In between the purely national and purely local, one finds a number of mixed objects that, while general in scope and pertaining to all individuals, need not be uniformly regulated. The example Tocqueville offers is the right to define the civil and political status of citizens. Since, on the one hand, any political association by definition must have control over the purely "national objects" and, on the other, local interests are of little import to the country at large, it is the intermediary acts of sovereignty that determine whether the ultimate authority rests in the center or remains in the member states. Put simply, the difference between unitary and divided sovereignty hangs on the relative degree of state centralization.[78]

Tocqueville's threefold classification of acts of sovereignty draws upon and complicates the distinction between governmental and administrative centralization introduced in volume one's account of the New England township.[79] This account is the locus classicus for Tocqueville's advocacy of local self-government as a crucial site of direct citizen participation. As in the discussion of federalism, the New England chapter champions two sets of political desiderata: first, the local self-government that enables vibrant pluralism, and second, capacious political union. To be free and strong, a democratic society requires both. In this context, Tocqueville praises American participatory practices and decentralized administration for its ability to reconcile these potentially competing objectives. With equal passion he excoriates the centralizing tendencies of his native France, in which he saw a foreshadowing of democratic despotism.

And yet, while a critique of *administrative* centralization is a central feature of Tocqueville's American analysis, Tocqueville declares in the same chapter that *governmental* centralization is indispensable for the stability and prosperity of any political body and blames "all the miseries of feudal society" on the insufficient concentration of governing power.[80] Pointing to the medieval principalities and contemporary German states (before their 1871 unification) as examples of a baneful lack of political centralization, he maintains that strong central authority is key to a functioning economy, effective foreign policy, and the rule of law. Modern democratic society in Tocqueville's view cannot exist without centralized government.[81] This simultaneous endorsement of administrative decentralization and political centralization shows that local self-rule need not—indeed *should* not interfere with the exercise of sovereignty by the central government. It also suggests that federalism, which connotes a partition of sovereignty, and decentralized institutions are not coterminous.[82]

Sovereignty and Peoplehood

Tocqueville's theory of sovereignty features two aspects worth highlighting. On the one hand, the exercise of public authority consists in a variety of acts and objects of sovereignty that can be discharged by different political and administrative units. On the other, while particular acts can be delegated to multiple agents the sovereign power itself, as a draft note puts it, is "always a single being." This being is the people.[83] In other words, though possible to delegate, sovereignty is indivisible. One can distribute governmental tasks and competences between various branches, design decentralized institutions, and carefully delineate levels of government and their relations. Even so, the center of gravity is one. Where this center is to be found, Tocqueville argues, depends neither on juridical fiat nor institutional calculus, but on the locus of civic attachment.

As Tocqueville's abstract considerations aim to clarify, what distinguishes a unitary government from a confederation is not *whether* there is sovereign authority but *where* this authority is located: in the constituent bodies or at the center. This in turn depends on the nature of the associates. National government is constituted by simple individuals; it is the political expression of a single people. The constituents of a confederation are peoples, each retaining its collective identity and the capacity to assert it. While national governments have a tendency to over-centralize and despoil localities of their "natural and necessary prerogatives," confederations tend "naturally" to dismemberment, forced apart by competing claims to autonomy.[84]

This alternative, Tocqueville claims, was well understood by the American framers who strove to give the federal authority "a separate existence and preponderate strength" or, in the language of the *Federalist*, to establish a supreme power. Their original intention notwithstanding, the founders

> were limited by the very conditions of the problem that they had to resolve. They had not been charged with constituting the

government of a single people, but with regulating the association of several peoples; and whatever their desires, they always had to end up dividing the exercise of sovereignty.[85]

In this partition, the states were charged not only with the conduct of strictly local affairs but with so-called mixed objects as well, which included the competence to define who could be a citizen.[86] In light of this division, Tocqueville argues, the seat of preponderant power remained in the states. Despite the Union's novel form, he diagnoses the American polity as a species of confederacy inherently liable to conflicts of sovereignty and potentially to dissolution. Although the ingenious institutional arrangement reduced the probability of such a conflict, it could not eliminate it. To explain why this is so, Tocqueville abandons the language of legal theory and explores the psychological effects of dividing the exercise of sovereignty: the split of citizens' allegiance. Underlying the juridical problem of sovereignty is the question about "the natural course of the human heart."[87]

In Tocqueville's account, while the Union is entrusted with the largest and most general interests of the polity—its independence and grandeur—these "have only a questionable influence over individual happiness." Though necessary in moments of crisis, the actions of the federal government are rare and its authority is little felt in times of prosperity and peace. The Union, moreover, rests on a complicated theory and "legal fictions" that are difficult to grasp. It "exists so to speak only in the minds."[88] The states, on the other hand, exert a direct influence on private interests whose importance and utility are palpable and easy to grasp. In contrast to the "artificial" and reasoned bond that ties Americans to the federal government, the states command a "natural" and "lively attachment," intimately linked with the patriotic "instinct" and self regarding passions of the citizenry. Much older and "born with the people themselves," the state governments have established "necessary relations" with their constituency and form an integral part of memories, sentiments, and habits. The direct control the states exercise over individuals' lives and fortunes secure them "the love and prejudices of the people."[89]

So while the Union is recent, remote, and abstract—or, as Tocqueville has it, an "ideal nation"—real political power resides in the states. What makes this power and grounds its sovereignty is not "money and soldiers," but received ideas, established practices, and deeply rooted attachments that fix the citizens' primary allegiance to the state governments.[90] For all its constitutional prerogatives, the Union is "by its very nature a weak government that more than any other needs the free support of the governed in order to subsist." Despite the efforts of the framers, in Tocqueville's judgment the federal authority has neither separate existence nor preponderant force: it is not sovereign.[91]

Tocqueville indicates that, so long as the Union remains a "legal fiction" unsupported by the instinctive loyalty and passionate commitment of the citizenry, it will lack the actual capacity for, if not the formal right to, self-determination. Contingent on the converging interests of the states and their unanimous will to remain united, the federal government's persistence will be "nothing more than a happy accident."[92] The long-term prospects of the federation, therefore, depend on its becoming the primary locus of citizens' allegiance. Tocqueville devotes the bulk of his reflections on the Union's future to studying the conditions that generate popular loyalty and shape its direction.

Forging Allegiance

Among the conditions that generate popular loyalty, the constitutional bond itself, though important, is not decisive. On Tocqueville's account, the federal form of government reflects the diversity of the original colonies and their unwillingness to relinquish their autonomy. Designed to protect this autonomy, the Constitution perpetuates existing sectional divisions. By recognizing the distinct identity of the states and endowing them with legal means to defend it, the federal elements embedded in the fundamental charter commit the Union to the partition of sovereignty and effectively reinforce its dependence on the interests and will of the states.[93]

To be sure, Tocqueville acknowledges the Constitution's success in tempering the centrifugal tendencies of American society, thus leaving "the new republic time to settle in."[94] Yet, by highlighting the extraordinary circumstances that assisted its ratification, he signals the contingent character of this success.[95] The Constitution works as a kind of palliative. It addresses the symptoms but not the causes of possible conflict over sovereignty. As Tocqueville's discussion of the nullification affair shows, in defending their autonomy, states elaborate constitutional interpretations that serve their sectional interests. In so doing, they weaponize the Constitution as an instrument in a political game, setting vital precedents in the process.[96] Put differently, although the federal constitution crucially facilitated integration and created the framework for peaceful coexistence, its viability depends on the norms and motivations, ambitions and capacity of political actors and their constituencies. The institutional arrangement alone cannot shape these motivations or foster the civic attachment and cross-sectional solidarity necessary to strengthen the Union and guarantee its future.

If the Constitution is not by itself sufficient to produce political integration, nor are economic or geopolitical interests. Surveying the fifty-year dynamics of the federal bond, Tocqueville shows that the states' perception of material interests varies according to circumstances. The rapid growth in wealth and the precipitous, "revolutionary" expansion of the Union had only made these perceptions less stable. While there certainly were economic arguments for declaring independence from Britain, and later for seeking a "more perfect Union," it was the sense of necessity or public danger, Tocqueville argues, more than the political or commercial advantage, that prompted the American people to "rise above itself" and extend federal authority.[97]

If the federal founding was crucially enabled by security concerns, the very success of the Union in addressing these concerns obscures its raison d'être and encourages a backlash of particularism—so much so that, in Tocqueville's view, "the greatest danger that threatens the United States arises from their very prosperity."[98] Though in fact useful to all its members, the Union seems indispensable to none of them. No longer perceived as necessary, the federal bond comes to be seen as a "nuisance":

> In general they desired to remain united, and in each particular fact they tended to become independent again. The principle of confederation was each day more easily accepted and less applied; thus the federal government itself, by creating order and peace, brought about its decline. As soon as this disposition of minds began to show itself outwardly, party men who live on the passions of the people began to exploit it to their profit.[99]

Tocqueville's analysis points out a profound paradox: the more successful the Union becomes, the less it is desired. This paradox seems to belie or complicate "one of the main tenets of political science" and of public policy: that political legitimacy rests on institutional performance. In light of this tenet, institutions need to deliver to be perceived as legitimate. The more they deliver, the greater the citizens' satisfaction with the political order, the more legitimate this order appears. Conversely, when crisis occurs, the tendency is to see it as a result of institutional incapacity.[100]

And yet, under certain conditions, the very opposite may be the case: the more the institutional order succeeds in the sense of empowering its constituencies, and making them feel strong and secure, the less indispensable it appears, and the more likely it is that it will be contested. Precisely this dynamic prompts Tocqueville to declare that material interests and instrumental loyalty, even when effective in promoting unity in the first place, may not be enough to sustain it.

The inhabitants of the United States speak a great deal about their love of country; I admit that I do not trust this considered patriotism that is based upon interest and that interest, by changing object, can destroy.[101]

But why are material interests insufficient? One reason Tocqueville gives is that, while all parts of the Union had grown in prosperity, they had not grown at the same speed. Differentiated progress is especially irksome in polities premised on equality and consent, and it poses distinct challenges to confederations. Since peoples "confederate only to gain equal advantages from union," unequal gain becomes a source of grievance that erodes public trust. A situation where some appear to benefit more than others undermines the federal bond and the states' confidence in the legitimacy of the institutional arrangement.[102]

Having noted the unequal pace of development, Tocqueville traces the reasons for that inequality to differences in mores. Probing the compatibility of what he calls "immaterial" or "non-material interests" between the states, he judges the American people—that is the white population that alone could claim civic membership—to be more unified and homogeneous than many an old European nation. Beneath the demographic and institutional diversity, he finds a great similarity of political, religious, and philosophical opinions, which he recognizes as distinctly American.

> From Maine to Florida, from the Missouri to the Atlantic Ocean, they believe that the origin of all legitimate powers is in the people. They conceive the same ideas on liberty and on equality; they profess the same opinions on the press, the right of association, the jury, the responsibility of the agents of power.[103]

Beyond common beliefs and political ideas, Americans are tied together by a shared sentiment of pride that separates them from all other peoples. While understanding their regime in terms of universal rights and "general principles that ought to rule human societies," they consider themselves "the only religious, enlightened and free people." Rejoicing in the success of their democratic institutions and seeing these as unique in the world, Americans "have an immense opinion of themselves, and they are not far from believing that they form a species apart in the human race."[104] Noting the intensity of national pride in America, Tocqueville claims that, however exaggerated, Americans' sense of exceptionalism and shared view of their uniqueness greatly reinforce their political bond—a point to which I will return in the following chapter.

Working against this widespread similitude of opinions, sentiments, and beliefs, Tocqueville observes a striking difference in moral character. Though joined in a commitment to the same republican principles and in a prideful sense of their national distinctness, owing to slavery, the Anglo-Americans stand divided into two diverging moral visions and markedly different social types. While slavery shaped institutional relations and economic life, in Tocqueville's diagnosis it is above all through the mores that the South's peculiar institution militates against the Union. Drawing the psychological profiles of the man of the North and of the South, Tocqueville puts on dramatic display the incompatible ways in which they view themselves and human life in general. Common cultural heritage, language, and allegiance to constitutional norms notwithstanding, he notes a profound difference in their disposition, mindset, and capacity, or what he calls "civilization."[105]

Whereas work, in the North, is synonymous with progress and well-being, slavery in the South puts a stigma on the very idea of labor. This prevents the Southern states from keeping up with the demographic and industrial boom of the North. The South's slower development manifests in its political influence as well. Having once been at the head of the Union, the slave-holding states grow indignant at their perceived decline, which they attribute to preferential treatment and domineering designs on the part of the commercial and manufacturing North. In effect, the confrontation of these two different outlooks on human life breeds a sense of inequality and with it distrust, envy, and hostile threats to exit the Union. In Tocqueville's account, differences in mores, perceptions, and passions—more than economic or political interests—endanger the integrity and future of the federation.[106]

Against this divisive tendency, Tocqueville detects a unifying countercurrent. Surveying the fifty-year history of the federation, he shows the ways in which decades of peaceful cohabitation have worked to the Union's advantage. The free circulation of things and ideas attenuates local prejudices, increasing the familiarity and interdependence between the various parts of the Union. The result is a significant degree of harmonization. From a merely imaginary and institutional being the Union gradually becomes a habit, a consistent aspect of the socioeconomic as well as the psychological reality. In addition, the mingling of populations and the constant stream of emigration from North to South "singularly favors the fusion of all provincial characters into one national character."[107]

In Tocqueville's account, while Americans progressively come to resemble each other, they do so not by blending into a composite mindset but by conforming to one predominant group: the North. The imperatives of commerce and the restless search for opportunity urge the inhabitants of New England to venture into the new territories of the West and spread throughout the Union.[108] As they migrate, Northerners bring along "their beliefs, their opinions, their mores." Serving as the commercial link that ties the states together, they gradually shape the federation in their own image. As Ralph Lerner puts the matter, by and by "the North colonizes the South."[109]

Tocqueville highlights this continuous migration from North to South and West as singularly favorable to the longevity of the federation. He attributes the influence of the North not only to expansionism and commercial strength, but also to the intellectual qualities and the moral vision that guides its way of life. Embodying most fully the distinctiveness of American society, "the civilization of the North seems destined to become the common measure against which all the rest must model themselves one day."[110]

Tocqueville's analysis of the prospects for the Union suggests that if the American republics remain united, their inhabitants will end up approximating the character of the Northerners. Not merely a consequence of their union, such convergence is also a necessary precondition for the United States to build a common destiny.

To sum up, Tocqueville views antebellum American federalism as inherently unstable and unlikely to last. While earlier in the work he describes the Union as charting a third way between national state and confederation, volume one's final chapter contends that, in the long run, the American Union faces a simple alternative: either to consolidate sovereignty and become one people, or wane into dissolution. To account for the practical political dilemmas of Jackson's presidency, Tocqueville elaborates a theory of sovereignty, defining it as the seat of "preponderant power." The fundaments of this power are neither material force ("money and soldiers") nor legal prerogatives, but mores and allegiance: the opinions, habits, and passions that make citizens recognize the government's authority and obey the laws. While pointing to the consolidation of sovereignty as a prerequisite for political longevity, Tocqueville's discussion of allegiance demonstrates that such consolidation cannot be achieved by political or legal means alone. As the American case substantiates, constitutional charters neither create nor destroy partitions of authority. At its best, the fundamental law gives institutional expression to and has moderating influence on powers and interests already present in society. Yet, if the fragmentation of sovereignty reflects existing divisions in the social body, this means that the unification of governing authority, and of the civic allegiance on which it rests, can only be achieved through processes of integration on the level of society.[111]

In Tocqueville's account the consolidation of sovereignty, and hence long-term political stability, depend on the possibility of harmonizing social differences and bridging political divides. As his comparative portrayal of the Americans of North and South illustrates, these divides are not primarily economic, ethno-religious, or racial. They have an ethical—what Tocqueville calls "immaterial"—dimension. By emphasizing the "immaterial" basis of people-building, his account of the American Union rejects the autonomy of law and politics as well as economics, and elaborates a sociocultural understanding of sovereignty. In light of this understanding, to raise the question of sovereignty is to ask what makes a people: How is a society held together as a viable political unit?

> What maintains a large number of citizens under the same government is much less the reasoned will to remain united than the *instinctive* and in a way *involuntary* accord that results from similarity of sentiments and resemblance of opinions.
>
> I will never admit that men form a society by the sole fact that they acknowledge the same leader and obey the same laws; there is a society only when men consider a great number of objects in the same way; when they have the same opinions on a great number of subjects; when, finally, the same facts give rise among them to the same impressions and the same thoughts.[112]

For Tocqueville, as for Rousseau, living under the same government and obeying the same laws is not enough to create or perpetuate a society. While necessary, these "intellectual bonds" are insufficient to bring about social cohesion or guarantee its persistence. Rather, the social glue needed for enduring coexistence issues from shared opinions, sentiments, and perceptions—in a word, mores—that bespeak tacit agreement about the purposes of communal life and the principles on which it rests. This convergence of passions and ideas across the social body is the effect of shared experience and habit rather than genes or deliberate choice. It issues from reciprocal action and living together, from mutual regard and interdependence, more than willful adherence to rational interest.[113]

Society, Tocqueville suggests, is the slow product of time. While it may well begin as a conventional arrangement or consideration of utility—as a social contract—for society to continue and achieve stability, the ties that hold individuals and groups together must become customary and spontaneous, hence, in a derivative sense, natural. Likewise, the political bond, beyond merely useful, must come to be perceived as necessary, and the association it represents must be seen as the "community of belonging *par excellence.*" Only by gaining primacy over particular interests and wills, thus transforming a political question into a social given, can the constitutional bond be shielded from opportunistic reconsideration and thereby endure.[114]

Tocqueville then seems to define society, and therewith peoplehood, as a political association that has become habitual, unreflective, and in a certain meaning of the word, involuntary. Made rather than born, it is the product of gradual convergence of perspectives and attitudes. Not an outcome of political deliberation and will, the social bond is the precondition for the existence of that will and the guarantor of its continuance. It results from abiding by the same laws and professing the same principles insofar as those principles and laws, while affecting the people as a whole, succeed in shaping what Rousseau calls "the State's genuine constitution," namely, the character and soul of the citizens.[115] Tocqueville's American analysis puts forward the formation of a distinctive moral character as a necessary condition of the people's existence, and of its enduring political and institutional expression.

As I discussed previously and return to in the following chapters, the convergence of character that Tocqueville postulates here need not mean substantive homogeneity or the absence of dissent. For society to be free, the consensus uniting different social groups can and, in Tocqueville's view, ought to include the right to contestation, as well as procedures that help negotiate and peacefully resolve disagreements. Indeed, the purpose of constitutionalism is to lay down both the parameters of consensus and the procedures that contestation should follow. Yet to ensure that pluralism and contestation do not result in debilitating polarization or separatist threats, there is a need for a broadly shared political identity and moral orientation.

Conclusion

Tocqueville concludes *Democracy in America*'s popular sovereignty chapter with a striking analogy: "The people rules the American political world as God rules the universe. It is the cause and the end of all things; everything arises from it and everything is absorbed by it."[116]

The people, Tocqueville seems to suggest, is to American democracy what God is to religion: the alpha and omega, its source and rationale. Not limited to America, this striking analogy elevates the people as a central category—and precondition—of democratic politics. It also suggests that, while faith in the people and its sovereignty is indispensable for democratic government, the way peoplehood and sovereignty are understood makes all the difference for the character and quality of popular rule. To understand the analogy as Tocqueville intends it, it may be helpful to recall how he viewed divine rule: not as a top-down imposition of a uniform design or an absolute principle, but as a plurality of ways and a diversity of means for achieving the same providential purpose.[117]

Likewise, sovereignty and its bearer the people need not imply a monolithic entity or homogenous institutional arrangement. It may well be articulated, as Tocqueville insisted it should be, into a great variety of different constitutional forms, applied "according to the necessity of the case," and adapted to a society's specific historical and cultural conditions. While advocating a diversity of forms and robust constitutionalism, Tocqueville's analysis makes clear that to be operative, legal norms and constitutional mechanisms depend on popular consent and the people's willing compliance with the constitutional process. Although institutions are crucially important for the viability and quality of popular rule, their power stems from shared opinion and trust. For institutions to be strong and stable, the opinions that support them must be integrated into the mores: that is in the common practices and self-understandings of the people. In this sense popular sovereignty, like divine sovereignty, is a regime of self-limitation: popular commitment to constitutional principles alone can limit the power of the people.[118]

Yet, as Tocqueville's account of the social state makes clear, a democratic society is not a static edifice but a dynamic set of processes, and a constantly shifting social reality. In such a society, the questions about the meaning of peoplehood and sovereignty are recurrent. Constitutions provide the frame and language within which to raise these questions, the concepts and mechanisms for addressing them. But they cannot settle them once and for all, constitutionalize them as it were. A democratic constitution, to generalize Chief Justice Marshall's point, is necessarily incomplete. This is why the people's authorizing power cannot be confined to the moment of ratification or constitution-making. Far from limited to a single constitutive event, securing broad-based appreciation of, and commitment to, the institutional frame is a recurring need and ongoing process.

On the other hand, democratic society, like any society, needs continuity and time. Though a work in progress, democracy requires an institutional and moral frame within which such progress can be imagined and pursued in a peaceful fashion. While the passion for equality ensures that the constitution is an ongoing quest rather than a date past, it is within the horizon of a historically constituted people that democratic equality as a fundamental principle and aspirational norm can attain political and social meaning. Even as Tocqueville advocates institutions and mechanisms that enable a vigorous civil society and competitive political process, his discussion of American federalism points to the need for a shared moral foundation that would keep competition in check and prevent society's disintegration. In other words, if institutional pluralism and political contestation are desirable, they are so only up to the point where they interfere with the government's capacity to guarantee the rule of law and general well-being. To be liberal, then, democracy needs to strike a balance between stability and change, pluralism and unity. Too much of either is threatening.

In light of Tocqueville's account, democratic sovereignty consists in a collective political capacity: the ability to set common goals and reach them through a process based on "reflection and choice," deliberation and consent, rather than through a hierarchical top-down enforcement. This capacity is contingent on a widespread perception of legitimacy—both of the goals set, and of the institutions and procedures that organize public life. As Tocqueville's Jacksonian analysis suggests, sovereignty is not only a matter of the government's ability to deliver security and economic benefits. It is inseparable from questions of identity and feelings of belonging. In the framework of constitutional democracy, legitimacy depends on a broad-based identification with the political order, its values and institutions. Sovereignty understood as collective political capacity is grounded in popular allegiance.

Sovereignty in that sense is synonymous with social integration and lies on a spectrum. It is manifested by the degree to which different parts of the social body come together in a shared agreement: not only about the *how*, but also about the *who*, and the *why* of political rule. In a democratic social state, this agreement is not set in stone but is the subject of a continuous quest and renegotiation. Sustaining this quest in a polity premised on equality and consent necessitates a relative convergence of mindsets and ways of life, what Tocqueville calls "homogeneity in civilization." As Tocqueville's poignant description of the civilizational differences between Americans of the North and of the South (and their historic clash) evidence, neither ethno-religious homogeneity nor shared commitment to republican principles were sufficient to reconcile differences and peacefully sustain the Union. Tocqueville's insistence on the need for a unifying principle and a coherent vision of "We the People" thus raises more questions than it answers: What kind of unifying principle? Where is it located? How to effect it? These are the concerns of the next chapter.

2

Nationalism and Democracy

THE PREVIOUS CHAPTER argued that the principle of popular sovereignty makes the people into a central category and, in a sense, the altarpiece of democratic politics. How the people and its sovereignty are construed, institutionalized, and practiced conditions the character of the political order, and whether or not it is liberal. This construction, moreover, is not a onetime event: in a democratic society, "We the People" is not only a constitutional faith or a foundational principle, but an object of ongoing political contestation. As Tocqueville's critical account of the antebellum American Union suggests, if this contestation is not to spiral into deepening polarization or civil war, there is a need for a shared sense of belonging, as well as of institutions, practices, opinions, and beliefs that mediate between individuals and groups, and help bridge differences at the level of society. Put otherwise, the possibility of sustaining a shared vision of, and allegiance to, the people is critical for the stability and long-term prospects of liberal democracy. This chapter aims to clarify why this is the case, what form of popular allegiance supports democratic freedom, and how it can be achieved.

I begin by discussing Tocqueville's understanding of the "people" as a concept and its relation to nationhood. Observing that Tocqueville uses "people" and "nation" interchangeably, I go on to clarify his comparative view of premodern and modern forms of nationhood, and his contribution to the vast literature on modern nationalism. For Tocqueville, I argue, nationhood defined as the moral bond that holds society together is a perennial phenomenon. Nationalism, by contrast, which is an ideology or doctrine that makes the nation into the primary object of civic allegiance is distinctively democratic and modern. I proceed to explore the affective foundation of this democratic allegiance through the distinction Tocqueville draws between different forms of public spirit. For all their differences, I argue, premodern and modern patriotism share profound similarities: while each relies on a distinctive social imaginary, both are grounded in mechanisms of identification and pride. I then turn to the paradoxes of democratic national identity in order to discuss, in my second case study, how these played out in one of the most heated moments in Tocqueville's political career: the 1840 dramatic reopening of the so-called Eastern question that occasioned Tocqueville's epistolary debate with J. S. Mill on national pride.

People vs. Nation

Grounded in a certain understanding of popular sovereignty, Tocqueville's conception of nationhood differs from other perspectives offered by legal theorists and historians, past and present. As discussed in chapter one, scholars of constitutionalism often focus on the formal meaning of "the people" and its function as a juridical person that replaces the monarch as the bearer of sovereignty. "The people" in this sense is a legal fiction, which, though endowed with formidable constituent power, appears to be void of an empirical reality. Further, as Dieter Grimm has pointed out, distinguishing between "people" and "nation," hence between national and popular sovereignty, was critical for the development of constitutional thought from the late nineteenth century onward. In this conceptual bifurcation, the *nation* refers to the collective subject existing across time and including past, present, and future generations. The *people*, by contrast, is understood as the totality of individuals that make up the political community as it currently exists.[1]

If constitutional theorists ask how the concept of the people helps sustain a certain legal order, the literature on nationalism studies the historical processes that underpin the formation of a bounded community, often insisting on the specifically modern character of these developments. Scholars of nationalism inquire into the social, economic, political, and psychological dynamics that allow a diverse constellation of populations and social groups to conceive of themselves as belonging to the same nation. In this context too, scholars have advocated the need to distinguish between "nation" and "people," hence between populism and nationalism, in order to reflect "fundamentally different, analytically independent phenomena."[2]

The debate about the relationship between "nation" and "people," though primarily concerned with analytical content and historical validity, has been further subject to "political evaluation." Next to conceptual and methodological considerations stand questions about rhetoric and the extent to which the analytical idiom we deploy in theorizing democratic phenomena enhances their emancipatory potential and shapes future developments. Assuming this discursive perspective, Bruno Bosteels argues that, even though a people is "constituted on the basis of a necessary exclusion," "people" as a concept seems distinct and preferable to the "nation," in light of the latter's fraught history of essentializing chauvinisms.[3]

It is important to note that Tocqueville makes no such distinction. Though mindful of the problem of rhetoric, and of the influence present modes of discourse can have over the future, Tocqueville follows Rousseau and the revolutionary tradition of the French constitutional debates, and speaks of people and nation interchangeably. Making no temporal distinction between the historic community and its current incarnation, Tocqueville's usage is ambiguous also in another sense: sometimes it refers to the people as the totality of citizens and at other times to specific classes. This ambiguity, I suggest, does not stem from methodological neglect or lack of intellectual and political sophistication.

As in his analysis of Jacksonian America, Tocqueville's hesitation to pin down the meaning of the people is likely intentional and part of a larger point. That he was fully aware of the issue is evidenced by the promptings of *Democracy in America*'s very first readers. "I keep repeating the same objection," states a marginal note by Count Hervé de Tocqueville (Alexis's father and unsparing critic) "for it strikes me at every step. What is "the people" in a society where, as much as possible, ranks, fortunes, and minds approach the level of equality? Assuredly, in the New World the word *people* has none of the same meaning as among us. I believe that a sense of this must be given somewhere."[4]

One such clarification opens Tocqueville's reflections on classical education in the second volume of *Democracy in America*:

> What was called the people in the most democratic republics of antiquity hardly resembled what we call the people. In Athens, all citizens took part in public affairs; but there were only twenty thousand citizens out of more than three hundred fifty thousand inhabitants; all the others were slaves and fulfilled most of the functions that today belong to the people and even to the middle classes. So Athens, with its universal suffrage, was, after all, only an aristocratic republic in which all the nobles had an equal right to government.[5]

Tocqueville's rumination on the ancient meaning of peoplehood, which goes on to include Republican Rome, underscores the differences between ancient republics and modern society, while also problematizing customary French usage. In the French usage, the word "people" typically refers to the lower strata of society, what the Romans called the plebs: a signification very different from the one invoked in the preamble to the United States Constitution. Yet, if in one respect the preamble hearkens back to ancient notions, in another it also breaks with them in a radical way. And Tocqueville's comment gestures both at the continuity and the difference.[6]

Whereas in ancient Athens suffrage was universal and all male citizens took an active part in the exercise of sovereignty by deliberating in the assembly and bearing arms in war, the Athenian demos was effectively an aristocratic governing class comprising, on Tocqueville's count, less than 10 percent of the whole population. The great majority of that population, which included not only slaves but also freemen and immigrants who together formed the mainstay of the economy, did not have political rights and for the most part could not attain them.[7] This contrasts sharply with the modern American and post-revolutionary French meaning of the people as a synonym for the whole society: a much larger collectivity that includes all members regardless of class or occupation. Nevertheless, by distinguishing the people from the middle classes, Tocqueville's comment also intimates that if the sovereign people in modern democracies is meant to comprise all individuals and social groups independent of wealth, origins, or profession, this inclusion is far from comprehensive. In the nineteenth-century, civic membership in the United States was limited to the white male population, and in Britain and France it was narrower still.[8]

Nor are the limits of political inclusion only demographic or gender based. As Tocqueville points out, if modern democracy aspires to comprehend and serve the interest of the whole, in reality the whole is at best a majority.

> The political form has not yet been found that equally favors the development and the prosperity of all the classes that make up society. These classes have continued to form *like so many distinct nations in the same nation* . . . The real advantage of democracy is not, as some have said, to favor the prosperity of all, but only to serve the well-being of the greatest number.[9]

This statement is notable for two reasons. First, it points out that every political system is only partially responsive. To serve the public good is to serve the interests of a part, the largest part though it may be, of the population. And this is because every society is a plurality that consists of a multitude of classes and interests, which "like so many distinct nations in the same nation" may not be mutually compatible and whose coexistence could be fruitfully compared to international relations.[10] Secondly, the analogy between classes and nations sheds light on the broader meaning Tocqueville ascribes to the word nation. In Tocqueville's usage, nationhood need not refer to ethnic or racial grouping but is more general, marking differences in ways of life, interests, and outlooks. Whatever the grounds for difference in society, or the organizing principle that unites the particular groups that compose it, the existence of diverse groups and classes is a source of tension, of which even the most inclusive political order is not free.[11]

On the other hand, if modern democracy is imperfectly inclusive, as I argued in the preceding chapter, it features a potential for inclusion that is inscribed in the very logic of its foundational principles. By declaring all to be equal, and the people to be sovereign, modern democracy empowers all members of society to seek and assert their rights of membership. The very cleavages and exclusions that remain offer opportunities for political contestation that push the boundaries of democratic membership, not least by redefining the meaning of the people. As Tocqueville observes in his brief account of the American Revolution, any tinkering with electoral qualification leads to the demand for further adjustments, and soon enough "there is no more stopping until universal suffrage is reached." Far from a self-evident truth, from its inception the American people was an essentially contested concept. And this observation applies, albeit in differing degrees, to any modern nation.[12]

In brief, what distinguishes modern nationhood is its aspiration to extend the principle of social and civic equality potentially to all classes, thus to include within its bounds all of society. While this promise is never perfectly realized, both its limits and potential are inscribed in society's legitimating principles and in the ways the people and its sovereignty as well as equality are understood and defined. And yet, while Tocqueville differentiates between the nature and meaning of modern peoples as compared to premodern ones, he also insists on a dimension of continuity and on the pertinence of nationhood to various historical contexts. This is evident in his frequent references to aristocratic nations or peoples.[13] In what follows I gauge these continuities and differences in order to clarify Tocqueville's understanding of the modern nation.

Nationhood vs. Nationalism

Nationhood for Tocqueville designates the principle of cohesion that makes collective life possible. It consists of a shared moral and political vision, rooted in what Tocqueville calls "immaterial interests": the norms and values that regulate public conduct and orient life's effort toward particular ends. Put differently, nationhood is the ethos that defines a given society and grounds its institutional order. This ethos is expressed in specific practices, customs, opinions, and beliefs that Tocqueville named mores and we today commonly refer to as culture. Insofar as every society, in order to exist, requires a shared moral compass and political culture, every society features a form of nationhood.

As noted above, Tocqueville's category of aristocratic nations lumps together various premodern societies, including the ancient republics and even the American South. Although premodern nationhood was historically varied, Tocqueville's model throughout *Democracy in America* is the feudal polity. In his account, this polity was articulated in a variety of orders or classes that were "prodigiously dissimilar." Each class, like a "small nation amid the larger one," was marked by its own "distinct passions, ideas, habits and tastes." The aristocratic nation thus formed a mosaic of diverse social orders and mindsets. What held this wide variety of human types and norms together was a permanent division of labor, social hierarchy, and, last but not least, religion.[14]

Tocqueville suggests that, though bound by "a very tight political bond," the aristocratic polity was an imperfect society. Founded by conquest, it was sustained by commanding will and material force, without which it would fall into anarchy.[15] The deep pluralism of ways of life precluded the possibility of mutual understanding and shared mores. As a result, rulers and ruled lived side by side. Though joined by "a long community of memories" and a sense of mutual belonging, they were "like parallel lines that never meet or separate." Nor do they have an awareness of forming one people. In fact, "they scarcely believe[d] themselves to be a part of the same humanity." This presence of deep divisions and irreconcilable outlooks necessitated external authority that would maintain the diverging social elements into a system of superiority and subordination. At the same time, owing to the rigid hierarchical bonds that attach each social stratum to its immediate superiors and inferiors, no part of the social body could perceive the whole, or take an interest in its political destiny. So there was neither a shared conception of the public good nor a truly national life, but instead a chain of personal relations of fidelity.[16]

Whereas the aristocratic nation preserved in its midst different principles of social existence—and with them the "seeds of revolution"—a democratic nation results from a process of consolidation and of society's emancipation from principles and forces perceived to be external to it. In the popular sovereignty chapter, Tocqueville observes that "in the United States ... society acts by itself and on itself. Power exists only inside it." Although there is still a plurality of interests and parties, the differences between them are much reduced to the extent that "those who govern have no interests contrary to the mass of the governed." And so, if aristocracy for Tocqueville "by nature always forms a minority" whose object is to monopolize wealth and power in the hands of a single class, democracy is defined by a broad (though never perfect) compatibility of interests between rulers and ruled. Tocqueville points to this compatibility as the first advantage—and precondition—of democratic government.[17]

Tocqueville's comparative account of democratic and aristocratic society offers two contrasting sociopolitical models of the nation. What distinguishes the old society from the new is not the fact of nationhood but the principle that grounds the social structure and legitimizes the institutional order: diversity and hierarchy in one case, and in the other similarity and agreement. In contrast to the aristocratic social bond, which is fundamentally based on constraint, a democratic nation explicitly rests on consent. Making voluntary agreement the principle of association implies the equal dignity and like standing of the associates, all of whom are presumed the best judges of their own interest. Accordingly, "inviolable privileges and exclusive categories" can no longer be established in principle. Likewise coercive institutions and practices cease to be perceived as legitimate.[18]

Elaborated throughout both volumes of *Democracy*, this new understanding of society has a number of momentous consequences. First among them is recognizing the people, understood as the whole of society and represented by a national majority, as the only source of public authority and the "law of laws" of the regime. Since broad-based agreement alone has the legitimate right to direct public life, eliciting such an agreement becomes critical not only for political stability but for society's very existence. It is perhaps because establishing social consensus is so critical to the existence of modern democracy that societies in the throes of democratic revolution undergo terror and purges, and the process of equalization often issues in outbursts of "xenophobic nationalism," even genocide.[19]

While sharing a moral outlook and "the same way of thinking and feeling" is indispensable for forming a majority, it is no less needed to ensure compliance with that majority. As Tocqueville notes, "when a nation is divided among several great irreconcilable interests, the privilege of the majority is often unrecognized because it becomes too painful to submit to it." His example is an aristocratic elite that believes itself to be permanently elevated above the social body. Yet without the recognition of the majority and voluntary compliance with its decrees, there can be no self-governing community, but only a part dominating the whole—an arrangement that no longer has a principled justification. And so, to prevent the minorities from being, or perceiving themselves to be, tyrannized over by the greater number, a degree of assimilation becomes indispensable. Put differently, in order for the greater number not to oppress and the smaller not to be oppressed (or, indeed, vice versa), they must share common principles and a sense of belonging to the constitutional order from which they all benefit.[20]

An egalitarian political system, then, rests on a foundation of similitude. This, however, need not mean uniformity. Tocqueville's discussion of religious difference clarifies this point. While celebrating the diversity of sects and religious opinions peacefully cohabiting in the United States, Tocqueville also unveils the mechanisms through which pluralism and unity can be reconciled. In America, the many different sects are harmonized not by forcing everyone to profess the same state-sponsored religion, but by separating religion and politics and making religious affiliation independent from political and civil rights. Unity out of plurality is achieved by two means: first, by recognizing each citizen's equal freedom of worship; and second, but no less importantly, by all coming to "perceive their religion in the same light:" that is as separate from, though an essential bulwark of, democratic politics. This shared perception shapes the popular view that, while worshipping in different ways, every citizen is a worshipper, and every worshipper is a committed American citizen.[21]

Further, in a political order where there is no exterior source of authority and all power emanates from society itself, the laws have to be stipulated in a manner congenial to the sentiments and understandings that predominate across society. In other words, a community that governs itself is a community governed by habits of mind and heart, of which the laws are more or less a direct expression. What rules this society is the moral vision of the majority. This is why Tocqueville argues that, representative institutions notwithstanding, in democracies "the opinions, prejudices, interests and even the passions of the people can find no lasting obstacles that prevent them from taking effect in the daily direction of society." Popular sovereignty is born and borne out as public opinion.[22]

The divergent levels of social integration that characterize the aristocratic and democratic nation determine the different self-conceptions of the people that make up each of these societies. In the old regime, every class insisted on its particularity and unique place in the social edifice. It formed in the eyes of its members "a sort of small country, more visible and dearer than the big one."[23] If aristocratic society formed a nation in the sense of a single political unit held together by a dominant ethos and institutional structure, it was not so in the self-understanding of its composite parts. Only upon overcoming the profound social differences, and weakening the moral valence of class distinctions, could the self-recognition of the people and their identification with the social order at large fully crystallize. Tocqueville's account thus distinguishes between the objective and subjective aspects of nationhood. When defined as a body politic held together by a specific moral vision and institutional framework, the nation is a transhistorical phenomenon, common to modern and premodern polities. By contrast, a nation whose every member shares a subjective identification with the people and the political order as a whole is a democratic phenomenon peculiar to the modern period.[24]

For Tocqueville, as for many a modern historian, modernization and nationalism are two sides of the same democratizing coin. Whereas nationhood, understood as the ethos that grounds the constitutional arrangement, is perennial, national*ism*, defined as an argument or ideology that equates the nation with the whole of society and makes it into the locus of civic allegiance, is distinctly modern. Nationalism is only possible in an egalitarian society and is uniquely necessary in a political order based on the principle of popular sovereignty.[25]

Patriotism in Democracy

Although Tocqueville, as I argue above, had a comprehensive insight into the phenomenon of nationalism, he did not have the word for it. He speaks of "patriotism" or "public spirit." Tocqueville elicits the distinctive features of the new democratic patriotism by comparing it to premodern forms of public spirit.[26]

Tocqueville's discussion "On Public Spirit in the United States" distinguishes between two types of allegiance: instinctive and reflective. The former is a "disinterested and indefinable sentiment that binds the heart of man to the place where he was born." Rooted in the love of family and ancestral land, instinctive patriotism "is a sort of religion ... it does not reason, it believes, it feels, it acts." By contrast, reflective patriotism is a calmer, "more rational" affection that stems from understanding the link between the advantages one reaps from society and the obligations one is called on to perform, or between civic rights and duties. While instinctive love of country is like the "sentiments of youth," reflective patriotism is "born of enlightenment" and, like knowledge, is cultivated and acquired. "[I]t grows with the exercise of rights and in the end intermingles in a way with personal interest."[27]

Tocqueville's distinction between instinctive and reflective patriotism anticipates contemporary conceptualizations of national allegiance that differentiate ethnic or pre-political loyalties rooted in common origins and cultural traditions from civic attachment based on political principles and rights.[28] Yet, in contrast to contemporary typologies, for Tocqueville both types are *political* attitudes with constitutional implications. When distinguishing instinctive and reflective public spirit, he calls the former "the patriotism of monarchy" and the latter "the patriotism of republics." Just as popular sovereignty is the more or less hidden principle underlying every regime, so too is patriotism the affective foundation of all political orders. Seconding Rousseau's critique of Montesquieu, Tocqueville claims that what distinguishes regime types is the object of public spirit and the different ways in which civic dedication is mobilized. While patriotic allegiance can take different forms in different constitutions, it is equally indispensable for political vitality and strength.[29]

Tocqueville presents the two types of patriotism not only as analytically distinct but as two moments on a temporal continuum. If, like the "sentiments of youth," monarchical love of country stems from simple mores, unquestioned beliefs and instinctive obedience, its republican counterpart issues from a period of revolution—an adolescence-like crisis of traditional authority and the loyalties to king and country. Once the legitimacy of the political order has been challenged, Tocqueville claims that "the most powerful means, perhaps the only one" of reconstituting civic allegiance is, as in America, by extending political rights and appealing to individual interests, in short, by giving the citizens a personal stake in public affairs."[30] Tocqueville's typology of patriotism thus suggests at once a historical and psychological progression: from monarchy to republic; from passionate obedience rooted in custom and faith to rational allegiance based on utility and rights; from credulous youth to enlightened maturity; from instinct to interest. It seems to assert that calculated loyalty is the psychological foundation of a free democracy. And this is how Tocqueville's account of public spirit is typically read.[31]

Yet, as we saw in the previous chapter, this reading is not without challenges. And the central one is this: in the critique of American federalism, which occurs four chapters after the thematic discussion of public spirit, Tocqueville disavows interested patriotism, and voices prescient doubts that this reasoned attachment would suffice to guarantee the longevity of the American Union. This tension in Tocqueville's presentation has prompted allegations of incoherence. It compels us to take a second look at his argument and to probe its psychological implications.[32]

Tocqueville illustrates the two types of patriotism with two examples: the French of the old regime and the Americans of his day. The French used to love their country by personifying it in their king. Although the great majority of them had no say in public affairs and were "delivered without recourse to the arbitrariness of the monarch," they felt "a sort of joy" and took pride in living "under the most powerful king of the world."[33] By contrast,

[t]he common man in the United States has *understood* the influence that general prosperity exercises over his own happiness, an idea so simple and yet so little known by the people. He has, moreover, become *accustomed to regarding* this prosperity as his work. So, in public fortune, he *sees* his own, and he works for the good of the State, not only by duty or by *pride*, but I would almost dare to say by *cupidity*.[34]

In Tocqueville's account, monarchical patriotism is a generalized sentiment of filial devotion based on love for the "paternal home." Like monarchy itself, it is rooted in the principle of heredity, namely of birth and belonging, and in fidelity to the paternal figure of the monarch. This way of seeing the world correlates with "a sort of joy": a prideful admiration for the political universe on which one has no influence.[35] Whereas monarchical patriots regard the polity as an unconditional given, the republican patriots treat it as an artifact and a corporation, whose fortunes can be enhanced and directed through industry and effort. If lack of political influence corresponds to the subjects' "fleeting" outbursts of selfless joy, having a vested interest in the political order stirs up the passions of ownership: a sense of responsibility and the corresponding ambition to increase the common stock and one's part in it—in a word, greed.[36]

Even while representing two distinct psychological profiles, the two kinds of patriotism, as Tocqueville describes them, have much in common. First, each relies on a habitual way of construing the political world. The French used to "catch sight" of their country in their king; the Americans are "accustomed to regarding" themselves reflected in the "public fortune." In that sense, both groups identify with a certain political imaginary, even if they imagine their community differently.[37] Further, just as the French under the old monarchy, so too modern-day Americans take pride in their country and its constitution. If in the French case this affection is disinterested in the sense that being "delivered . . . to the arbitrariness of the monarch" cannot be said to serve the subject's interests, it is not without its pay-offs. For the glory of the king glorifies the subjects and elevates their self-esteem, much in the same way as the nation's prosperity and greatness grant the democratic citizens opportunities for self-congratulation.[38] Conversely, if American patriotism is more reasonable because it serves the citizens' interests more directly, it is no less morally ambiguous. Once integrated into the citizens' self-image, this proud and greedy love of country transcends what is rational or useful. Closing his thematic discussion of public spirit, Tocqueville satirizes the "irritable patriotism of the Americans" who go so far as to defend their country's "climate and soil . . . as if they had taken part in their formation."[39]

For Tocqueville, then, citizens and subjects alike come to see the public weal, or the glory and power of the nation, as their own. In so doing, they affirm the political order and take pride in belonging to it. Although the two types of patriotism issue from two different ways of seeing the political world, the psychological effect is similar: by collapsing the distance between public and private, patriotic attachment prompts a prideful endorsement of society's values and institutions. By signaling that both types of civic spirit rely on the mechanism of identification and the sentiment of pride, Tocqueville shortens the distance between them.

Further, if both kinds of patriotism are grounded in identification and pride, to be efficacious, both must become habitual and internalized and, in that sense, "instinctive." In his critique of American federalism, Tocqueville claims that without the conversion of utilitarian commitment into instinctive allegiance, the political order would be precarious.[40] In volume two, he praises free institutions and participatory practices in America precisely for their capacity to effect such a conversion:

> It would be unjust to believe that the patriotism of the Americans and the *zeal* that each of them shows for the well-being of their fellow citizens have nothing real about them. Although

private interest directs most human actions, in the United States as elsewhere, it does not rule all . . .

The free institutions that the inhabitants of the United States possess and the political rights of which they make so much use recall to each citizen constantly and in a thousand ways that he lives in society . . . One is occupied with the general interest at first by *necessity* and then by *choice*; what was *calculation* becomes *instinct*; and by dint of working for the good of one's fellow citizens, one finally picks up the *habit and taste of serving them*.[41]

Tocqueville advocates civic associations as core institutions of a free democracy and the "great schools, free of charge" of democratic freedom. Associations bring home the benefits of liberty and teach the citizens how to protect those benefits through concerted action. By reminding "each citizen constantly and in a thousand ways that he lives in society," they provide daily demonstrations of the coincidence of duty and interest. Active engagement socializes selfish passions and fosters civic dedication, at first as a matter of necessity, but soon as an informed preference and "instinct." What begins as self-serving calculation is by means of continual practice transformed into a "habit of benevolence" and "taste" for public service. In effect, participatory practices help blend public and private not merely on the level of reason and interest, but also of habits and ultimately of moral character. Here, as elsewhere, Tocqueville emphasizes that the strength and durability of liberal democracy depend on the conversion of instrumental involvement into spontaneous identification with the community and its way of life.[42]

From Interest to Instinct

Tocqueville's analysis suggests that while democratization transforms instinctive belief into rational interest, for democracy to be free a reverse formation is likewise necessary. Rather than a stable attitude, democratic patriotism is a process of turning interest into instinct and of blending, through civic practice, society's values into the pride and self-conception of the people. This process, however, is not limited to a single historical moment. Democracy, to recall, is at once a social state and a dynamic of equalization fueled by the passion for equality that continually triggers social change. If modern democracy is, so to speak, an institutionalized revolution—a kind of dialectic of stability and innovation, of settled principles and their contestation—Tocqueville's account of its psychological basis reveals the need for a similarly dialectical attachment. Democratic patriotism is an ongoing questioning and remaking of civic allegiance in which the idea of rights and the "norm of self-interest" play a mediating role.[43]

As discussed in chapter one, modern democracy is premised on the moral equality of human beings and the recognition of each individual's right to shape her own life. For Tocqueville, popular sovereignty and the individual capacity for self-direction are "correlative" ideas. In contrast to aristocratic society, which was held together by subordination, and considered hierarchy and obedience as "the immutable order of nature," the democratic social bond is grounded in the implicit primacy of the individual. To be lawful, authority must be seen as supportive of and instrumental to individual pursuits. Contractual bonds thus appear as the foundation of social life. Utility and consent come to be viewed as the "natural limits of obedience." In effect, self-interest becomes the chief reference point and authoritative guide to human conduct.[44]

Tocqueville claims that this way of construing the political and social world at once supports and threatens liberty. On the one hand, the nature of the democratic social bond invites contestation of authority, which nourishes self-reliance and infuses society with activity and the "manly habits" of independence. As a check on social tyranny and pathological forms of collectivism, self-interest is a crucial safeguard that protects individual dignity and freedom. On the other hand, the democratic tendency, indeed compulsion, to perceive society and one's role in it in terms of self-interest alone can lead to a misguided view of individual independence. As a dogmatic affirmation of self-interest, democratic individualism invites a radical understanding of personal autonomy that poses unprecedented threats to the social order. By devaluing spontaneous impulses and exalted sentiments, individualism erodes the instinctive identifications on which, Tocqueville claims, both social vigor and robust individuality depend.

These identifications, then, are in need of constant remaking. And Tocqueville extols civic associations in America precisely for their capacity to reproduce such identifications. As I argued in the preceding chapter, broad-based popular participation in the task of governing is indispensable for sustaining the political capacity of citizens and their continued dedication to democratic forms and constitutional values. Vibrant civil society is also Tocqueville's primary means of inspiring modern democratic citizens with the "spirit of the city," and balancing the solidarity deficits produced by the self-interested logic of democratic individualism.[45]

However, while civic participation is critical for boosting democracy's public spirit and liberal character, in democracy this participation cannot be taken for granted. Far from easy or spontaneous, associating is "an art" that requires skill as well as institutional and moral incentives to sustain it. Among the institutional means, Tocqueville highlights decentralized administration, a model for which he finds in New England. Readily conceding that decentralized decision-making may not result in orderly procedures or well-executed public works, Tocqueville commends "the political effects of decentralization," highlighting its capacity to foster patriotic attachment and a sense of belonging. In Tocqueville's account, decentralized institutions trigger a virtuous circle: by taking part in the public business, "[t]he inhabitant becomes attached to each of the interests of his country as to his very own." The psychological investment elevates the citizen's self-esteem and facilitates effective civic action. This, in turn, helps sustain the people's commitment to the democratic order and their self-understanding as being in charge. Tocqueville's analysis underscores this double impact: on the one hand, decentralized institutions strengthen society by diffusing energy and activity; on the other, they enhance individual agency and cultivate able and assertive citizens.[46]

And yet, though necessary, decentralized administration and participatory practices are not enough to produce the public spirit a free democracy requires. As already touched upon in the previous chapter, even while extolling the necessity for civil society and participatory practices, Tocqueville signals that they are insufficient. By claiming that local institutions "are to freedom what primary schools are to knowledge," he points to their limitations. They are, after all, just a primary school and do not by themselves complete a nation's political education.[47]

One reason for this is their narrow scope. The American example shows that local patriotism and provincial attachments may fail to extend to the country as a whole and thus guarantee national unity. Indeed, the more vigorous sectional loyalties are, the more exclusive and dangerous they become. The trouble with federalism is that strong regional bodies, especially when endowed with a degree of political autonomy, can forestall the formation of wider loyalties, thus vitiate the project of "a more perfect union." Whereas participatory practices pluralize the public space, and create the conditions for vibrant political life, they also fragment it. Guarding against oppressive majorities, they run the risk of entrenching minorities and impeding their recognition of majority rule. Yet, forming a majority is of existential importance for democratic society. Though a democratic majority is always in danger of turning tyrannical, the inability to elicit majoritarian consensus leads to political paralysis and social malaise that may easily turn violent. To be free, then, democracy must steer between two rocks: lack of consensus and too much of it.

If the threat to unity is most obvious in the case of robust local associations, a similar difficulty inheres in national organizations, such as political parties.[48] In his discussion of the American political system, Tocqueville likens the party to "a separate nation inside the nation, a government inside the government" that has a material existence and moral force of its own. While political parties cut across regional, economic, and other divides, they create centers of allegiance and power that become divisive and polarizing in their own right. Local associations, then, exemplify the more general problem of factionalism in democracy—a problem that has vexed democratic theorists, both ancient and modern.[49]

Madison's famous solution to that problem outlined in the *Federalist* no. 10 is not to suppress factions, which would be tantamount to extinguishing freedom, but to pluralize them. The greater the diversity of interests and opinions that acquire voice and representation, the lesser the chance that any single one of them would consolidate into an oppressive majority or become strong enough to threaten the integrity of the political order. And the key to achieving plurality, as James Madison argued, is greater territory: small unitary republics are more likely to fall prey to factionalism and majority tyranny than are larger federal ones.[50]

Tocqueville's defense of decentralized institutions echoes Madison's proposed solution, yet it raises questions about the conditions that enable and sustain a pluralist civil society. Tocqueville indicates that the civic spirit and vigorous participatory engagement he witnessed in America rely on a particular set of circumstances: geopolitical situation, and a legacy of mores and religious beliefs that work both to support and regulate local freedom. He thus indicates that the Madisonian solution is not self-sufficient. Size and institutional levers are not enough. Not a mechanical system, the liberal polity is made possible by a delicate balance of social and political forces and the corresponding mores and self-understanding. While crucially perpetuated by a shared commitment to constitutional principles, this equilibrium likewise depends on the possibility of sustaining a broadbased agreement on the meaning of peoplehood and national identity.[51]

Tocqueville's analysis of the young American Union points to the necessity of cultivating national sentiments and identification that by balancing regional and partisan attachments and the great diversity of interests and opinions commit the various parts of the country to a common political project and a shared vision of "We the People." It also raises questions about how this can be done. If integrating the public interest into the citizens' self-understanding is key to socializing human selfishness, for the democratic order to subsist this interest and identification must include the nation as a whole.

Paradoxes of National Identity

Identity, an all-too-common word today, is a term Tocqueville rarely uses. He does so once in *Democracy in America* in the context of reflecting on the probable effects of the Union's disintegration on American commerce:

> It is clear that whatever happens the commercial states will remain united. They all touch each other; among them there is a perfect identity of opinion, interests and mores, and alone they can make up a very great maritime power.[52]

Identity here is a synonym for likeness: Tocqueville claims that the commercial states of the North were perfectly alike when it came to "opinions, interests and mores," which put their enduring unity beyond reasonable doubt. Earlier in the same chapter, he contrasted the characters of North and South and worried about the strain the discrepancies in disposition and moral outlook (irrespective of shared ethno-religious origin) put on the constitutional bond. As I discussed in the preceding chapter, the trouble with the Union, in Tocqueville's view, was that its citizens did not seamlessly share a political identity and self-understanding.

To share an identity, then, is to be alike or to believe to be alike in aspects held to be relevant. And yet, alongside similarity, the word identity also indicates difference. The identity of a person or a group consists of a set of distinctive characteristics, which this person or group hold as definitive of their being. As Tocqueville comments in a marginal note: "What makes [the Americans'] common bond is what separates them from the others."[53] Neither of those senses—the perception of a group's internal similarity or of its distinctiveness from other groups—needs to be fully based on objective fact. As Tocqueville's psychological analysis indicates, in a fundamental sense it cannot be. One reason for this is that identity, both in the sense of who we believe we are and what distinguishes us from others, is rooted in pride.

Pride for Tocqueville is an integral aspect of the human condition. It is a theme that runs through all of his works.[54] Tocqueville's reflections on pride draw on the French moralist tradition, especially on Rousseau and Pascal, whom (together with Montesquieu) in a letter Tocqueville names as his daily interlocutors. As in the tradition, so too in Tocqueville's rethinking of it, pride is an indelible aspect of the human psyche. It is moreover a site of an unresolvable moral conundrum:

> You can change human institutions, but not man. Whatever the general effort of a society to make citizens equal and similar, the particular pride of individuals will always try to escape from the level, and will want to form somewhere an inequality from which it profits.[55]

Tocqueville defines pride as the sentiment of one's distinctiveness. This sentiment thrives on forming inequalities and making distinctions. Requiring an *other*, or others, with whom to compare itself, pride is relational, an inherently social passion. It is also moral: a perception not only of differences but of "profitable" differences, it relies on assumptions about value and worth. Pride, in Tocqueville's view, is a claim not merely to uniqueness but to superiority: it is the aristocratic passion par excellence.[56]

Tocqueville acknowledges that, as an urge to assert one's superiority and difference, pride is a vice: it tends to cloud reason and silence the heart. On the other hand, as an affirmation of one's own worth, pride undergirds human dignity. As Tocqueville argues, the exalted sentiment of one's value is not simply the effect of individual merit and achievement, but in considerable measure their precondition. The humbler one's self-conception, the less ambitious the undertakings and lower the goals one sets out to attain, the more limited one's energy for self-improvement. And vice versa: a sense of entitlement and prideful self-respect often leads to the exercise of faculties and the accomplishment of deeds that justify the opinion of one's elevated standing.[57] Pride, then, is both a source of moral threat and a psychological foundation for democratic liberty. Understood as an unqualified assertion of superiority and difference, it is politically dangerous and morally unsound. At the same time, as a constitutive element of subjectivity, pride plays a crucial role in conditioning the aspiration and efforts to live in freedom. Seeing pride as the common source of both great virtue and cardinal vice, Tocqueville lists elevated self-conception and moderate pride among the psychological and moral prerequisites for self-government.[58]

Like the pride of individuals, national pride is a site of moral paradox. Though universally human, it assumes specific features in democratic society. Tocqueville's Americans offer a case in point. The intensity of American national pride is among the first things Tocqueville notes on his transatlantic journey. It is also a recurrent theme in *Democracy in America*.[59] Tocqueville finds American pride, though "often exaggerated," to be "almost always salutary."[60] His celebrated discussion of the New England township presents the citizens' pride in themselves and in their institutions as a key ingredient of and important motivator to civic life. By bolstering a belief in the legitimacy of the political order, prideful self-regard facilitates civic action. This in turn helps sustain the people's trust in the institutional arrangements and empowers their sense of being in charge.

Observing that the civic pride of the Americans is a premise as much as an effect of their vigorous public engagement, Tocqueville traces its sources to the Americans' sense of distinctness. While professing a commitment to universal rights and "general principles that ought to rule human societies," the American people presume nonetheless that they are uniquely predestined to be religious, enlightened, and free. The novelty and unprecedented success of their institutions elevate their self-conception even to the point where "they are not far from believing that they form a species apart in the human race." Tocqueville further suggests that the Americans' idea of their exceptional place at the forefront of human civilization sustains their confidence in democratic institutions and their willingness to take their destiny into their own hands. It makes the strength as well as the substance of their political bond.[61]

And yet, though often salutary, the national pride of the Americans has dark sides, which Tocqueville explores at length in the chapter on the three American races. Touching on the problem of pride, the race chapter canvasses in poignant detail the temptations and consequences of essentializing difference: the dehumanization of native and African Americans and the looming sectional crisis that posed existential threats to the integrity and future of the American Union.[62] Tocqueville's probing analysis thus points to the deep tensions that underpin American and—by implication—democratic national identity: though affirming equal rights and universal values, a democratic nation nonetheless craves particular recognition for its exceptional standing. While a democratic people's sense of its own distinctiveness fuels its civic spirit and helps sustain its political culture, it can also lead to chauvinistic excess and mistreatment of others.

Tocqueville explores this tension further in volume two's thematic chapter on national sentiments. By contrasting American national pride with that of the English, he underscores the relative and relational character of national sentiments in democracy, and points to the main stage where they play out: international relations. Sketching memorable portraits à la Jean de La Bruyère, the chapter anticipates the epistolary debate on national pride (recounted below) between Tocqueville and J. S. Mill.[63]

The Englishman of Tocqueville's day harbored no doubt about the uniqueness and value of his country. His national pride is a "peaceful sentiment of superiority," which he feels no need to defend or establish. He neither recognizes others nor expects their recognition in return. "He maintains vis-à-vis the entire world a reserve full of disdain and ignorance. His pride does not need to be fed; it lives on itself." The reason for this, Tocqueville explains, is constitutional: England is a country still ruled by an aristocracy whose "insouciant and haughty" pride sets the tone for the nation as a whole. The elevated posture of the aristocratic ruling class is predicated on its uncontested social and political preeminence, which it mistakenly considers to be "a sort of natural right" inherent in itself. Aristocratic pride in Tocqueville's view is fundamentally based on ignorance. Unaware of its relative status and dependence on others, it is a calm persuasion of natural superiority.[64]

In contrast to the self-contained (and ignorant) pride of the English, the national passions of the Americans are unstable and in constant need of external validation. As if uncertain of their country's merit and doubtful of its importance, Americans "want to have its picture before their eyes at every instant." The reason for this too is constitutional:

> In democracies, since conditions are very mobile, men almost always have recently acquired the advantages they possess; this makes them feel an infinite pleasure in putting them on view ... and since, at every instant, these advantages can happen to escape them, they are constantly alarmed and work hard to demonstrate that they still have them. Men who live in democracies love their country in the same way that they love themselves, and they transfer the habits of their private vanity to their national vanity.[65]

Unlike aristocratic society, where ranks are fixed and one's sense of worth is rooted, as it were, in "the immutable order of nature," in democracy social status is mobile. With the egalitarian rejection of inherent differences and permanent social roles, the citizens' sense of self is no longer based on stable hierarchy and birthright, but essentially depends on social recognition.[66] At the same time, social mobility and a growing awareness of the flux of human affairs make this recognition uncertain: one's worth is in constant need of confirmation and display. Sensitive to its relative standing and reliance on others, democratic pride thus becomes jealous and petty vanity. "It seeks compliments and is quarrelsome at the same time."[67]

Tocqueville's comparison of English and American pride illustrates the urgency and other-directedness of national sentiments in democracy. By disallowing a host of social categories that used to ground individual and group self-conceptions, the democratic social state makes the desire for distinction more pressing while rendering its object less determinate. Stripped of the institutional and moral support that previously upheld one's sense of self, democrats launch on a restless quest for recognition. In effect, vanity and a constant need for validation become the "natural condition" of the democratic soul, a condition reflected in the restlessness of private and civic passions alike.[68] Disabused of the aristocratic fallacy of taking conventional distinctions for natural ones, democrats run into the opposite confusion losing sight of legitimate differences. Identity, both personal and national, becomes an urgent need and permanently open question.

To be sure, this modern condition in which self-worth is no longer inherited but must be earned has positive dimensions. In Tocqueville's account, the uncertainty of merit correlates with the universal activity and the unleashing of productive energy that characterizes democratic society. While previously the permanence of social roles resulted in ignorant self-satisfaction that kept the greater part of society poor, the mores harsh, and the institutions immobile, now the need of external support and validation tempers morals and fuels an unceasing effort to improve one's condition by winning the help and approval of others.[69]

Nevertheless, Tocqueville cautions that the pervasive insecurity and the imperative to prove one's standing that accompany the rising tide of equality lead to pathologies of a new kind. The citizens' awareness of their need for social acceptance enervates their capacity for independent judgment. The anxieties of democratic life, and the sense of individual disempowerment that often arise amid relentless competition and quick-paced social change, render the pressures to conform to a powerful majority or to follow a strongman almost irresistible. What is more, the instability of individual self-worth makes the yearning for national pride and collective self-definition all the more urgent. In order to prevent democratic peoples from falling into, or oscillating between the extremes of tyrannizing cohesion and identity crisis, or contempt for others and paralyzing self-doubt, Tocqueville calls on moralists and statesmen to elevate democratic ambition and cultivate pride:

> So far from believing that humility must be recommended to our contemporaries, I would like you to try hard to give them a vaster idea of themselves and of their species; humility is not healthy for them; what they lack most, in my opinion, is pride. I would willingly give up several of our small virtues for this vice.[70]

In the remainder of this chapter, I explore the practical implications of Tocqueville's paradoxical advice and his own efforts to broaden the moral and political vista of his contemporaries by revisiting one especially troubled moment in Tocqueville's parliamentary career: the 1843 crisis in the Middle East that strained Anglo-French relations and prompted his exchange with J. S. Mill on national pride.

Case Study 2: The Eastern Question and the Politics of National Pride

Tocqueville's parliamentary speeches, especially those concerning France's foreign policy, are the site where his theoretical reflections on democratic nationhood meet the exigency of political action. Although tailored to particular French circumstances and a pressing rhetorical purpose, these speeches often transcend their historical and national context. As André Jardin has observed, a hallmark of Tocqueville's oratory is its attempt to raise the level of debate by discussing general principles. Along with specific policy goals, Tocqueville pursues larger objectives: by enhancing the political understanding of his audience, he aims to consolidate at home and to project abroad a vision of a democratic and liberal France.[71]

In his political interventions, as in his analytical writings, Tocqueville highlights the persistence of illiberal mores as the greatest obstacle to securing a constitutional order in France. How to remedy the popular ignorance of and disinclination to self-government? How to establish a free democracy in the context of a centuries-long absence of such an inclination in the popular mind? Both Tocqueville's theoretical agenda and his statesmanship are oriented around the practical political question of reeducating national mores. In analytical argument and edifying speech, Tocqueville points to revitalizing the nation's self-understanding and redirecting its pride as indispensable elements of that education.[72]

1840, the year the second volume of *Democracy in America* appeared, was as eventful for European politics as it was for Tocqueville's own career. In the summer of that year, Russia, Prussia, Austria, and England signed a secret treaty on England's initiative to settle a burgeoning crisis in the Middle East. The crisis was caused by the pasha of Egypt Mehmet Ali's invasion of Syria, then an autonomous region within the increasingly dysfunctional Ottoman Empire. The secret treaty included an ultimatum to the pasha, France's long-time ally, to either pull out of Syria or face the joint attack of European powers—a threat which was made good later that summer. The news about the secret agreement caused a vehement reaction in France. By excluding the French government and menacing its client, the treaty was seen as an attempt to isolate France internationally and challenge her status as a great power. Recalling the 1815 humiliation of Napoleon, the press stirred public indignation and Anglophobia. The Chamber of Deputies, France's parliamentary body, followed up with a vote to mobilize the military and make preparations for war. That fall, however, King Louis-Philippe dismissed the bellicose Adolphe Thiers ministry and appointed a new cabinet to work out a rapprochement with Britain. In November the new foreign minister François Guizot gave a speech in the chamber maintaining that France had neither a formal commitment to the pasha of Egypt, nor a vital interest in the Middle East that would justify compromising Anglo-French relations.[73]

It is in this context that Tocqueville, who had been elected deputy in 1839, delivered his second speech in parliament.[74] Echoing the outcry in the press and the popular sentiments on the streets of Paris, he called on the government to defend France's honor and assume a resolute stance against the anti-French coalition by living up to its obligations to Egypt. Drawing a suggestive picture of the world-historical situation, Tocqueville argued that the events in the Middle East were of crucial importance to France's position as a world power, and that France should uphold this position if she had self-respect.

Tocqueville pointed to his country's isolation as inevitable: owing to the principles of her revolution, France was an offense in the eyes of the old monarchies of Europe that could not but conspire against her. At the same time, what isolated France was also what shored up her moral standing as the vanguard of democratic equality. Not military strength but the universal creed France had proclaimed to the world, and the high regard of the peoples of Europe (as distinct from their governments), were the foundation of France's power and of her bid for honor and global leadership.[75]

Tocqueville insisted that France should strive to protect her great power and cultivate world opinion even at the risk of going to war with a Europe united against her. At the same time, he urged that sending a clear message about France's determination to defend her position was more likely to prevent hostilities than to invite them. A politics of appeasement, by contrast, would signal France's weakness and encourage future arrogance from abroad. Worse still, it would demoralize public opinion and deepen the gulf between the monarchy and the French people.[76] In an impassioned finale, Tocqueville indicted the government's position on the Eastern crisis for being driven by fear of internal instability. He claimed that embracing the nation's sentiments and demanding foreign recognition for the "legitimate" and "holy" grievance of the country was the only way to prevent the revolution the government dreaded. Precisely because of France's precarious internal situation, a disadvantageous war was less to be feared than a "peace without glory."[77]

Tocqueville's speech produced an international sensation. Across the Channel his uncompromising stance and severe criticism of "the peace party" in power won him an instant reputation as a belligerent hothead. It also occasioned a heated exchange with his English friends and correspondents including, notably, J. S. Mill. If the reaction of the English press was scathing, that of modern scholarship has not been kinder. With a few exceptions, Tocqueville's speech and his position on the Eastern crisis has been read as emotional, chauvinist, and "warlike in the extreme." Adding a personal touch to the political drama, scholars have suggested that the relationship between Tocqueville and Mill, whose correspondence petered out after 1843, was fatally damaged by the incident. A beautiful intellectual friendship crushed on the rock of national pride.[78]

All these statements need to be qualified, and in part they have been. A closer look at Tocqueville's letters and notes reveals a deliberate strategist behind the fervent orator. Both in the speech on the Eastern crisis and the correspondence it occasioned, Tocqueville described his position as moderate, equally opposed to a "violent and unjust war" as to "undignified peace." Distancing himself from the hawks à la Napoleon Bonaparte and from the doves obsessed with material security, Tocqueville contended that, though backed by no political party, he spoke for France herself and represented the nation's legitimate sentiments. In the so-called "war speech" itself, he highlighted the strategic advantage of the appearance of strength and the "utility" of saving the nation's face for the sake of preventing military hostilities as well as revolutionary turmoil.[79] When considered in this light, the rhetorical effort of a first-time politician to channel popular mood and cut a figure at home and abroad appears more tactical than belligerent. Nor did the friendship with Mill break over the incident: despite interruptions, their correspondence and the tone of mutual regard continued until Tocqueville's death.[80]

To be sure, even if Tocqueville's position on the Eastern crisis was more deliberate than the English press at the time and much of modern scholarship has allowed, this does not make it beyond reproach. In fact, Tocqueville himself reproached it: a decade later, after another revolution that he had predicted put an end to the July regime, Tocqueville described Thiers' warlike attitude in 1840 (and by implication his own) as "madly risky." In retrospect he saw things differently, as do historians.[81] Notwithstanding these revaluations, I propose that Tocqueville's stance on the occasion of the Eastern crisis reflects enduring dilemmas of liberal democratic government: How to translate theoretical insight into workable policy, especially in volatile circumstances? How to foster national feeling potent enough to bridge internal divides and to offset radicalism while resisting nationalist excess? How to craft political speech that successfully addresses both domestic and international audiences? Calling attention to popular appeal and to a certain kind of emotional investment as a necessary dimension of liberal politics, Tocqueville's speech on the Eastern crisis and the reaction it provoked still resonate today.

This so-called war speech inaugurated the political rivalry between Tocqueville and his once much-admired teacher François Guizot.[82] An eminent historian of French and European civilization, Guizot was a dominant presence in French politics prior to the revolution of 1848, and a leading figure of the liberal mainstream. Tocqueville's quarrel with Guizot was not about *whether* but *how* to ground a moderate liberal order and thus extricate French society from the cycle of violent upheavals that had convulsed it periodically since 1789. Although Tocqueville pledged loyalty to the July revolution that ousted the Bourbons and embraced its charter of 1830 as an important step on the path to constitutional democracy in France, he consistently opposed the way the regime strove to realize its social and political program. The strategy of the July Monarchy, of which Guizot became in Tocqueville's words "one of the principal apostles," was to focus public life and the nation's energies on economic development. In Tocqueville's view, crippled by fear of dissent and by mistrust of its own power, the government sought to substitute material interests for "the moral and political interests of the country," thus pushing citizens further down the path of "narrow and crude individualism."[83] Against this economic strategy, Tocqueville insisted on stimulating political life and the citizens' public engagement as indispensable for reforming France's political culture. Inveighing against the nontransparent practices and patronizing tone of the ruling party, he urged the government to inform public opinion and to foster rather than suppress national sentiments as a means to creating political consensus.[84]

> In fact, Gentlemen, for a nation as for a man, the best means of acting is the knowledge of the real situation, it is knowing precisely on what to count; this is good for all peoples, but particularly for free peoples.
>
> A despotic government has its own force. Secrecy often serves it, it is often in its interest that the people it governs, it dominates, that this people does not know what [the government] is going to do, what it must do, because, I repeat, its force is in itself. But among free peoples where *the force is not in the government but in the opinions and in the sentiments of the nation,* it is necessary that the nation be informed about what it should wish, about what it should feel, so that the force, which it has in itself, is communicated to its government.[85]

Stressing the need for an open communication between government and people, Tocqueville's oratory, more emphatically than his analytical works, highlights the centrality of passions in political life and the need to sustain and actively encourage emotional commitment to the institutional order. Not replacing passions with reasoned interests, but resonating with public emotions and orienting them toward a higher object is, in his view, the essence of liberal democratic government:

> Do you believe that you can govern free people by canceling and enervating all their passions? For my part I am convinced of the contrary. I think that in a people constituted as ours, there is only one means of taming bad passions: it is by countering them with good ones.[86]

As in his analysis of American democracy, so too in his parliamentary speeches Tocqueville underscores the irreducible importance of civic passions and identification for political legitimacy. He claims that embracing "the patriotic spirit" and the "generous" and "honorable sentiments" of the country would allow the July regime to establish itself as the representative of the nation. It is also the most effective means of combating the upsurge of revolutionary extremism, which, Tocqueville concurs, posed a real threat. Only by promoting a shared vision and reuniting the country behind a national cause of which it can be proud, could the ruling elite successfully confront the disaffection and anarchic impulses roused by "the enemies of order." Conversely, if the Monarchy continued to defy the tide of public feeling, it would undermine its own foundation and run the risk of revolutionary overthrow.[87]

Along with briefing the party in power on the general rules of popular governance, Tocqueville also reveals the specific French inflection of this political grammar. If making passion counteract passion is a universal maxim of the art of ruling, the intensity and kind of sentiments at play depend on circumstances and historical conjuncture. In his oratory and correspondence, Tocqueville repeatedly comments on French pride and the concern for honor and on the need to address this concern as a prudent approach to policy.[88] His standing indictment of the July government is that, by offending sentiments dear to the French, it manifests its ignorance of the character and predilections of the people:

> Do you know the pride of this people, this pride nourished by so many victories, by so many triumphs, by triumphs of so diverse kinds that have succeeded each other for two hundred years? Don't you know that among all the broken ties that lie scattered on the surface of this country, there is one, only one perhaps that is whole and strong, this is the pride of the name we bear? Such is the sentiment, the only one perhaps, which keeps this great society together. Do not offend it, for it is stronger than you.[89]

In his speeches, Tocqueville instructs France's political class to conciliate public opinion not by defying but by directing its instincts, that is, by recognizing and addressing the values of the people it is trying to govern. In the concrete situation of mid-nineteenth-century France, he sees mobilizing national pride as a necessary means to spur and moderate civic passions. As a safeguard against revolutionary radicalism on one hand, and against apathetic retreat from political life on the other, national sentiments are a vital support for the liberal constitutional order.[90]

However, while recognizing the need to give public sentiments their due, Tocqueville did not simply advocate that the government become a puppet of popular passion. In *Democracy in America*, he praised the "unyielding character" of George Washington for resisting the outcry that swept the country at the outbreak of the French Revolution demanding that the newly founded United States declare war against England. Just as uncompromisingly, Tocqueville condemned Andrew Jackson, who actively courted popular support, as the majority's slave.[91] These assessments suggest that for Tocqueville whether to humor or resist public opinion very much depends on the content of that opinion and on particular circumstances. In other words, how to handle popular sentiments is a judgment call—a judgment, moreover, that may well be easier to make with the benefit of historical or geopolitical distance. Be that as it may, both in his oratory and correspondence, Tocqueville insisted that democratic politics must be grounded in civic passions and he spelled out the dilemmas this involves.

Late in the fall of 1840, commenting on the critical condition of Anglo-French relations, Tocqueville writes to Mill:

> I don't need to tell you, my dear Mill, that to sustain a people, and especially a people so mobile as ours, in a state of soul that would make it do great things one should not let it believe that it must resign itself to insignificance. After the manner in which the English government has acted toward us, for politicians not to show how aggrieved we are would have been to hurt and extinguish a national passion which we may need one day. National pride is the greatest sentiment that we have; *one must doubtless seek to regulate and moderate it in its aberrations* but one should beware of diminishing it.[92]

In this letter, which initiates the two thinkers' epistolary debate on national pride, Tocqueville argues that nationalist sentiments are a necessary moral and political resource, yet one to be tempered and regulated.[93] He also points to the behavior of politicians (possibly including himself) and their effort to represent popular sentiment as instrumental to safeguarding this emotional resource. And yet, though needed in a free democracy, Tocqueville acknowledges that national passions and emotional investment are also dangerous and, once inflamed, can lead to "aberrations." Later in the letter he voices his concern "not only for the good of our nations but for the good of all Europe."[94]

In the course of the exchange, Tocqueville grants Mill's objection that, if left unrestrained, the national pride he has commended as France's only generous sentiment can deteriorate into a far less generous amour propre. By conjuring up the ghost of the empire, the urgent demand for national prestige, instead of elevating sentiments, might bring the country down before another

Napoleon.[95] For his part, Mill concedes the benefits of striving for esteem: "Most heartily do I agree with you that this one & only feeling of a public, & therefore, so far, of a disinterested character which remains in France must not be suffered to decay." While partly granting Tocqueville's point, Mill insists nevertheless on the peril of sacrificing liberty at home for a symbolic satisfaction abroad. As if echoing the discussion of national pride in the second volume of *Democracy in America*, Mill accuses the French of the restless vanity that Tocqueville ascribed to Americans and democrats in general. He further contends that the nation's desire for prestige is precisely what needs redirection, and charges that "posterity have a right to expect from such men as you . . . that you should teach to your countrymen better ideas of what it is which constitutes national glory & national importance."[96]

While hinting that the French "solicitude about the world's opinion" is an all too democratic lack of national confidence, Mill's own position, allegedly espoused "even by the most stupid and ignorant" Englishman, bears many an aristocratic feature. Mill claims that more than outward recognition, the "real importance of a country . . . really depends upon the industry, instruction, morality & good government"—that is, on its intrinsic merits and hard-won achievements. Criticizing French insecurity, his letter implies that England's standing in the world was the result of her just deserts rather than geopolitical scheming. Although dispatched from India House—the London headquarters of the East India Company where Mill was employed for thirty-five years—Mill's missive glosses over the imperial dimension of English self-confidence, and the empire's role in upholding not only Britain's material well being, but her identity as well, and the public trust in the constitutional order.[97]

The main issue between Tocqueville and Mill, much like the one between Tocqueville and the Guizot ministry, was not *whether* but *how* to impart "better ideas of . . . national glory & national importance" and thus to reform public sentiments and mores, which both thinkers recognized as the main source of France's malaise. Although concurring in principle with Tocqueville's diagnosis of French democracy and, to a degree, with his defense of national pride, Mill recoils before his proposed cure: a responsive government and transparent foreign policy. Alarmed by the wave of pubic feeling in France, he argues for the need to shelter foreign affairs and European politics from popular involvement and the surge of nationalist passions. "Without this," Mill urges, "Europe will always be on fire."[98]

A "steadfast warrior in the cause of Radical reform," when it comes to international politics Mill explicitly champions top-down technocratic policies. His position in the debate with Tocqueville parallels his unapologetic defense of the East India Company a decade and a half later, and the claim that India is better governed by an expert bureaucracy than by parliament and the public.[99] Mill argues that the task of governing a remote dependency, and by implication foreign policy tout court, requires expert knowledge of intricate social and cultural conditions and practical experience that, while eluding the general public, are likely to be weaponized by its representatives for partisan gain. Though not without merit, Mill's recommendations on India, and the idea that foreign policy can and ought to be placed on a different footing than domestic affairs, call into question parliamentary accountability, the very bedrock of the British constitutional system.[100]

In his exchange with Tocqueville, Mill admits that his approach comes at a cost that is not insignificant. As he comments in an earlier letter,

> I agree with you in thinking our ministry very culpable, but our people are not to blame. You know that the English public think little & care little about foreign affairs & a ministry may *commit them beyond redemption before they are aware*. If the Tories had been in power they would have been suspected of anti-French predilections, they would have been watched ... But the ministry being liberal ... the public looked on in confidence that all was right, and that Palmerston knew more about the matter

than they did, never dreaming that they have been brought to the brink of a war until it was revealed to them by the manifestations of feeling in France.[101]

As Mill indicates, the English public's insouciance about foreign policy went hand in hand with its trusting the government's expertise and commitment to do the right thing. Public confidence left the ministry a free hand: a greater leeway for maneuver and, potentially, for abuse. It also left the public ignorant and helpless. Not only did the lack of meaningful debate over foreign policy rob the nation of learning opportunities and prevented it from grasping the complexities of its situation. Reducing foreign affairs to strategic or technical questions to be handled by experts behind closed doors runs the serious risk that the people and their representatives may find themselves committed "beyond redemption" to an international standing attained, as it were, in a fit of absentmindedness. It directly impacts their sovereignty.

For Tocqueville, by contrast, if the government is to be both liberal and democratic, involving the people in external affairs is no longer a matter of choice, but of double necessity. An alert and enlightened public opinion serves to uphold the legitimacy of the institutional order and provides an indispensable corrective to the government's action. As Tocqueville conjectures (and Mill concurs), had the English public been involved, the Eastern crisis could have been averted. What is more, alongside providing policy correctives, informing public opinion about external affairs is a vital opportunity to shape national identity and thus sustain the moral preconditions for political freedom.[102]

As in his polemics against Guizot, so too in his debate with Mill, Tocqueville denies that exclusive preoccupation with domestic affairs or with increasing individual and public prosperity suffices to generate civic life in democracy, let alone reeducate popular habits. Beyond "building railways and making prosper in peace ... the well-being of each individual," fostering a prideful sense of collective mission and dedication to the principles of national life is needed to shape a democratic people's self-understanding, and build solidarity across social divides. And while Tocqueville and Mill agree that national passions must not only be stimulated but above all instructed, they differ, on some points profoundly, about the format and curriculum of national instruction.[103]

In *Democracy in America*, Tocqueville appoints legislators and religious leaders as the custodians of the public spirit and mores. His work, while offering a comprehensive analysis of democratic society and propaedeutic into the new science of politics, can be read as a manual on how to govern and sustain popular regimes. In a similar fashion, Tocqueville's oratory instructs the French political class to direct patriotic passions and, by keeping "a proud attitude," to elevate the country's aspirations and image of itself.[104] Infused with patriotic declamation and appeals to national honor, Tocqueville's speeches not only prescribe but exemplify such an attitude. Depicting in lofty language France's historic mission and democratic calling is the hallmark of what Ralph Lerner has called "Tocqueville's political sermon." Presenting himself not as party man, but as "l'homme du pays" whose cause is the nation itself, Tocqueville holds up the universal ideals and the liberal principles of the French Revolution as the substance and justification of French national pride.[105]

Yet pride, as discussed above, is a relative sentiment that crystallizes in comparison to and distinction from others. Unlike aristocratic government, which was permanently elevated above the social body and could understand itself in contrast to it, the popular sovereign includes in theory, if not in actual practice, all of society. As democratic equality presses against and gradually invalidates internal social differences, the citizenry's pride and confidence in the political order cannot be grounded or sustained simply from within. Though decentralized institutions and associational practices are indispensable for invigorating public spirit and strengthening local attachments, these institutions alone are insufficient to foster commitment to the principles and interests of the country as a whole, and may in fact work contrary to this purpose. Often obscured in the contest between local and partisan agendas, national purpose and pride take shape first and foremost in an international context. It is in relation to other peoples that the democratic nation stands "as one and the same individual," its distinctiveness comes to the fore, and its principles are tried and applied in practice.[106]

Democracies, in short, are in special need of turning outwards in search of a coherent self-definition. If local institutions and participatory practices are the primary schools of political freedom, Tocqueville points to foreign relations as the arena where the highest form of national instruction can take place. In his view, just as participation in political life broadens and informs individual self-conception, so too are national sentiments and the pride the citizens take in their country educated and adjusted through active engagement in international politics. As the next chapter will show, Tocqueville looks to the experience gathered through energetic involvement in external relations both as an incentive for democratic patriotism, and a necessary corrective to the aberrations of national pride.[107]

On the other hand, while Tocqueville views the cultivation of national pride as indispensable for modern society, he indicates that equality, which is this society's "first principle and symbol," inevitably undermines the legitimacy of national distinctions.[108] Not only global commerce and intensified communication between all parts of the world, but also the very logic of the egalitarian creed work to assimilate cultures and attenuate national differences. Contemplating the advent of what we today call globalization, Tocqueville recognizes that under the pressure of democratic equality, national identity just as personal identity can no longer be based solely on exclusive categories or permanent differences. This creates a challenge for liberal democracies. If preserving a sense of national particularity and civic pride is a condition of possibility for a liberal democratic society, this society's distinctiveness must be articulated in terms of universal ideals and egalitarian principles appealing to, if not accepted by, the universality of humankind.

For Tocqueville, then, the means to foster democratic patriotism and national pride is not only by cultivating local traditions or wearing strange hats—as Rousseau counseled the Poles—but also by championing universal causes and striving to be an example to all.[109] While democratic national pride stands in need of outward recognition, the only valid bid for recognition is a claim to advance the cause of human dignity and progress—a claim that must prove its merit and win acknowledgement "in the eyes of the world."[110]

Conclusion

Nationhood for Tocqueville is the moral bond that holds a polity together. Though pertaining to premodern and modern societies, it manifests differently in democratic social orders. Likewise patriotism and civic pride are the affective foundation of every political order, even though different regimes focalize and mobilize these affects differently. In premodern society their locus was the ruling body or the king; in modern democracy it is the people defined as the whole of society. The democratic social state at once throws into relief and modifies the character of civic passions.

The democratic polity is premised on the equal value and like capacity of individuals. Although there still are and, as Tocqueville famously argues, need to be intermediate associations and social identities of various kinds, the people as a whole emerges as the principal political identity, hence the main source of collective values and moral distinctions that shape citizens' self-understanding. The stability of democratic society requires that the people or nation become the primary locus of civic loyalty and pride. Tocqueville's analysis thus indicates that popular allegiance and the mobilization of national pride are not only the likely effects of democratization, but its very prerequisites. Democracy's stability and freedom crucially depend on how the people, and membership in the people, are experienced and understood.

And yet, as discussed in the preceding chapter, because democratization is not a single event but a continuing process, the question of who "We the People" are cannot be answered or constitutionalized once and for all. Although, the institutional order, once it is in place, becomes a major factor in addressing issues of membership and popular self-definition, it alone cannot decide them. Nor is constitutional patriotism enough, when it is defined as commitment to universal principles or abstract legal norms.[111] In order to function the institutions need to be grounded in "shared ways of thinking and feeling": that is in collective passions and self-understandings that serve as the moral foundation of coexistence. To be liberal, in other words, democratic society requires not only a declaration of the formal principles of government, or a shared conception of justice, but also a story about the particular collective that is entitled to govern itself, and to make these principles its own.[112] Yet, just as the individual identity under modern conditions is no longer simply given but must be achieved, so too is the quest for national identity and institutional stability ongoing. In democratic society, a society on the move, the boundaries of membership are not always in question. But thanks to the principle of and passion for equality, they can always be questioned. When this happens, and the meaning of peoplehood becomes the explicit ground for political contestation, a "populist moment" is born.[113]

In an effort to handle one such moment in the tumultuous history of his country, Tocqueville advanced arguments that still resound today. Chief among them is that a certain kind of patriotic discourse and national feeling—one oriented by a combination of historical resonance, particularist narrative, and universal ideals of equality and self-rule—is a vital prerequisite for democratic liberty. Popular sentiments and affirmations of national identity are indispensable to balance solidarity deficits and contain the disaffection that threatens to upend democratic stability. They help prevent the individualistic decline of civic spirit that exposes modern societies to the twin dangers of despotic oppression and revolutionary extremism.

At the same time, though a necessary feature of the new politics based on the principle of popular sovereignty, national identification and allegiance pose dangers of their own. These, however, cannot be forestalled by suppressing national sentiments, any more than a house can be protected from fire by drawing out all its oxygen. Tocqueville agrees with Mill that national pride, especially when wounded, can turn pathological, but he argues that it must be educated and managed, rather than repressed. Local institutions and participatory associations are an integral part of this education that fosters—and pluralizes—the sense of belonging, and brings home the know-how of democratic self-rule. Yet they are not sufficient. Tocqueville's proposed antidote to the excesses of national pride is to educate national feelings and self-conceptions in the "rude school" of international politics, notwithstanding the risks this involves.[114] As I discuss in chapter three, just as the citizens' participation in political life socializes their individual pride and adjusts their self-understanding, so too is their collective pride and the idea they have of their country corrected and refined in active engagement with other nations and political orders. It is for these reasons, among others, that Tocqueville advocates an active foreign policy and involving the nation at large in the affairs of the world.

3

Whither Globalization?

CHAPTER TWO ARGUED that democracies need a coherent national identity, which they cannot achieve simply from within. The dynamics of the egalitarian social bond impel modern societies outward in the search for dignity and self-definition, as much as for economic opportunity and political influence. Put differently, democracy's outward orientation issues from the internal as well as the external dimensions of popular sovereignty: that is, from each people's need for a coherent self-understanding, and from the desire to be recognized as a sovereign member in the community of nations. Developing this argument, this chapter contends that in Tocqueville's account, the quest for equality is the main driver behind the complex phenomenon we have come to call globalization.

Globalization is a new word that gained currency in the decades after World War II. It does not, however, name a new thing. The manifold processes now collectively referred to as globalization have been centuries in the making and have long commanded the attention of political thinkers. This chapter aims to show that, even though Tocqueville does not speak of globalization any more than he does of nationalism or populism, both his analytical works, and especially the policy writings, elaborate profound insights into the nature and mechanisms of global transformation. Integral to Tocqueville's "new political science," these insights are still a largely untapped resource that offers an instructive perspective on the modern world.[1]

Tocqueville defined the modern world through the soon-to-be global rise of democratic civilization. As in a national context, so too in the international one, he viewed democratization as an irresistible, longue-durée phenomenon driven by a conjunction of religious, technological, economic, and political developments. Among these many factors, Tocqueville highlights the imperial rivalries of the eighteenth and nineteenth centuries as the motor behind the global movement toward equality. His analytical and practical engagement with European expansionism probes its social, ethical, and political ramifications. Offering a clear-sighted analysis of the global dimensions of the democratizing process, Tocqueville indicates its likely denouement.

In what follows, I sketch Tocqueville's vision of globalization by comparing it to one of its most influential alternatives: the one outlined in Karl Marx and Friedrich Engels's *Communist Manifesto* (1848). Marx and Engels envisage globalization as a process of convergence that by undermining political or national differences consolidates classes, thus leading to a final clash between the bourgeoisie and the proletariat. Tocqueville, by contrast, claims that the spread of equality brings about the erosion of class differences and the crystallization of national identities. His account points to international politics rather than economic relations as the main locus in the struggle for global democracy.

With this framework in mind, I go on to examine Tocqueville's theory of international relations. Drawing on *Democracy in America* as well as on his foreign-policy writings, which remain largely unavailable in English and are generally less known to Tocqueville readers, I probe Tocqueville's analysis of the specificity of democratic foreign policy and the geopolitical dimensions of democratization. Against this analytical backdrop, I discuss as my third and final case study the most controversial aspect of Tocqueville's political career: his official involvement in France's colonization of Algeria as a privileged instance of the effort to spread democratic norms and institutions. In the final section of this chapter, I recapitulate Tocqueville's analytical and practical understanding of the colonial experience and what it suggests about the future of globalization.

Honor, Nationhood, Globalization

Democracy in America heralds the irresistible rise of democratic equality throughout the world. As discussed in the preceding chapters, it also redefines the meaning of democracy. More than an institutional arrangement or a political order, democracy for Tocqueville names a dynamic condition that progressively remolds along egalitarian lines every aspect of collective life, from political institutions and social practices down to the prevailing mentality and the "manner of thinking and feeling." Explored at length in the book, the trajectory of the democratizing process finds a systematic recapitulation in the chapter "On Honor in the United States and in Democratic Societies."[2]

Tocqueville defines honor as the ethical system in light of which a society considers human action. In his account, social life necessitates a moral compass: that is shared principles and standards that regulate conduct and orient individual efforts toward particular ends. Alongside "the simple notions of the just and the unjust" that are common to all human collectivities, each society is characterized by conventions and valuations specific to itself that distinguish its particular way of life and reflect its self-understanding. These Tocqueville calls *honor*. Honor, then, is inherent in social life: every association obeys a code of honor that constitutes its cultural and moral outlook. While the phenomenon of honor is universal and pertains to society as such, its concrete manifestations differ vastly across time and place. In the body of the chapter Tocqueville labors to show that, far from arbitrary, society's morals are grounded in particular needs and evolve in complex interrelation with the physical environment, material conditions, and political context. As Céline Spector observes, in doing this, "Tocqueville pursues Montesquieu's project," even while disagreeing with Montesquieu.[3] I return to this disagreement later.

Toward the end of the honor chapter, in summarizing its argument, Tocqueville highlights the "tight and necessary relation" between honor and inequality of conditions. Honor stands in a twofold relation to inequality. As the criterion that distinguishes public virtue and vice, it is the source of moral cleavages *within* society. At the same time, lying at the core of cultural particularity, honor discriminates *between* societies or social groups. It marks the frontiers between classes and nations. Tocqueville outlines the effects of democratization on these frontiers:

> Ranks mingle, privileges are abolished.... and you see successively vanish all the *singular notions* that each caste called honor; honor now derives only from the particular needs of the *nation* itself; it represents its *individuality* among peoples.[4]

As discussed in chapter two, for Tocqueville, aristocratic society is divided into classes or castes, each characterized by "singular notions" of honor and a particular ethical perspective. What unites these "prodigiously dissimilar" social bodies are permanent social hierarchy and division of labor, as well as a shared belief in the inequality of human beings and groups.[5] Against this vision of society, articulated into diverse manners of life and superimposed social strata, Tocqueville depicts democratization as a two-pronged process.

On the one hand, the gradual equalization of conditions levels classes and assimilates moral outlooks. As "privileges are abolished," the corresponding "singular notions" of honor weaken or disappear. Belonging to the nation rather than to a class or family becomes the principal source of the moral valuations that shape the citizens' self-conception and orient their way of life. On the other hand, as class distinctions within democratic society weaken, the differences *between* societies or nations become clearer. "The particular needs of the nation" come to define society's identity and "represent its individuality among peoples."[6]

Democratization then issues in two seemingly opposed phenomena: while the frontiers between classes blur, those between nations crystallize. National differences surface as the main resource for individual and collective self-definition. As chapter two argued, for Tocqueville equalization and nationalism are the two sides of the same democratizing coin.[7]

Tocqueville's account of democratic modernity can be usefully compared to the vision outlined in the *Communist Manifesto*. Marx and Engels define modernization as an inexorable process of global transformation, critically driven by international trade and the dynamism of the British Empire. Viewing political and social relations as a byproduct of underlying economic processes, the *Manifesto* anticipates that in the search for global markets capitalism will "melt into air" the seemingly solid national bonds and reduce the multiplicity of political units and cultural values to an ultimate antagonism between the bourgeoisie and the proletariat. For Marx and Engels, religious and national differences progressively dissolve into more fundamental class or economic differences.[8]

While Tocqueville too notes the interrelation between material and moral factors, he grants relative priority to the latter.[9] In his view, the social system is defined less by what people possess or how they produce it than by what they esteem and hold dear, that is by *honor*. Whereas for Marx and Engels modernization is headed to a planetary struggle over the distribution of material resources, for Tocqueville the fundamental fault lines are cultural and moral. Group divisions are first and foremost ethical divisions: less about what we have than about who we are and what makes a human life worth living.

And so, while both *Democracy in America* and the *Communist Manifesto* sketch modernity as a global process of convergence, the two analyses differ significantly. Marx and Engels view globalization primarily as the effect of commercial expansionism that undermines nations or political units and consolidates classes. Resolving social relations and "personal worth into exchange value," and imposing a uniform materialist perspective on human life, the global rise of capitalism deepens economic inequalities and class polarization, thus paving the way for a final showdown between the haves and the have-nots of the world. Tocqueville, by contrast, claims that democratization leads to the erosion of class differences and to the attendant intensification of national consciousness. More than class or economic status, nationhood with its diversity of cultural norms and ethical perspectives emerges as the ultimate obstacle to the universalization of equality. At the same time, Tocqueville acknowledges that, far from stopping at national borders, democratization presses against them. Universalist ideals, as well as economic and cultural developments, intensify patterns of interdependence and level differences between societies.[10]

Tocqueville's analysis of the dynamics of equality thus points to the realm of international relations as the emerging theater in the battle for democracy. How does democratization affect national differences? Can it cross the frontiers between peoples and countries? And what, in Tocqueville's view, are the long-term prospects of the struggle for equality?

The following sections seek to answer these questions by examining Tocqueville's analytical understanding of international relations and the global dimensions of democratic freedom. This understanding, I argue, underpins Tocqueville's qualified endorsement of the French colonial mission in Algeria. It also informs his view of its likely outcome. Tocqueville's colonial writings show that, *pace* Marx and Engels, globalization is not a uniform or linear development. It tends in two seemingly opposite directions simultaneously: toward a universalization of equality and growing interdependence on the one hand, and toward affirmation of cultural differences and resurgence of particularism on the other. In other words, democratization advances not by eliminating cultural differences and reducing all peoples to the same materialist horizon, but by equalizing different peoples' capacity to affirm and defend their cultural particularity and normative perspective. Though precipitated by European expansionism, this global democratizing process is not synonymous with imposing European ways or with achieving universal consensus. So long as diverse peoples exist history's end is not in sight.

Democracy and International Relations

In *Democracy in America*, his main analytical work, Tocqueville says comparatively little about foreign relations. As he judges, it was the American Union's geopolitical fortune and considerate policy to stay clear of international entanglements. At the same time, while he credits the country's protected isolation with the success of the federal Constitution and its "prodigiously decentralized" system of administration, Tocqueville forecasts America's future role as a great power and reflects on the distinctively democratic approach to external affairs. Advancing, in Stephen Garrett's words, "a general theory of democratic foreign policy," Tocqueville's reflections shed light on his own lifelong preoccupation with international politics.[11]

In *Democracy*'s first volume Tocqueville pinpoints the realm of diplomacy and external affairs as the Achilles' heel of popular regimes. This vulnerability stems from the peculiar character of democratic politics. The instability of public life in democracy, driven by the contest of parties with competing objectives, makes the formulation and pursuit of a consistent strategy difficult. Competitive party politics prioritizes internal improvements and often instrumentalizes national security for domestic political gains, thus subordinating foreign relations to shifting domestic and partisan agendas.[12]

Beside the incapacity to "settle on one plan," democracies tend to judge poorly their interests abroad. This, Tocqueville claims, is because "the people feel much more than they reason." Prone to abandon a matured purpose in order "to satisfy a momentary passion," the popular sovereign and its "prophet" public opinion are rarely able to take the long view and to see clearly into the future.[13] To illustrate this irrational bent, Tocqueville recalls the controversy that erupted in the newly founded United States at the outbreak of the French Revolution. With popular sympathies vehemently in support of revolutionary France, it took "the unyielding character of Washington and the immense popularity he enjoyed" to restrain the Union from declaring a war on Britain (which it could not finance) and from getting embroiled in a conflict that would soon drench Europe in blood. Were it not for the constitutional powers and personal authority of the first president, "the nation would have done then [in the 1790s] what it condemns today [in the 1830s]."[14]

Weighing democracy's strengths against its weakness, Tocqueville concludes:

> In a democracy, experience, mores, and education almost always end by creating the sort of everyday practical wisdom and the skill in the small events of life that is called good sense. Good sense suffices for the ordinary routine of society.... But it is not always so in the relations of one people with another.
>
> Foreign policy requires the use of almost none of the qualities that belong to democracy and, on the contrary, demands the development of nearly all those qualities that it lacks.[15]

Democracy's second volume reflects at length on the qualities and drawbacks of the democratic mindset. Tocqueville argues that the passion for equality strengthens the perception of similitude not only among the classes of each nation, but also between nations, thus bringing to light "for the first time" the idea of universal humanity. The rising ideal of human fellowship fosters an attitude of "general compassion for all members of the human species." Tocqueville credits this modern attitude with softening mores, and moderating the relations between peoples. "At the time of their greatest enlightenment," he notes,

> the Romans cut the throats of enemy generals, after dragging them in triumph behind a chariot, and delivered prisoners to the

beasts for the amusement of the people. Cicero, who raises such loud cries at the idea of a citizen crucified, finds nothing to say about these atrocious abuses of victory. It is clear that in his eyes a foreigner is not of the same human species as a Roman.[16]

Censuring Cicero's reticence about the atrocities of Roman triumph, Tocqueville praises modern compassion and its effect on international relations. Yet he also warns about its dangers. The democratic impulse to sympathize with others carries an equally spontaneous inclination to misunderstand them. Sympathy, Tocqueville argues, is premised on similarity. By assuming human beings to be equal, the compassionate democrat believes "he can judge in a moment the sensations of all the others: he glances quickly at himself; that is sufficient." Taking all humankind to be alike—and all like themselves—democracies often fail to acknowledge differences and have difficulty comprehending alterity as such. Their relative inexperience with otherness renders them especially insensitive to the complex and arcane issues of international politics.[17]

In short, Tocqueville points to a limited understanding of foreign policy as a "natural vice" of democracy. Politically savvy at home, popular regimes are considerably less able to discern their long-term interests abroad, or pursue them with consistency and vigor. Public opinion, which is the driving force of political life in democracies, is at best a clumsy and often a dangerous guide to international affairs.[18] As discussed in chapter two, while agreeing with J. S. Mill on this score, Tocqueville nevertheless denied that a democratic government could dispense with consulting popular opinion on foreign-policy questions, or on any others. Rather than removing foreign affairs from public contestation and debate, and entrusting them to unaccountable experts, public opinion must be enlightened. It is to the weakness in discerning and negotiating the necessities of the international environment that leadership efforts must be directed. Tocqueville stresses the indispensability of enlightened statesmanship that strives to guide popular opinion and inform the nation about its interests and international standing. His view of the specific challenges of democratic foreign policy also helps explain why, in entering political life, Tocqueville put special emphasis on foreign affairs.[19]

Tocqueville's Grand Strategy

From his very first speech in the chamber, Tocqueville made foreign policy the main focus of his political career.[20] Spanning more than a decade, his career culminated in a brief tenure as a foreign minister of the Second Republic. As evidenced by his notes and edifying rhetoric, Tocqueville saw his role in the legislature as an exponent of the "natural and permanent interests" of the nation. Decrying a lack of foresight and a coherent vision of international affairs, his foreign-policy speeches trained the chamber's attention on international relations questions of the highest order, seeking to explicate the country's situation, clarify its political priorities, and formulate policy tasks.[21]

Tocqueville's extensive pronouncements on national security and international relations were prompted by five major issues: the so-called Eastern question, discussed in the previous chapter; the subsequent heated debates over the right of search; the Spanish succession; the alliance with England; and what Tocqueville called France's "greatest affair": the colonization of Algeria.[22] A characteristic feature of these interventions is Tocqueville's attempt to broaden the debate by addressing not only the immediate political conjuncture, but also general principles and enduring concerns. Sovereignty and isolationism, the extent to which international commitments can and should be binding, the compatibility of liberal principles and national interests, as well as France's identity and role in the world are recurring questions in Tocqueville's oratory that motivate his stance on foreign affairs and inform what Paul Carrese has called his "grand strategy."[23] Often overlooked by scholars, Tocqueville's speeches on foreign affairs shed bright light on the complexities of international politics and the global prospects of democratization.

Sovereignty and Isolationism

Alongside the general critique of democracy's capacity for prudent diplomacy, particular French circumstances urged Tocqueville to turn his attention to foreign relations. His public addresses, as well as his letters and private notes, reveal his sensitivity to France's humiliation in the Napoleonic wars and her diminished status as a great power. Tocqueville was especially concerned with the far-reaching implications of his country's disengagement from European affairs. More than the loss of international prestige, he feared the degrading effects of a policy of isolationism on the political and moral life of the nation.[24]

The second volume of *Democracy in America*, published a year after Tocqueville entered the Chamber of Deputies, analyzes the dangers of individualism and the apolitical tendencies that arise with the spread of democratic equality. The individualist mentality, Tocqueville warned, is presentist and utilitarian. Fixated on narrowly defined interest and bolstered by a presumption of self-sufficiency, it carries with it the temptation to disengage from public life. This withdrawal weakens the individuals themselves as much as it depletes society of its vitality and strength.[25]

In a similar vein, Tocqueville decries in his oratory France's isolationist policies and the individualistic mindset of the country as a whole. He insists that, as in the case of selfish individuals, a self-absorbed nation runs the risk of languishing. A polity that willingly ignores the affairs of the world and refuses to undertake great tasks beyond its immediate utility or interest is set on a path of decline.[26] Alongside the loss of France's global status with its moral-psychological effects, Tocqueville cautioned against the threat he perceived to her sovereignty. In his view, the country's passivity on the international stage would not only detract from her reputation and confidence as a world power. It would also menace France's independence:

> A nation that allows the greatest thing of the century to happen without her falls into the second rank; a nation which is content with not losing, but allows her neighbors to grow prodigiously in force ends up finding herself in their dependence.[27]

In his parliamentary speeches, as in the analytical works, Tocqueville analyzes states with categories he applies to individual agents. The frequent parallels between man and nation suggest that, in his view, the world of global politics is governed by psychological and moral determinants analogous to those of interpersonal relations.[28] In the international context, particular nations act as persons striving for freedom and flourishing. National sovereignty like individual freedom is to a greater or smaller degree externally determined. Next to the country's own resources, it is contingent on the equilibrium of powers and the complex web of dependencies that create the dynamic field of international politics. As Tocqueville argues, in the case of nations and of individuals, it is above all by participating in political life that each agent's liberty is upheld and safeguarded. If sovereignty names the capacity to set and follow a self-chosen course of action, what fosters this capacity is not isolation from but an active engagement with others. Conversely the isolationism of states, like the individualism of persons, is an inherent threat to sovereignty, for it proceeds from—and reinforces—a misguided notion of independence. Just as the citizens' political disengagement can compromise individual freedoms by leaving the door open to an enterprising tyrant or the impersonal despotism of the state, so too will nations that withdraw into their domestic lives, unconcerned with the world at large, soon find themselves at the mercy of more expansive players. Not only a matter of national self-esteem or vainglory, having a say in the world's affairs is a crucial condition of self-determination.[29]

Tocqueville's argument that foreign relations are essential to maintaining democratic freedom in general, and France's liberty in particular, parallels his advocacy of vigorous associations on the level of domestic politics. In both cases, his advocacy rests on a set of presuppositions regarding the moral prerequisites for self-government. In *Democracy* Tocqueville argues that local freedoms and civil rights are maintained by actively involving individuals and groups in political life, thus reminding "each citizen that he lives in society." Simple citizens learn "the art of being free" above all by meddling in the public business and directly partaking in the task of governing. Likewise, Tocqueville's foreign-policy speeches contend that the great liberty of the nation can only be sustained by vigorous engagement in international politics. It is by acting on the world stage and claiming responsibility for world affairs that nations improve their self-understanding, gauge the realities of their own situation, and acquire the skills to deal with these realities. As I argued in chapter one, in Tocqueville's view, democratic sovereignty is the ability to set common goals and reach them through a collective process based on deliberation and consent. Throughout his political career, Tocqueville points to energetic foreign policy as indispensable for advancing his country's political and moral outlook as well as its material prosperity, and, by the same token, for enhancing France's sovereignty.[30]

Balance of Power

While the very concern with sovereignty prescribes an active involvement in external affairs, the mode of this involvement and its specific objectives depend on conditions that are only in part, if at all, of one country's making. More often than not, a country's foreign policy and strategic priorities are dictated by the international environment and geopolitical conjuncture. Precisely because these priorities are in significant measure beyond one's wish or control and involve a range of more or less undesirable choices, they are often difficult to discern and to resolutely pursue.[31]

In his foreign-policy speeches, Tocqueville presents Europe's global expansion as the most significant development in world politics and "the movement of the century." A historical and geopolitical given, the construction of colonial empires is, moreover, a critical factor behind the providential rise of equality to which Tocqueville's analytical work bears witness. Like Marx and Engels would later do, Tocqueville assigns a special role in this development to the unrelenting dynamism of the British Empire and its former colonies. His analysis also calls attention to the decline of the Ottoman Empire and the rise of autocratic imperial Russia as critical factors for French and European politics.[32] Put otherwise, Europe's global rise and the democratic movement to which it gives impetus cannot be arrested or steered otherwise than by partaking in it. This is why, I suggest, Tocqueville cautiously embraces his country's colonial vocation and urges France to play an active role in "the great affair of the century." A matter of necessity, more than of choice, participation in that historic movement is the only reasonable and honorable course of action that would counterbalance British predominance and safeguard France's influence in the affairs of the world.[33]

If European expansionism is the historical and political backdrop for Tocqueville's foreign-policy vision, striving for global equilibrium is the fundamental principle of that vision.[34] As a legislator, Tocqueville insists on maintaining a power balance both as a prerequisite for sustaining the global conditions of liberty and as a main objective of French foreign policy. A discarded passage originally concluding his observations on American commerce in the first volume of *Democracy in America* shows that this pragmatic position was not simply born of the particular geopolitical conjuncture. Tocqueville writes:

> France is called to be always one of the great maritime powers, but she can never become the first except by chance. Since France cannot hope to dominate the sea in a lasting way, her visible interest is to prevent another from dominating there ... and to make the most liberal maxims as regards commerce prevail in the whole world ...

It is from this point of view that France is the *natural enemy* of England. She will always be so ... as long as England is able to impose its laws on the ocean. America is at present in a position analogous to that of France. It is powerful without being able to dominate; *it is liberal because it cannot oppress.*

So America is the *natural ally* of France, in the same way that England is its enemy.... If maritime forces come to reach a balance between England and America, which will happen I think in a period that is not far away, the role of France will be, by going *alternately to the side of the weaker*, to prevent either one of them from entirely dominating the sea and thus *to maintain liberty* there.[35]

Expressing views conveyed elsewhere, Tocqueville's discarded reflections on maritime commerce articulate with striking directness his view of the agonistic character of interstate affairs and of politics in general. Note the language of "natural" friends and foes. For Tocqueville, England is an enemy of France not because of incompatible interests, differences of creed, or historical entanglements—nor because, as he once claimed in a speech, rivalry with England is the genius of the French—but because of the actual power distribution that is likely to change over time.[36] Likewise, France's "natural" friendship with the United States appears independent of ideological common ground, or historic ties and obligations. Drawing a parallel between the principles of domestic constitutionalism and those that govern global affairs, Tocqueville suggests that freedom in the international context, as in the national one, depends on the existence of checks and balances that pose structural constraints on the hegemonic aspirations of particular agents. Far from condemning such aspirations, he recognizes the desire for power and independence, and the urge to extend the sphere of one's control, as the intrinsic ends of political life. Given these ends, the possibility of liberal politics, on a global as on a local level, depends on the plurality and balance of active forces and wills. It also implies the instrumental character of political alliances.[37]

This is not to deny that common objectives and shared principles can sustain long-term partnerships. Surely international treaties and legal agreements provide guarantees that may stabilize the international order for a time. Yet, the complexity and competitiveness of the global environment—an environment comprising a multitude of unequal states, each oriented by incommensurable values—ensures that no such order can endure indefinitely. Given this inbuilt instability and changing constellations, the idea of unconditional loyalty and open-ended commitment is equally at odds with the sovereignty of any one country as with the liberty of all. In order to ensure that structural checks are continuously in place, each country's national interest must be informed and enlightened both by a prudential recognition of mutual dependence and by an abiding concern for global equilibrium.[38]

Nothing better illustrates Tocqueville's adherence to this vision of international politics than the position he took in the controversy over granting England the so-called right of search. Having banned the Atlantic slave trade in 1807, throughout the nineteenth century Britain pursued the suppression of the slave trade as a top foreign-policy priority, resorting to force or diplomacy as circumstances demanded. A crucial diplomatic instrument of the antislavery campaign were bilateral agreements that granted Britain the right to search in the high seas for foreign ships suspected of transporting slaves for the global markets.[39] A committed abolitionist and lifelong Anglophile (to the point of taking an English wife against his family's wishes), Tocqueville endorsed the ends, yet protested the means. Urging France to join the cause of abolition, he vehemently opposed what, in a letter to a newly appointed American secretary of war, he calls Britain's "dangerous and distressing dominance" and the threat it posed to the freedom of the seas.[40]

Tocqueville points to England as an object lesson and practical example of the rules that govern international affairs. In his analysis, Britain's pursuit of abolitionist policy was driven both by the humanitarian demands of domestic public opinion, and by the urge to project abroad her political and economic power.

Anticipating Marx's critique of imperialism and a current of contemporary scholarship, Tocqueville argues that Britain's imperial expansion was a matter of economic necessity more than choice. Likewise, the British campaign against the slave trade was informed by political and economic calculation as much as an earnest commitment to humanitarian principles. While commercial and political needs pushed England to be not only powerful but all-powerful, the right of search and the abolitionist regime it served to establish were privileged means to that end.[41] Tocqueville, in short, recognized in British abolitionism a mix of philanthropic and self-interested motives, as well as a bid for global dominance. The campaign against the slave trade served to legitimate at home and extend abroad the British Empire.[42]

If striving for domination was a natural consequence of Britain's political and economic orientation, it was just as natural for other countries to resist her hegemonic aspirations. For, however well-intentioned, a political actor that acquires the capacity to wield unchecked power will sooner or later be tempted to put that power to oppressive use. In Tocqueville's account, it is not only in the interest of other countries but also in her own that England must not be allowed to become the world's master and policeman. Commenting on the international reaction to the 1857 Sepoy Mutiny—an uprising of the East India Company's Bengal army that escalated into a civilian conflict so considerable that it has been dubbed India's first war of independence—Tocqueville states that Britain's very hegemony denied her the compassion and good will of other nations. Giving rise to grievances at home and abroad, the political and commercial dominance of England restricted her moral sway in world affairs.[43]

In sum, for Tocqueville, maintaining the power balance and the resources necessary to sustain it is the first condition of national sovereignty and of freedom in the international realm. It is also the backbone of Tocqueville's grand strategy. While political actors naturally seek freedom and strive to expand their sphere of control, in the international context as in the national one liberty crucially depends on limiting each agent's capacity for domination. This understanding of the preconditions for liberal politics highlights the interrelation of national interests and international concerns. It also intimates the broader implications of the principle of national sovereignty. While one country's self-assertion may be intended to serve its national interests, if it contributes to the power balance, it also helps to promote international stability hence the common good of all.[44]

And yet, though seeing freedom as the effect of structural constraints that regulate the agonistic behavior of expansive and self-regarding agents, both in internal and foreign relations Tocqueville repudiates a purely pragmatic approach to policy. His analysis suggests that unless grounded in norms and informed by a larger vista of human affairs, a politics of crude national interest is likely to issue in reckless action or imprudent disengagement that threatens to compromise the global equilibrium. Calling for ongoing vigilance and flexibility of means, Tocqueville insists that foreign policy can only succeed if it is based on clear principles and exalted ends. Not simply debunking Britain, his foreign policy analysis shows that Britain's global status and aspirations are not reducible to economic or material interests for which humanitarian commitments serve merely as a front. Emphasizing time and again the moral foundation of power, Tocqueville argues that, unlike domination, legitimate authority is based on opinion and consent, hence on an appeal to ideals and shared norms. Legitimacy at home and maintaining the power balance abroad both require not only military force or the attainment of economic resources, but crucially a competition for "moral capital" as well.[45]

Liberty and Greatness

There are people who think that nations should retire in themselves and live, in a way, in a narrow and sterile egoism. I don't hesitate to say it, Gentlemen, I myself am not of this school and I dare add that my country is not of it either. No, Gentlemen, nations, be sure of it, do not do great things without perceiving something greater than themselves.[46]

As I have argued, Tocqueville regarded Europe's global expansion as the most significant development of his time and a critical factor behind the providential rise of democratic equality. He urged France to partake in and help steer "the movement of the century," which he saw as a precondition both of French sovereignty and of global liberty.[47] Stressing the need to uphold the global power balance and to confront steadfastly the reality of European expansionism, Tocqueville strove nevertheless to embed France's exterior politics in a long-term view and a principled approach to foreign policy.[48] His parliamentary oratory and journalism summoned France to recognize liberal democratic principles as the foundation not only of domestic political culture, but also of her international standing and mission as a modern nation. As an 1845 speech proclaimed,

> If France were governed as she ought to be she would sense that her principal interest, her permanent interest, is to make liberal institutions triumph in the world, not only out of love for these institutions, but even out of care for her force and for her grandeur . . . The great interest of France is to substitute everywhere despotic institutions with liberal ones; this, I dare say, is France's capital interest.[49]

In like spirit, in an 1843 series of articles titled "Emancipation of Slaves," the very ones that dissect the complex motives behind British abolitionism, Tocqueville exhorted his compatriots to live up to "our principles" by abolishing slavery in the old colonies:

> These notions of freedom and equality that are weakening or destroying servitude everywhere: who spread them throughout the world? This sentiment, disinterested and yet impassioned with the love of men, which all at once made Europe hear the cry of slaves—who propagated it, directed it, illuminated it? We were the ones. Let us not deny it. It was not only

our glory but our strength ... Thanks to us, these ideas have become the symbol of the new politics.[50]

Tocqueville insists that France should strive to counterbalance "the political, commercial and industrial influence of England" first and foremost by emulating British efforts. While opposing England's demand for the right of search, he argues that it is not by abandoning the abolitionist cause, but by reclaiming it as her own that France can hope to regain her international standing. Failing to do so would amount to self-abdication. Tocqueville points to the ideals of the French Revolution, which made that Revolution a world-historical event, as the mainspring of France's power and bid to world leadership. Invoking glory and national honor, he contends that only a policy oriented by universal creed and liberal principles can restore the nation to her global status and make France great again.[51]

Tocqueville's approach to foreign policy has been characterized as a nationalist argument for humanitarian ends. In his oratory and journalism, Tocqueville plays up France's vocation as a great power by redefining the nation in liberal terms and attaching, in Cheryl Welch's words, "the notion of French grandeur to the spread of democratic liberty."[52] In Tocqueville's telling, not military conquests but greatness of soul and the *"sublime faiblesse"* to labor for the emancipation of humankind are the fundaments of French power and grandeur. Nor is this grandeur a privilege of birth or a historic necessity. Rather, it is a merit and responsibility that demand sustained commitment and expenditure of "great efforts." The principles of the French Revolution, Tocqueville contends, made France great in the eyes of the world. It is by a renewed commitment to these principles that she can maintain her greatness. His appeal to greatness aims to stimulate France's engagement abroad as well as to shape the character of this engagement.[53]

By tying France's mission in the world to the "notions of freedom and equality," Tocqueville highlights the coincidence of national honor and humanitarian creed. Rather than permanently opposed, national interest well-understood and liberal democratic principles can and should be reconciled. Not only is it possible to harmonize the conduct of external affairs with the liberal and egalitarian values cherished at home. It is necessary to do so if France wishes to uphold her status as a global leader and beacon of modern civilization—an aspiration Tocqueville consistently encouraged.[54]

To recapitulate, Tocqueville's foreign-policy speeches appeal to French glory and national honor in order to advance an image of liberal democratic France and promote policy orientations at home and abroad.[55] Underscoring the tight relationship between national identity and foreign policy, and between domestic principles and global standing, Tocqueville points to international politics as the ultimate school of democratic liberty, and as a privileged setting for the ongoing task of enhancing France's self-understanding and her sovereignty as well. Tocqueville's grand strategy for France thus combines what contemporary international relations theory calls idealist and realist dimensions.[56] The realist aspect consists in recognizing the agonistic character of international relations (and of politics in general), and the necessity to project power abroad in order to maintain domestic stability and the global power balance. The idealist dimension comes to light in Tocqueville's untiring insistence on the moral foundations of power, and on the need to reconcile liberal democratic principles espoused at home with foreign-policy objectives. Distinct though they are, these realist and idealist dimensions could be seen as mutually supportive. Democratic freedom cannot be established or sustained without power or material resources. Tocqueville remarks in *Democracy in America* that "for nations, strength is often one of the first conditions of happiness and even of existence." At the same time, as Tocqueville's theory of democratic sovereignty posits and his analysis of England corroborates, in foreign as in domestic affairs, strength and legitimate authority are based on opinion and consent more than "money and soldiers." They consist in the ability not to compel obedience but to inspire it, thus to lead by exerting moral influence rather than force. Though necessarily including a material dimension, legitimate power vitally depends on the capacity to win the battle for hearts and minds at home and abroad.[57]

Tocqueville's theoretical and practical engagement with international politics culminated in his brief tenure as a minister of foreign affairs from June to October 1849. Occurring near the end of his political career, which was cut short by the 1851 coup d'état of Louis Napoléon, Tocqueville's mandate as a foreign minister was too short to make a difference in the country's orientation or exemplify his own. As I have suggested, Tocqueville's decade-long grappling with the conundrums of French colonial policy, more than his time in government, epitomized and put to a practical test his foreign-policy vision.[58] In the remainder of this chapter, I revisit the rationale and main dilemmas of Tocqueville's colonial policy. By shedding light on what I argue are its inherent contradictions, I seek to discern Tocqueville's view of the trajectory and long-term prospects of globalization.

Case Study 3: Colonizing Algeria, or Grand Strategy in Practice

Colonization is a theme that runs through all of Tocqueville's writings. From his early travel notes and unpublished sketches, through *Democracy in America*, to the parliamentary oratory, political journalism, and extensive correspondence, European expansionism and its defining significance for the modern world are at the center of Tocqueville's attention. Tocqueville views colonization and the bringing face to face of diverse populations and ethical perspectives as a crucial factor that propels the global rise of equality, and shapes its social and political trajectories. For it is in the cohabitation and rubbing together of different modes of life that the question of universal norms and common humanity arises in all its urgency and practical significance. Informing both Tocqueville's analytical work and his understanding of foreign affairs, the link between colonization and democratization underpinned his qualified support for the French colonial empire and his efforts (for the most part unsuccessful) to shape French policy in Northern Africa. Declaring the colonization of Algeria France's "greatest affair" and principal interest, Tocqueville made this affair the main feature of his statesmanship. As the most salient— and controversial—of his political causes, Tocqueville's involvement with Algerian colonization throws into stark relief his vision of international politics and the challenges of reconciling realism and idealism in the emerging global order.[59]

Tocqueville penned his earliest sustained reflections on French colonial policy, the 1837 *Letters on Algeria*, in the context of his first electoral campaign. Printed in a local newspaper, the *Letters* survey the history of France's engagement in northern Africa, its political and social context, and main policy dilemmas. In 1841 and 1846, Tocqueville made two visits to Algeria, which resulted in a body of writings on the political, social, and economic condition of the colony. These writings include drafts and travel notes, an unpublished policy brief, two official reports for a parliamentary commission on the colony, two parliamentary interventions and extensive correspondence with French and British colleagues. Reaching for a comparative perspective, Tocqueville also studied closely and began to draft a work on British India that remained unfinished.[60]

Tocqueville's colonial writings elaborate on themes first broached in his American analysis. Key among them is the confrontation of diverse peoples and ways of life that colonization brings about. *Democracy in America*'s chapter on the three American races reflects at length on this confrontation. Though claiming to consider subjects particular to America, Tocqueville's account has broader implications. These are signaled by its focus on race: a term that, for Tocqueville, marked cultural rather than natural differences, and carried a range of meanings from class and people to humanity as a whole. As scholars have pointed out, beyond its historical and local specificity, Tocqueville's reflections on the meeting of the three American races illustrate the worldwide effects of Europe's encounter with non-Europeans. Canvassing in poignant detail the consequences of this encounter, the image Tocqueville paints is that of the "European race" reigning "tyrannical" over the others. Whether in "removing" the Indians or enslaving the Blacks, this tyranny works above all by breaking up the bonds of family and language, custom and religion that hold societies together. It ends up dissolving cultures and peoples that cannot defend their claim to equality and perpetuate their way of life.[61]

In Tocqueville's telling, though in many ways exceptional and marked by new racial hierarchies, the collision of the three American races is not sui generis. Historical particularity notwithstanding, this collision is comparable to that between the American North and the South, or between the French and Spanish with the Anglo-Americans. Along with the irresistible ascent of a democratic way of life, these fateful confrontations reveal, as a footnote states, "the destructive influence that very civilized peoples exert on those who are less so."[62] Tocqueville's striking claim is that, in the North American context this "destructive influence" is not necessarily the result of military conquest or physical violence. Rather, it is brought about by the coming "face to face" of diverse cultures and ways of life.[63]

Tocqueville's analysis of the nature and effects of North American colonization marshals a host of contemporary sources and legislative documents. Silently but no less crucially, as Spector has argued, it relies on Montesquieu's distinction between territorial and commercial empire. While differentiating between two forms of empire, Montesquieu critiques the former for being imbued with a spirit of conquest that results in despotism and slavery. Pointing to the ancient Romans and to their modern imitators, the Spanish and the French, Montesquieu charges that by militating against human diversity territorial empire is as pernicious to the power that pursues it as to its unhappy subjects. Yet Montesquieu also imagines a different kind of empire, which he saw embodied in the exploits of Alexander the Great and in modern sea-faring England. Pursuing commerce more than domination, and preserving rather than suppressing the diversity of human ways, maritime commercial empire is poised—under certain conditions—to enhance human prosperity and freedom. It can bring civilization and improvement rather than misery and enslavement to the vanquished.[64]

As Spector points out, Tocqueville's discussion of American colonization blurs this Montesquieuan distinction and calls into question the implied humanity or beneficence of commercial empires. Citing official documents, Tocqueville shows that in their own self-understanding, the Anglo-Americans were waging a war of conquest by commerce. Appropriating the land through skilled diplomacy and legal purchase, their aim was to displace America's native inhabitants in a manner that "is more agreeable to justice and more merciful than to assert their possession by the sword." As I discuss in chapter one, the federal government's attempt to control this process and protect the Indian populations, even when sincere, was powerless to oppose the concerted effort of the states and the restless spread of European settlers.[65]

Collapsing the distinction between conquest and commerce, the problem Tocqueville identifies is intimately connected with what he views as the virtues of American colonization: its bottom-up, popular, and federal qualities that distinguish it from statist projects à la France or Spain. While this mode of colonization has helped create unusually self-reliant colonists—a democratic citizenry par excellence—it also set firm limits on what the federal government could do to protect the native peoples. Bringing up the Cherokees as a case in point, Tocqueville's indictment is not so much that the federal government was acting in bad faith, but that it was impotent to act. It could only do as much as the popular mandate allowed, which historically meant removing the natives.[66]

Having described the situation of America's native peoples, Tocqueville goes on to assert that, for all its atrocities, the Spanish *conquista* was less successful in wiping out cultures and peoples than the commercial and legalistic Anglo-Americans. In contrast to the violent incorporation of the Spanish colonies and their "monstrous crimes without precedent," the story of the three American races puts on dramatic display how peoples can be subdued or annihilated "without violating a single one of the great principles of morality." The Indians, Tocqueville claims, were being destroyed "calmly, legally, philanthropically," while the enslaved Africans were brought to American soil as a result of a legal trade that flourished for centuries under the auspices of European powers.[67]

Scholars have pointed out that both in *Democracy in America* and in later references to the American experience, Tocqueville downplays the violent character of interracial relations in the United States. While Tocqueville's account may be factually debatable, its rhetorical effect is striking. In what reads as a direct riposte to Montesquieu and an anticipation of Marx and Engels, Tocqueville claims that trade was more efficient than military violence in dispersing and annihilating native cultures. Calling into question a fundamental tenet of classical political economy, his American analysis prompts us to recognize the destructive effects of economic affairs on human diversity. It suggests that, in the realm of international relations, trade could be equally—perhaps more—devastating than war. As Tocqueville claims, engaged in a contest "with the most civilized and, I shall add, the greediest people on the globe," the Indians and the Blacks (and to an extent Southerners, French, and Spaniards) succumb to a "destructive competition." His account thus raises vexing questions about the preconditions for mutually beneficial economic and cultural relations, and for the possibility of justice among nations.[68]

Whereas Tocqueville's account of the three American races offers a model of racial and civilizational conflict, and reveals its importance for democracy's future, it is in his political involvement in Algeria that this model is elaborated into a full-blown institutional and policy analysis. Tocqueville's colonial works expound on cultural confrontation as both a crucible of and barrier to social and political equalization. They substantiate, more fully than his stylized American account, Tocqueville's vision of the mechanisms and paradoxical dynamic of globalization.

France's occupation of the Ottoman regency of Algiers began in July 1830 with a punitive expedition targeting, in Ann Thomson's words, "the most powerful and intractable of the Barbary states" that for centuries sponsored piracy and the slave trade in the Mediterranean. The Barbary states were autonomous provinces of the Ottoman Empire, inhabited by Arab, Berber, and Jewish populations, and governed by a small Turkish elite. Although run by, and in the interest of, a foreign power, the Ottoman institutions and practices succeeded in accommodating local customs and enjoyed a degree of religious legitimacy.[69]

Launched on the pretext of a diplomatic blunder, France's invasion of Algiers was an opportunistic effort by the embattled Bourbon monarchy to avert a political crisis at home. At the same time, the Algerian campaign was the culmination of a European cause célèbre dating back to the mid-seventeenth century that called for the abolition of slavery and corsairing in the Mediterranean—a cause to which the young American republic had made a contribution of its own.[70] Armed with revolutionary arguments and relying on leadership and military strategy developed by Napoleon, the French invasion was originally aimed at political and economic reconfiguration rather than permanent occupation. Yet the fall of the Bourbon government and the dynastic change in France triggered a vigorous debate on the mode and objectives of France's presence in Northern Africa.[71]

Tocqueville's official involvement with the African colony began nearly a decade after the capture of Algiers at a point when the French occupation was a fait accompli and a political consensus in favor of colonization was crystallizing. Throughout this involvement, Tocqueville steadfastly repudiated territorial expansion for its own sake.[72] He likewise opposed the alternative scenarios championed by the critics of colonization, namely "maritime occupation without colonization" or of pulling out altogether. Emphasizing the geostrategic and political importance of the lands that in 1838 the French government would officially name Algeria, Tocqueville argued that without an effort to modernize the ethnically divided and economically underdeveloped territory (to engage in nation building in today's terms) occupation would be pointless. Unless Algeria was made to flourish on its own, France's presence in Northern Africa would be "ruinous for the treasury, destructive of our influence in the world, and above all precarious."[73]

Although a policy of colonization was the emerging consensus in France, the question of how to colonize was a major political battleground, with Saint-Simon–inspired generals commanding the field.[74] Siding with the proponents of colonization, Tocqueville insisted that France must take political and historical responsibility for the territories and populations that had come under her power. Against the variety of socialist proposals, however, he strove (with limited success) to endow France's colonial efforts with a liberal orientation, for which the American and the British experience more broadly served as a model as well as a warning.[75]

Tocqueville admonished the French government to prevent Algeria's native populations from meeting a plight similar to those native to America. Writing admiringly about the Arab religious and military aristocracy, and the proto-republicanism of Algeria's Kabyle people, he urged the French to show due regard for indigenous customs and institutions.[76] At the same time, Tocqueville viewed the "tribal organization and nomadic life" of the native peoples as a challenge to setting Algeria on a path of self-improvement. He claimed that, so long as this mode of social organization persisted, there would be no hope of initiating political and economic development with the help of local powers. Yet changing that organization, which he called "the most tenacious of all human institutions," was not up to France. It would require a social revolution "whose work," as he put in a letter, would be slow and "very painful"; and about which, he believed, France "can do nothing for a very long time, perhaps ever."[77]

This is why from the outset of his involvement with the colony Tocqueville supported a program for settling the African territory in the ancient Roman or modern American way: by attracting agricultural colonists from Europe who would commit their destiny and fortune to developing the land. As scholars have argued, Tocqueville's support for colonization was based on his belief in the crucial importance of an agricultural proprietary class for the success of American democracy and its westward expansion. His colonial policy sought to replicate that success in Algeria.[78] However, as Tocqueville well knew from the American experience, settler colonization was anything but unproblematic. Bound to intensify local resistance and incite inter-group violence, introducing European colonists would entail the "unfortunate necessities" of an all-out struggle for pacification.[79] Along with the immediate challenges to peaceful coexistence, colonization also creates the long-term problem of integrating in the same territory and under the same government profoundly different and, soon enough, mutually hostile modes of life. Fully aware of these repercussions, in the "Essay on Algeria," drafted after his first African visit, Tocqueville notes repeatedly that renouncing colonization would greatly facilitate maintaining French control. "But such domination would always be *unproductive* and *precarious*."[80] Legitimacy and development appear as two mutually incompatible objectives.

If governing the Indigenous peoples was one part of the colonial conundrum, the French made up the rest. Perusing the official documents from the first decade of the conquest, Tocqueville notes in dismay:

> It is inconceivable that in our times, and coming from a nation that calls itself liberal, near France and in the name of France, a government is established that is so disorderly, tyrannical, officious, so profoundly illiberal even in the portion where it could safely afford not to be such, so estranged from the elementary notions of a good colonial regime ... one sees generals and

administrators, who, having suffered at home the yoke of public opinion, the application of the principles of liberty, and the rule of law, seize with delight the occasion to act freely at last, and to satisfy passions and tastes spurred by the restraints, in a country whose exceptional situation serves them as pretext.[81]

Tocqueville's travel notes from his first trip to the colony paint no less distressing a picture. They diagnose in anecdotal detail the hostility between European colonists and the native populations, which mapped onto the persistent animosity between the civilian and military mandates of the colonial administration. These multiple tensions issued in a complex matrix of contending political interests and cultural fault lines that enduringly shaped—and bedeviled—French rule in Algeria.[82]

As Tocqueville contemplates in these early notes and will reiterate in public later on, the French presence in Algeria creates opportunities to indulge motives and behavior normally repressed at home. Rather than civilizing the colony, the military regime installed in the first decades of the conquest brings out the worst of the mother country. Tocqueville reserves his harshest critique for the army. In a frequently cited passage, he confesses to have returned from Africa "with the distressing notion that we are now fighting far more barbarously than the Arabs themselves. For the present, it is on their side that one meets with civilization. This manner of conducting war seems to me as unintelligent as it is cruel . . . It was certainly not worth taking the place of the Turks to recreate that aspect of their rule that deserved the world's abhorrence."[83]

As Margaret Kohn has argued, viewing the French regime in Algeria as a protracted state of exception, Tocqueville dedicated his efforts to replacing military rule with a civil government based on the same liberal institutions and legal procedures that applied in France.[84] And yet, removing the military government, which Tocqueville made into his primary political objective, would hardly be a silver bullet. As he openly acknowledged, the army, whose leadership was trained and advised by the so-called Bureaux Arabes—intelligence units staffed with Arab speakers and expert ethnographers—was intimately familiar with the local populations. Though wielding arbitrary authority, it often acted in their defense. The colonists, on the other hand, perceiving themselves in direct competition with both the army and the native peoples, were soon possessed of genocidal ideas and racist attitudes that pervaded the civil administration as well. In short, the efforts to replace "the rule of the sabre" with the rule of law in Algeria urged the critical question: whose law?[85]

As in America, so too in Algeria, Tocqueville recognized the vital importance of regulating the interactions between colonists and native populations, as well as the monumental challenges that stood in the way of such regulation. The official reports, which he drafted on behalf of a parliamentary commission reviewing the 1848 budget for the colony, highlight the relation with the native peoples as the centerpiece of French colonial policy and the key to its success:

> The commission is convinced that the future of our domination in Africa depends above all on our manner of treating the indigenous population . . . for in this matter the questions of humanity and budget are joined and mingled. We believe that in the long run a good government can lead to real pacification of the country and a considerable diminution of our army.
>
> If, on the contrary, without saying it—for such things are sometimes done, but never admitted—we act so as to demonstrate that for us the ancient inhabitants of Algeria are but an obstacle that has to be removed and trampled underfoot; if we surrounded their populations, not to lift them in our arms toward well-being and enlightenment but to destroy and smother them, the question of life and death will pose itself between the two races . . .
>
> Let us not, in the middle of the nineteenth century, begin the history of the conquest of America over again. Let us not

imitate the bloody examples that the opinion of the human race has stigmatized. Let us bear in mind that we would be a thousand times less excusable than those who once had the misfortune of setting such examples; for we are less fanatical, and we have the principles and the enlightenment that the French Revolution spread throughout the world.[86]

As this passage intimates, in Africa just as in Europe not military force but moral authority is the solid basis for governing power and the sole guarantee of political stability. Pointing to America as an example to shun, Tocqueville argues that moral authority—hence durable peace—can only be achieved by showing genuine concern for the native populations, thus winning their recognition and consent over time. This concern for the "well-being and enlightenment" of the Indigenous peoples motivates his endorsement of a strong central government with extensive administrative competences. The reports demand empowering the central government to intervene between colonists and native population in order to safeguard the rights and interests of the latter. They charge the French state with conciliating the Indigenous inhabitants, taking them under its "tutelage," and gradually introducing them to the basic institutions of modern society. And yet, if the need to protect the native populations prompts Tocqueville's advocacy for a strong centralized government, his colonial writings also abound in the emblematic Tocquevillean critique of the pitfalls of centralized administration and its inability to handle its responsibilities. As in America, so too in Algeria, governmental capacity and liberal orientation proved difficult to reconcile.[87]

Tocqueville is often portrayed as an "avid colonizer" and "militant imperialist" advocating violent conquest.[88] An attentive reading of the colonial works suggests, however, that throughout his official involvement in Algeria, he was an ambivalent friend and a stern critic of French colonization. True, in the heated debates about Algeria's future, Tocqueville defended colonization as the only viable way of building a modern society on the shores of

Northern Africa. In contrast to the elegiac tone of the chapter on the three American races, his colonial writings struck a pragmatic note. Geared to the practical objectives of governance and reform, they seem less intended to raise moral questions than to promote political solutions. Nevertheless, even while lending political support to the French imperial project, Tocqueville's public pronouncements and to a greater extent his private notes and correspondence offer a sobering analysis of the French colonial regime. As Tocqueville stated in the posthumously published "Essay on Algeria," he harbored "no illusion about the nature and value" of French domination. Indeed, "even if we handle it in the best possible way, we shall never create anything but an often troubled and habitually onerous government there." Tocqueville's insight proved prophetic, yet again.[89]

It is crucial to note that, for Tocqueville, the difficulties of Algerian colonization stemmed not only from the economic and social conditions of the native peoples, or from the incapacity of the French.[90] If France's efforts in Algeria were particularly vexed (not least due to the peculiarities of French political culture), Tocqueville's comparative analysis suggests that the decisive challenges inhered in the very structure of colonial rule, which brought different political and moral systems face-to-face.

Tocqueville's first Algerian writings sounded a tone of hopeful optimism about a cultural amalgamation of Christian and Muslim societies. Published in the context of his first bid for election, the *Letters on Algeria* insisted that France's purpose should be to weld Europeans and the native peoples into "a single people" and claimed "that this possibility is not as chimerical as many suppose." By the time of his 1841 visit to the colony, however, Tocqueville was convinced that such optimism was a "chimera."[91] The hatreds born of the iniquities of conquest and sustained by discrepancies in mores and ways of life raised enormous barriers between settlers and native peoples. As Tocqueville had observed in the confrontation of the three American races, the asymmetry of power, principles, and modes of life—what he termed "civilization"—proved extremely difficult to overcome. Not only does this asymmetry invite abuse, exploitation, and cruelty. In a culturally divided society, even a well-intentioned attempt to bridge social cleavages was inevitably tainted with violence:

> The indigenous population has the greatest need of tutelage at the moment when it comes to mix with our civilian population and finds itself, partly or completely, subjected to our officials and our laws. It is not only violent behavior that it has to fear.... The same rules of administration and justice that seem to the European to be guarantees of liberty and property, appear to the barbarian as intolerable oppression.... The forms that we call tutelary, they name tyrannical, and they would rather withdraw than submit to them. This is how, without drawing the sword, the Europeans of North America ended by pushing the Indians off of their territory.[92]

Referencing once again the North American experience, this passage from the first *Report on Algeria* spotlights the central contradiction of colonial rule: the tension between legal norms and moral dignity. In the presence of profound social and cultural divisions rooted in different moral understandings, insisting on uniform rules and legal equality ends up instituting moral tyranny. It imposes norms and practices that are seen not merely as foreign, but as sacrilegious and incompatible with deeply held beliefs about what constitutes a dignified and righteous human life. Napoleon III's attempt two decades later to extend "perfect equality" to Algeria's native inhabitants corroborated Tocqueville's point. Proclaiming Algeria "an Arab kingdom" and himself the emperor of the Arabs and the French, Louis Napoleon offered full citizenship rights to all native Algerians who would renounce their religious status and accept French law. In historian Charles-Robert Ageron's words, "the requirement to abandon their status under Islamic and Jewish law meant in effect that neither Muslims nor Jews applied for the full citizenship on offer."[93]

Tocqueville's rich appreciation of the colonial dilemma underpinned his outspoken opposition to a policy of legal or cultural assimilation. Rather than imposing French institutions, Tocqueville championed the creation of a differential legal system that would respect religious and legal differences, and work toward integration incrementally by fostering an indigenous path to modernity.

> It is not along the road of our European civilization that they must, for the present, be pushed, but in the direction proper to them ... Islam is not absolutely impenetrable to enlightenment: it has often permitted certain sciences and certain arts. Why not seek to make these flourish under our empire? Let us not make the indigenes come to our schools, but let us help them rebuild their own, multiply teachers, educate men of law and men of religion, without which the Muslim civilization cannot do any more than our own can.[94]

Throughout his involvement in Algeria, Tocqueville expounded on the social and political importance of Islam and criticized the adverse effects of French presence on Muslim society. In an impassioned speech of 1847, he castigated the government's "unjust and impolitic suppression" of religious foundations as a result of which "the Muslim cult ... has fallen into a misery that casts shame not only on France but on all civilization." Staining the honor of France, this suppression detracted from her moral power, "the first among the powers of this world."[95] Once again, Tocqueville highlighted the coincidence of justice and expedience: a policy of religious pluralism that showed genuine concern for the cultural identity of the native peoples was not only liberal and good in itself but also in France's best interest. By contrast, destroying monuments, "ruining temples, letting schools decline" could not but undermine French authority and feed the resistance to it.[96]

This is not to suggest that Tocqueville was sanguine about reconciling traditional Islam with modern democratic values. Early in his engagement with Algeria, he immersed himself in a study of the Koran and of Islamic institutions, which he considered central to understanding the mores of Algeria's native peoples. As Kahan has shown, in the course of this study Tocqueville's view of Islam grew increasingly critical. The core of Tocqueville's criticism concerned the lack of separation between secular and sacred realms. As a brief passage from volume two of *Democracy* puts it: "Mohammed made not only religious laws, but also political maxims, civil and criminal laws, and scientific theories descend from heaven and placed them in the Koran."[97]

For Tocqueville this imbrication of secular and sacred is "the first cause of despotism" and the main obstacle to social and political change in the Muslim world. While proclaiming Christianity's superiority in this respect, Tocqueville was well aware that the separation of church and state, virtually absent in colonial New England and still incomplete in the France and Europe of his day, was a hard-won historical achievement attained in the protracted religious and political conflicts that ushered into the modern age. Even if Islam had hitherto failed to separate secular from sacred, as Christianity had for most of its history, this did not preclude the possibility of a future separation. By calling on the French to promote Islam under their empire, and to support native religious and educational institutions while taking a firm hold on the government, Tocqueville gestured at the role France might play in encouraging the separation of religion from politics, thus in liberalizing Algerian mores.[98]

And yet, if imposing legal equality and cultural *assimilation* was inevitably perceived as morally oppressive, this alternative approach—which in French colonial jargon came to be called *association*—was bound to produce legal inequality and social segregation. Although it protected religious and cultural differences by diversifying the justice system, such segregation undermined the principle of social equality and was bound in time to radicalize the subject populations.[99] Tocqueville vividly captured this colonial conundrum in an 1858 letter to Henry Reeve, his English correspondent and the first translator of *Democracy in America*. Responding to Reeve's article on India published in the aftermath of the 1857 Sepoy uprising, Tocqueville grants its central claim: that Britain "cannot retain India without the consent, at least tacit, of the Hindus." Yet, pointing to the insurrection, he explains why and how colonial rule puts this consent out of reach. Tocqueville blamed the insurgence of the Hindu army not on poverty or oppression, but on the lack of camaraderie between soldiers and captains. The "real or pretended superiority" of the Europeans mortifies the self-respect of the Hindus, and "the resulting anger is much greater than any political oppression can produce." Differences in civilization and "race," as well as the exceptional pride of the English—a haughtiness, he added, "intimately tied to their great qualities"—introduced insurmountable distance between the two peoples, and daily reminded them of their inequality.[100]

Analyzing the colonial question in psychological terms, Tocqueville's letter to Reeve suggests that colonialism is unsustainable not only, or not primarily, because it violates rights, but because it offends against pride, and against the dignity and self-understanding of the subject peoples.[101] In another letter of the same year, addressed to Adolphe de Circourt, Tocqueville states that the Sepoy rebellion is more than *a* rebellion. It reveals "a new and general *fact*: a universal reaction against the European race ... [which] is occurring everywhere and is the common cause of a thousand different effects." While too weak at present, it was only a matter of time before this "universal reaction" seeks to dismantle Europe's domination.[102]

Globalization's Paradox

Democracy in America's chapter on honor concludes with the following reflection:

> If it were finally allowed to suppose that all races were blended and that all the peoples of the world had reached the point of

having the same interests, the same needs, and of no longer being different from each other by any characteristic feature, you would cease entirely to attribute a conventional value to human actions; everyone would envisage them in the same light . . .

It is the dissimilarities and the inequalities of men that created honor; it grows weaker as these differences fade away, and it would disappear with them.[103]

As this passage suggests, honor, and with it the distinction between peoples and races, is conventional: it is based not on physical fact but on social agreement to live in a certain way and value certain actions. Did Tocqueville expect that "the dissimilarities and the inequalities of men," which result from such social conventions, would eventually vanish? Could "all peoples of the world" come together as "one equal civilization" in which all would view human life in the same light? Or is our human condition, as he states elsewhere, to be confounded by a plurality of moral views, and divided by language and country?[104] As Tocqueville's analysis of international politics and his grappling with colonial practice suggest, the global rise of democratic equality follows a paradoxical dynamic that points in two opposite directions simultaneously: global convergence on the one hand, recurrent differentiation on the other.

For Tocqueville, I have argued, the rise of modern colonial empires was instrumental in propelling the global movement toward equality.[105] Neither in Europe, nor anywhere else was this democratizing movement quick, spontaneous, or peaceful. In *Democracy in America*, Tocqueville claims that American society saw "the results of the democratic revolution . . . without having the revolution itself." Nevertheless, his account indicates that the political culture of the Anglo-American settlers was attained in the "rude school" of centuries-long partisan and religious conflict. It points to the colonial experience and its racial confrontations as a crucible of democratization. Rather than a "natural and tranquil development," equality is born in the throes of prolonged social and political struggles spurred by the conflict of classes and the rivalry of states.[106]

Just as in *Democracy in America* Tocqueville declares the spread of democratic equality "irresistible," so too in the colonial works he considers Algeria's entering the equalizing process as an irreversible fact. By removing the Ottomans, France's intervention in Northern Africa had opened a pervasive power struggle that precipitated revolutionary change in the life of the native populations.[107] Prompted by the fall of their centuries-old Ottoman rulers, local elites availed themselves of the "arts and even the ideas of Europe" in order to fight a two-front battle: to resist the French, on the one hand, and to transform the traditional structure of their own societies, on the other. Emir Abd-el-Kader, in whose regime Tocqueville recognized the most ambitious attempt at erecting Islamic sovereignty on Algerian territory, epitomized this two-pronged struggle. While claiming to defend the ancestral way of life, the Emir strove to consolidate power by reducing the hereditary aristocracy and undermining the hierarchies that sustained the tribal orders. Sketched in phrases borrowed from Machiavelli, Tocqueville's account of Abd-el-Kader is among the first to recognize in this brilliant new prince a fully modern leader. According to Tocqueville, France's intervention and proximity had contributed to a political and social transformation "very much like that which took place in Europe at the end of the Middle Ages." Once brought into the ambit of European politics and the global power balance, Algeria would be neither able nor willing to leave it: for the very forces that resisted the French had benefited from the French presence and power.[108]

Tocqueville signals that a major effect of France's invasion was to put the native populations on the path to democratic modernity by revolutionizing their social and political relations.[109] While calling on France to manage this revolutionary transition and orient it toward liberal ends, he did not view the colonial relationship as a one-way street. Tocqueville notes that, just as native leaders learned from European ideas, so too did the French take more than one lesson from Abd-el-Kader's military leadership.[110] His policy recommendations insisted on expanding this education to the areas of civil government as well. Tocqueville identified in the colonial debates and administrative conundrums the very contest of liberal and socialist ideas that convulsed public life in France. Castigating the taste for uniformity and the collectivist underpinnings of French colonial practices, Tocqueville's colonial works highlight a central tenet of his new political science: the need "to adapt government to times and places; to modify it according to circumstances and men." They reveal how much had France yet to learn about the art of government, and about the sources and depth of human diversity.[111]

For Tocqueville, in short, the attempt to build a modern society in Northern Africa could succeed only if it redressed the ignorance and advanced the political understanding not of isolated individuals but of the nation at large. Like the Saint-Simon–inspired socialist reformers, but in a liberal way, Tocqueville believed that the Algerian experience could serve to enlighten public opinion and thus to reform France's own political culture.[112] While doubting the colony's long-term future, he wagered that Algeria could provide the budding French democracy with an education it very much needed. Arguably, it is because Tocqueville sought to mobilize domestic attention and political commitment to the colony that he repeatedly called Algeria the "greatest task" and national interest, on which hung France's role in the world and—"most formidably"—her honor.[113]

For Tocqueville, then, as a result of France's invasion, and of the larger context in which it took place, Algerian and French interests had become intertwined. And it was on the long and rocky path to modern democratic civilization that they might be reconciled—a path along which, Tocqueville reckoned, France and European powers in general could be a force for good in fostering the development of non-Western societies, even while advancing their own.[114]

And yet, while pointing to the gradual spread of democratic equality as the civilizational horizon of modern history, Tocqueville's colonial writings caution against jejune optimism and unwarranted hopes for the future. These writings expound, more expressly than the analytical works, on cultural differences as both a crucible of, and greatest challenge to, social and political equalization. "With a brutal clarity," as Cheryl Welch puts it, Tocqueville brings to light not only the failings of France but also the structural and moral contradictions that turned colonial society into a dystopia and compromised its future.

> There is no government so wise, so benevolent, and so just that it can suddenly bring together and intimately unite populations whose history, religion, laws, and practices are so profoundly divided ... We believe it would be imprudent to think that we can manage easily and in so little time to destroy in the heart of the indigenous populations the blind hatred created and sustained by foreign domination. It is therefore necessary, whatever our conduct, to remain strong.[115]

As this recommendation implies, Europe's attempted dominion over the world recalls the characteristics of aristocratic rule. Both have their origin in conquest and were based on force. Violence and domination are the likely effect of the asymmetries of power and civilization, and the coming face to face of moral differences. Yet, as Tocqueville's account of feudal society makes clear, though established through force, and in part maintained by it, the aristocratic polity managed, over time, to gain stability and enlist the tacit consent of its subjects. Entering into habits and mores, it replaced physical coercion with the authority of law and opinion: the shared opinion about the inequality of persons and groups, and a divinely ordained hierarchical order. No such prospect was open to modern European empires not least due to the very ideals of equality and freedom that animated colonial projects and served as moral justification of modern imperialism.[116]

On Tocqueville's account, colonial society is unsustainable first and foremost because it is not a society in the modern egalitarian sense: that is a people constituted by free citizens equal before the law. Lacking consensus on the norms that should direct human life and define the public order, colonial populations were differentiated into personal and group statuses, with one set of laws applying to those deemed capable of being citizens and another to "the natives." Mirroring in this way the corporate structure of aristocratic society, colonial regimes were a combination of modern and premodern elements. To legitimize themselves and resolve their contradictions, Western empires construed the colonial divide as a merely provisional step on the way to modern civilization. Rather than being stuck in their subaltern condition for eternity, the native populations, like nonage children, were placed under temporary tutelage whose overt purpose was to bring about their eventual enfranchisement. And yet, while colonial rule was legitimized by the promise of integration and the attainment of full de jure citizenship down the road, the native peoples could not attain this status without abjuring their cultural identity—a step the great majority of them were not willing to take. Colonialism, in other words, was based on principles it could not realize in practice. For the realization of those principles would require the abolition of the very cultural differences that necessitated and entrenched the colonial divide.[117]

And so, the European empires' attempt to unite and hold together vastly different cultures and modes of life could only be based on inequality and coercion. In the context of colonial society, for coercion to be superseded by the rule of law and the government of opinion, by moral equality and persuasion, a considerable assimilation of fundamental ideas and ways of life would have to take place. Yet, precisely that which makes assimilation necessary, also stands in its way: the sense of national distinctness and the prideful attachment of both colonists and native peoples to their particular manner of life and its ethical perspective, or to what Tocqueville calls *honor*. Tocqueville's colonial writings caution against the tenacity of cultural and moral divides whose deep roots—in collective memory, identity, and national pride—frustrate, even as they give impetus to the process of civil and political equalization. As long as these cultural divisions subsist, there can be neither moral justification for colonial rule in the eyes of those subjected to it, nor the possibility of an all-encompassing community of ideas and practices. While in Tocqueville's *Letters on Algeria* he suggests that achieving such a community is a question of "time, perseverance, ability and justice," taken as a whole his colonial works indicate that all these resources would likely be in short supply.[118]

Tocqueville, in short, balanced his support for colonization with a clear-sighted assessment of its probable future. Charging France with the responsibility to disseminate liberal democratic principles abroad in the interest of sustaining them at home, he confronted in colonial practice the difficulties of this dissemination, and its enormous moral and material costs. He also anticipated its likely denouement: rather than crush or assimilate subject peoples, Tocqueville expected European powers to mobilize their sense of cultural distinctness, and hand them the means of successful resistance. Already in the late 1830s, his analysis of Abd-el-Kader's leadership—the fiercest opposition the French encountered in Algeria before the Front de libération nationale that ended their rule in 1962—highlighted the chief among those means: political centralization and nation building. Tocqueville's analysis points to the rise of Arab nationalism and of political Islam that mobilize religious passions in order to bridge centuries-old ethnic divisions and thus consolidate political power. Likewise, in the drafts for a book on British India he never completed, Tocqueville states that sooner or later "the English will end up putting the Hindus in a position to resist them."[119]

As a whole, Tocqueville's colonial works signal that the most likely result of European expansionism is neither integration, nor lasting imperial domination, but wars of decolonization and the making of new nations. The coming together of civilizations and diverse ways of life that globalization brings about does not simply assimilate peoples, or force them to imitate each other. Stimulating differentiation as much as convergence, it also prompts them to strive for a more robust cultural and political self-definition, and to assert their "individuality among peoples."[120]

For Tocqueville, then, modernity's globalizing current both issues from the confrontation of cultural differences and reinvigorates these differences. Produced by the struggle of particular visions, it is productive of that struggle. Likewise, while set in motion by Western expansionism, and triggered by the often-violent meeting of civilizations this expansionism brought about, the global democratizing process is not synonymous with Westernization. The simultaneous universalization and individuation, the bridging and corroborating of cultural and moral differences that makes up globalization's paradoxical dynamic, comes to the fore, once again, in contrast to the Marxian vision.

Whereas both Tocqueville and Marx understand history to be spurred by conflict and the struggle of contradictions, for Marx these contradictions can and will be overcome—and "the riddle of history solved"—in the beatific state of fully achieved communism. Though Marx never elaborates how this state may come about, his early writings pinpoint its precondition: abolishing the grounds for human difference. For Tocqueville, by contrast, the human condition seems to be marked by a permanent tension between the abiding passion for universal equality, and just as abiding desire for individuality and difference, whose main symptom is pride. Although Tocqueville depicts modern democracy as a "world entirely new," whose future cannot be discerned from the past, so as long as these anthropological givens endure, history's riddle appears insoluble.[121]

CONCLUSION

Sustaining Liberal Democracy

THROUGHOUT THIS BOOK I have argued that three vital issues—sovereignty, nationalism, and globalization—have come to define the contemporary world and configure current political dynamics. The preceding chapters aimed to show that these issues are also pivotal (if often neglected) aspects of Alexis de Tocqueville's work. Clarifying Tocqueville's view of these crucial dimensions of modern democracy is indispensable for gauging the originality and depth of his liberalism. It also provides a powerful framework for understanding our current situation and the dilemmas of liberal democracy in the twenty-first century.

I want to conclude my inquiry and recapitulate the book's main findings by imagining how Tocqueville would understand our current situation and respond to questions raised by contemporary analyses. I begin with a discussion of Steven Levitsky and Daniel Ziblatt's *How Democracies Die* as one prominent and distinctive voice in the current debate. The book's argument, I will show, has multiple affinities with what I take to be Tocqueville's vision—affinities that make the differences all the more striking and worthy of consideration.

In *How Democracies Die*, Levitsky and Ziblatt draw lessons from history in order to illuminate the prospects of democracy in the United States and the world. As the book's title intimates, democracies are mortal, and they die in one of two ways: either collapsing quickly in a violent coup, or eroding "gradually, subtly, even legally" in the hands not of generals but of elected leaders. Today, Levitsky and Ziblatt warn, democratic backsliding is likely to begin at the ballot box and to proceed without violence or drama. "Constitutions and ... democratic institutions remain in place. People still vote. Elected autocrats maintain a veneer of democracy while eviscerating its substance."[1] One prominent example is Venezuela: Latin America's oldest and most successful democracy has descended within less than two decades into a dysfunctional autocracy. Training their analytical lens on the United States, Levitsky and Ziblatt ask whether the world's oldest and most stable constitutional democracy can withstand erosion any better than Venezuela did. Skeptical about American exceptionalism, they warn that democracies, no matter how old or well constituted, are vulnerable. This warning comes with a promise: history shows that democratic erosion can be resisted. To learn from the past, however, we must give up our exceptionalist presumptions—that our time is unprecedented and our society unique—and with them two cherished democratic myths.

The first myth Levitsky and Ziblatt aim to revise concerns the critical importance of constitutional design. Constitutions, they contend, are not by themselves a sufficient guardian of democratic norms. To work well, a constitutional system of checks and balances relies on informal practices and "unwritten laws." While the two examples of "unwritten laws" explored in the book—mutual toleration and forbearance—are drawn from the practice of party politics, the analysis makes clear that partisan fair play is shaped by a wider range of social and cultural factors. Levitsky and Ziblatt trace the regression of constitutional norms and public discourse in the United States to a disintegration of the public sphere into warring camps pursuing diverse existential visions and prepared to use any means—constitutional or not—to promote them. "When partisan rivals become enemies, political competition descends into warfare, and our institutions turn into weapons."[2] If the election of Donald Trump accelerated this polarization, it did not cause it. In the world's oldest liberal democracy, Levitsky and

Ziblatt diagnose, support for constitutional norms and democratic conventions has been eroding for decades.

Having qualified the importance of constitutionalism, the book identifies another fallacy that stands in the way of properly appreciating and adequately addressing our current situation:

> We like to believe that the fate of democracy is in the hands of its citizens. If the people hold democratic values, democracy will be safe. If citizens are open to authoritarian appeals, democracy will be in trouble. *This view is wrong*. It assumes too much of democracy—that "the people" can shape at will the kind of government they possess.[3]

If questioning the role of constitutional design in a functioning democracy is provocative, this claim is more radical still. It calls into question the people's capacity to shape policy and direct public life. Indeed, putting "the people" between scare quotes casts doubt on the possibility of a collective will and the very existence of popular power. Levitsky and Ziblatt challenge the view that in a democracy the people are in charge in order to advance their main claim: that authoritarianism never comes into power with majority support. Democracies, they argue, die not by popular fiat but due to the "abdication of political responsibility by existing leaders," so-called gatekeepers. Yet, the effort to absolve the mass of ordinary citizens—the people—from political responsibility comes at a high price. In defending their main claim, Levitsky and Ziblatt call into question the core legitimating principle and normative ideal of modern democracy: popular sovereignty.[4]

How Democracies Die contends that in America today, or in any Western-type political system, neither constitutions nor people are sovereign. More than institutional arrangement or popular power, the one thing needful to resist democratic erosion is the gatekeepers' political good will to reach across party lines and uphold democracy's normative guardrails. Never mind what their constituencies may demand of them, or how the party base might vote in the next election. If only the political elites could be persuaded to stop treating each other as enemies and to embrace the spirit of cooperation and compromise, backsliding would be contained and democracy saved.

And yet, can a society whose health signally depends on the civility and enlightened will of elites be properly called democratic? If one questions that "the people" can have the power to shape their government, in what sense is one still a defender of democracy? Is it possible to defend democratic norms or work toward their preservation, yet deny popular agency and the responsibility that comes with it? While assuming that democracy is worth saving, Levitsky and Ziblatt omit to explain why this is the case, or indeed what it is they mean by "democracy."

This book's premise and the starting point of my inquiry is that, in order to safeguard Western-type constitutional democracy and revive a broad-based commitment to its principles and institutions, we must raise and address the questions Levitsky and Ziblatt gesture at but leave out of their account: What is liberal democracy, and why should we wish to preserve it? What are the cultural assumptions and unwritten norms that ground liberal constitutionalism? Under what conditions can institutional dynamics and competitive party politics protect rather than erode these norms? How can these conditions be sustained in the twenty-first century? In other words, withstanding democratic erosion and what looks like a global wave of illiberalism requires that we reexamine the intellectual foundations of liberal democracy and the preconditions that make it work. The main purpose of this book has been to contribute to this task of reexamination by drawing on the analytical oeuvre and political practice of Tocqueville. In what follows, I recapitulate the book's main findings by way of reconstructing Tocqueville's answers to the questions raised by Levitsky and Ziblatt, putting these answers in conversation with other contemporary analyses. In doing so I hope to show how Tocqueville can help us deepen our understanding of the present challenges and illuminate a way forward.

Democracy vs. Liberalism?

The relationship between institutions and political culture is a core concern of Tocqueville's work. One stated purpose of his American analysis is to demonstrate the relative priority of unwritten norms, habits, and preconceptions—what he called *moeurs*—over laws on one hand, and over geographic and historical circumstances on the other. Tocqueville, then, would concur with Levitsky and Ziblatt that institutions are not self-sustaining but rely on common practices and understandings, and on shared standards of behavior that help to ground the institutional edifice. Indeed, *Democracy in America* could serve as an authoritative reference for this thesis.[5] However, while agreeing with the first premise of Levitsky and Ziblatt's analysis, Tocqueville would question the second: the unreality of popular rule. As chapter one above sought to show, Tocqueville's contention about the secondary importance of law in a democratic republic is precisely what prompts him to affirm the principle of popular sovereignty. The subordinate role of constitutional design is both evidence for and the primary meaning of popular sovereignty.

As a philosophical principle, the sovereignty of the people points to a general if obscure fact: that every authority depends on popular acceptance, and no institutional order could long endure without the voluntary compliance of those subject to it. Political regimes, in other words, are never simply based on domination. Nor is leadership a one-way street. To be viable and lasting, institutional orders require a critical mass of supporters as well as a community of opinions and sentiments. In Tocqueville's telling, the main effect of the Atlantic revolutions of the seventeenth and the eighteenth century was to call attention to this fact, thereby changing the character of modern politics and of political science as well.

Tocqueville, I argued, distinguishes two facets of popular sovereignty as a principle. The first is the universal insight into the foundation of political life, namely, that every regime is, in some sense, based on consent. The second is the historically distinct character of modern republicanism that turned this privileged insight into a common sense and global opinion. From Tocqueville's perspective, the novelty of modern democracy resides not in the nature of its legitimating principle, but in the extent to which the popular principle has become accepted and widespread and its meaning explicitly contested. Modernity can thus be described as the comprehensive transformation that the recognition (and contestation) of popular sovereignty set in motion. One crucial aspect of this transformation is that democracy has come to be viewed as the only legitimate political order. This is the starting point of Tocqueville's analysis.

It would not be difficult to show that, far from dying an imminent death, democracy today is on the ascendant, certainly as a political aspiration and slogan (and perhaps also more than that). As Levitsky and Ziblatt observe, if endangered in some parts of the world, democracy is reclaimed in others: "for every Hungary, Turkey and Venezuela there is a Colombia, Sri Lanka or Tunisia—countries that have grown *more* democratic over the last decade."[6] Moreover, even in Hungary, Turkey, and Venezuela, to which one could add Russia, China, Iran, and North Korea, governments claim to be authorized by their people and go through elaborate rituals in order to demonstrate their democratic legitimacy. Rare exceptions notwithstanding, peoples and governments the world over prize democracy, technocrats and autocrats pay lip-service to it, elitists and populists alike invoke it, academics write books about it, the antiliberals on the left and right swear by it. As Tocqueville anticipated two centuries ago, we are all democrats now.[7]

And yet, if democracy is on everyone's banner, not everyone means the same thing by it. While nearly all modern governments claim the mantle of democracy and profess to rule by popular consent, regimes differ a great deal in the way they institutionalize popular power and construe the consenting people. In other words, though democracy is universally embraced, its institutional and ethical meaning is contested. That meaning is the very ground on which the great political battles of the past centuries were fought. Whereas the fall of the Berlin Wall appeared to put an end to the history of contesting democracy, thus to equate once and for all democracy with Western-style liberal constitutionalism, in retrospect that appearance proved misleading, and the confidence in a global liberal future it had inspired turned out to be a mere "confidence trap." Just as for most of its modern history, so too in our time democracy's meaning is in question.[8]

The reopening of this question invites us to appreciate that democracy and liberalism are analytically and historically distinct, and it urges us to rethink the conditions of their union. It also suggests that what may be in danger today is not democracy as such, but liberalism, or the long and not always happy marriage between the two that has defined the political West for the past two and a half centuries.[9] Drawing on Tocqueville's theory and practice, this book sought to shed light on this troubled relationship in order to diagnose illiberalism's root causes and identify the preconditions for sustaining liberal democracy today. Crucial among those preconditions is how we understand and grapple with the synergies and the tensions between popular sovereignty and equality: the two foundational principles of modern society.

Equality and Popular Sovereignty

For Tocqueville, I have argued, one cannot fully comprehend modern polities without the principle of popular sovereignty, any more than one can conceptualize democracy without reference to equality. Yet, these two principles of modern society are both mutually constitutive and in tension. Democracy cannot be liberal if either of those elements is missing. But their combination generates frictions and fault lines that propel social dynamics and shape the stakes of modern politics.

Tocqueville shows that, historically, equality and popular sovereignty developed hand in hand, and he points to the American Revolution in order show how they can be mutually reinforcing.

In Tocqueville's account, American independence enacted the aspiration to two kinds of equality: the right of a people to assume an equal station among nations, and the individual right of each member of the people to equally enjoy the advantages of membership. This twofold equality corresponds to two aspects of sovereignty. Externally, sovereignty is synonymous with the self-assertion of the community as a distinct people entitled to determine its fate. Internally, it bespeaks society's capacity for collective self-rule. This capacity is underpinned by the citizens' self-understanding as belonging, in some fundamental respects, to one and the same nation, thus sharing the benefits and duties of equal freedom.[10]

Both the United States and France, the world's first modern constitutional regimes that drew explicit legitimacy from the principle of popular sovereignty, were founded on declarations of rights: not the historic rights of the French, or particular rights claimed by the newly minted American people, but abstract universal rights that pertain to human beings and abstract citizens. Mobilized to dislodge the corporate logic of feudal society and to endow individuals with a new sense of worth, this appeal to natural law and transhistorical rights redefined the meaning of the people: from a lower, disenfranchised class to the ruling sovereign; and from the monarch's loyal subjects to a self-governing republican citizenry. The American and French Revolutions charted, in effect, a new vision of humanity that soon became a major export item and a forceful claim to global leadership.[11]

The rise of popular sovereignty as legitimizing principle and "the law of laws" of modern society set in motion a democratizing dynamic that Tocqueville declared "irresistible." In order to share the benefits of democratic equality one needs to be recognized as a member of the people, and the self-evident truth of human equality serves as a standing claim to such recognition. Democratization thus proceeds by means of extending constitutional guarantees and equal protections to ever-wider descriptions of persons who would thereby become full-fledged members of the political people. Membership in the people is both the instrument and precondition of attaining equal rights.[12]

However, though equality and popular sovereignty can be seen as two moments in democracy's emancipatory logic, they are also distinct and potentially in conflict—a conflict that can, as Tocqueville warned, precipitate illiberal outcomes. While proclaimed as a universal right, political and social equality was, and in crucial respects continues to be, limited to members only. To enjoy equal rights under the law of the land and to be fully entitled to society's advantages and protections, one must be recognized as a citizen of a particular polity, not simply as human. Although all individuals are declared to be universally equal or equally entitled to live as rights-bearing citizens, the concrete parameters of that equality differ greatly from country to country. And so, while proclaimed as universal, equality often stops at the border, which belies its claim to universality. Insisting on its universality, on the other hand, calls into question not only particular borders, but the very idea of border and the legitimacy of the system of nations and states by which the world is governed.

Put differently, because modern democracy takes its ethical bearings from universal rights—that is rights that pertain at once to "man and citizen" with no clear distinction between them—this gap between abstract human being and a member of a particular polity, already put into sharp focus by Aristotle, acquires new urgency in the modern world. The chasm between the universalist principle and the particularist practice is experienced as an affront to our democratic sensibilities. Heightened to the point of impasse by the contemporary debates about immigration and the ravages of economic globalization, this gap is a source of profound psychological and moral tension—a tension that, as Tocqueville predicted, would grow more unbearable the more equal we become.[13]

If this tension between equality and peoplehood is most obvious in the relations between countries and political systems, it is no less present within any modern polity no matter how homogeneous, wealthy, or advanced. This is because every society is a plurality encompassing many groups and citizens that are, as Tocqueville put it, "like so many distinct nations in the same nation." This plurality manifests itself in different beliefs and customs, languages and modes of life, and in a diversity of administrative practices and institutional arrangements as well. Often this variety is the result of a deep-rooted historical legacy, but not always. As Tocqueville points out, democratic individuals seek fresh ways to distinguish themselves from the mass by claiming recognition for their particular identities and fashioning new modes of self-expression. This democratic urge toward distinction comes precisely out of the equality of rights and the promise of individual flourishing that democracy postulates. Both as individuals and as collectivities, we strive to be recognized for our distinctive and unique contributions. Moreover, this desire for recognition and the affirmation of personal and group identities are key motivators for civic participation. Not merely an empirical given, or a sociological fact to be managed, diversity is a democratic aspiration and a desideratum to be cultivated.[14]

A free democracy, then, needs both equality and difference. Socially, as well as institutionally, it strives, as the American motto has it, to form unity out of plurality and, conversely, to maintain and foster plurality in unity. Yet this condition of being both one and many, equal and diverse is shot through with tensions and contradictions that put pressure on sovereignty as well as peoplehood, on the institutional structure as much as on the self-understanding and allegiance of the citizens. Just as on the international level, so too on the domestic one, equality and diversity often collide.

Tocqueville's complex account of state centralization illustrates this collision at the institutional level. As I argue in chapter one, Tocqueville views centralized government as a core achievement of modern society. Without an energetic and potent central power, legitimized by the broad-based consent of the citizenry, there can be neither rule of law and a stable economy, nor a sufficient guarantee for equal rights and freedoms. Governmental centralization, in other words, is both an institutional expression of popular sovereignty and a logical extension of each individual's equal right to self-direction.[15] Conceptually as well as historically, individual freedom is consistent with popular rule. And yet, while a strong central power is needed to assert and protect the equality of rights, centralized government and the social leveling it requires pose a standing threat to these rights. This threat proceeds from majoritarian pressure and direct administrative encroachment, but also from the indirect psychological effects of equalization: the declining motivation to exercise civic freedoms that Tocqueville discusses under the rubric of individualism and diagnoses as democracy's most dangerous ill.[16]

It is to balance the coercive tendencies and psychological ramifications of state centralization and of national sovereignty that Tocqueville famously insists on the indispensability of free associations and a vibrant public sphere. As chapter one argued, the existence of such a sphere and its institutional precondition—decentralized administration—is the hallmark and very substance of democratic freedom. More than a constitutional bill of rights, the active exercise of those rights is the criterion that above all differentiates a free from an illiberal democracy. Beyond merely symbolic authorization, the citizens' actual participation in the formation of popular will and in contesting and constituting the public interest is the touchstone of democratic legitimacy.

Yet, if broad-based civic participation is popular sovereignty in its strongest and most precise sense, Tocqueville shows how robust participation can clash with equality and call its meaning into question. As chapter one sought to show, while celebrating the participatory spirit of antebellum American federalism and the "prodigiously decentralized" public administration that made it possible, Tocqueville's unsparing account of its racial policies reveals its failure to protect the rights of racial minorities, or to conceive of them as equal members of "We the People."[17] This failure was in part due to the weakness of the federal authority, which, more than good will, lacked essential prerogatives or the real power to assert them.

For Tocqueville, in short, diversity and equality, though entwined, are in tension. On the one hand, collective sovereignty and its hallmark—centralized government—necessitate a degree of social harmonization and overcoming of diversity when this diversity interferes with the equality of rights. On the other, a meaningful exercise of civic rights and freedoms implies a plurality both of institutional settings and of moral opinions. Offering space for what Jason Frank has called "insurgent citizenship," participatory freedoms help foster visions and projects that can interfere with the institutional status quo; indeed, whose very object is to effect such interference thus generating social conflict that can erode the moral foundation of the institutions.[18]

Without quite thematizing this tension, Levitsky and Ziblatt offer a striking illustration. Tracing the current erosion of unwritten democratic norms to the rise of "extreme partisan polarization," they show that this deepening division is in many ways a consequence of the civil rights movement and of democratic gains. "America's efforts to achieve racial equality," they argue, has precipitated social fragmentation and "an existential conflict over race and culture." Their analysis thus points to a paradoxical dynamic that would not surprise Tocqueville: the progress of equality seems to go hand in hand with a loss of a shared sense of membership in the people. Then again, in telling the story of how "the unwritten rules of American politics" were first attained, then lost, and rebuilt after the catastrophe of the American Civil War, Levitsky and Ziblatt claim that in the United States, partisan comity and respect for unwritten democratic norms have often been achieved on the basis of shared white identity and at the price of racial exclusion. And they highlight the difficulty of reconciling democracy with diversity as the very challenge we face.[19]

As Tocqueville was among the first to argue, having emancipated individuals from traditional sources of moral or political authority, modern society needs to find fresh ways to mobilize their civic passions and motivate them to play their part in upholding the democratic order. This, as contemporary studies show, is a deepening challenge in advanced democracies.[20] Yet, drawing individuals into the public sphere and goading their political engagement is not the only precondition for sustaining freedom. For a democracy to remain liberal it must also guard against the factionalism that can arise from such political engagement. Under certain conditions, active civil society and vigorous contestation can deepen legitimacy deficits and create political antagonisms that erode the trust in democratic norms. Nor is the outcome of civic contestation necessarily liberal. As recent work reveals, the rise of Viktor Orbán's Fidesz party in Hungry and its conquest of state institutions was enabled by a civil society campaign that was as broad-based as it was skillfully organized.[21]

To sum up, although popular sovereignty and equality, are grounding principles and necessary dimensions of modern society, there are ways in which they find themselves in unresolvable tension. The viability of liberal democracy depends on how the contradictions between these distinct democratic imaginaries and the policy dilemmas behind them are navigated. This, in turn, is conditioned by the way "the people" is defined and understood. If the proper functioning of constitutional democracy depends, as Levitsky and Ziblatt ascertain, on unwritten norms and mores, Tocqueville shows that a crucial element of mores is the sense of belonging to "We the People" and a shared vision of what that belonging means. For liberal society to forestall the twin dangers of social atomism and ideological polarization, and to sustain both the civic engagement and solidarity that a free democracy requires, shared popular allegiance is a sine qua non.

Why Nationalism?

The challenge of reconciling democracy and difference, political self-rule with the equal right to individual self-direction brings to light a third dimension of popular sovereignty: alongside governmental centralization and robust civic participation, there is a need for fostering broad-based solidarity and allegiance. Liberal democracy, in short, needs a form of nationalism—a vision of who we are as a people and why we belong together—that fleshes out and motivates the attachment to the constitutional order.

There is no clearer illustration of this pressing need than postelection rhetoric. A conventional genre given to clichés, this rhetoric assumed special pathos in the context of the long-unresolved 2020 American presidential election. In the wake of the protracted vote count, president-elect Biden called on American citizens to cool off the heat of partisanship and calm down its adversarial spirit. Electoral campaigns, he acknowledged, entail viewing political opponents as enemies in battle. Yet, once the outcome becomes known and the electoral dust settles, winners and losers must find a way to reconcile, to "come together as a nation" and recommit to a shared civic life. Unless they affirm that "what brings us together is so much stronger than anything that can tear us apart," the constitutional order is at risk.[22]

What does it take to rise to such an affirmation? As chapter two argued, running through Tocqueville's account of America is the claim that a free democracy combining centralization and decentralization, popular legitimacy and contestation, requires not only a diversity of associations, interests, and identifications that can draw citizens into the public sphere, but also a common allegiance of a particular kind. It presupposes a sense of shared destiny that would enable individuals and groups to recognize one another, despite vast disagreements, not as enemies but as fellow citizens.

This contested election put on dramatic display that such a sense of shared destiny implies a great deal more than instrumental loyalty to the procedures of democracy, or to abstract constitutional provisions. Relying, as Abraham Lincoln once put it, on "bonds of affection" and "mystic cords of memory," it evinces a comprehensive *we*: an affirmative story of "one nation under God, indivisible" that anchors constitutional loyalty and renders the political process and the norms that govern it acceptable and trustworthy. Put differently, the citizens' attachment to constitutional principles and to the particular people that espouse them are mutually constitutive. They are two sides of the same liberal democratic coin.[23]

Peoplehood for Tocqueville, as chapter two showed, is not a natural or genetic phenomenon, but a cultural and constructed one. To use a well-worn expression, it is an "imagined community" bound together by shared experience and ethical horizon. A people is the historical result of practices of coexistence and of ongoing efforts to craft shared norms that sustain social trust. Rooted in a vision of human life and oriented by a set of civic principles and existential values, peoplehood delineates the social space within which practices and norms have become acceptable and where political consensus can take place. Again, the shared sense of being part of the same people is a fundamental form and primary meaning of democratic equality. It is also the common ground of solidarity on which political union can be achieved, and where the disagreements that issue from differing visions of the public good can be negotiated peacefully and allayed in a constitutional fashion.

A necessary bridge across social and ideological divides, the shared loyalty to the nation also serves as a lever for motivating civic participation. Tocqueville's account of public spirit in America shows that identification with the people is a crucial dimension and enabling condition of democratic citizenship. By fostering psychological investment in and commitment to the democratic community, a robust national identity helps galvanize individual efforts on its behalf. The citizens' sense of belonging to the political order—and to "We the People" as its physical and spiritual embodiment—is the psychological root of democratic legitimacy and the moral foundation for institutions. And yet, while a form of nationalism is a necessary precondition for a free democracy and a vital source of the solidarity and trust that sustain democratic norms, it is also a peril. As Tocqueville was only too aware—and his epistolary exchange with J. S. Mill showcases—though a necessary resource, nationalism defined as a quest for social cohesion and collective political identity spells out many a danger for democratic freedom. One set of dangers, discussed in chapter two, flows from the pressure to conform to the national majority and to toe the political and cultural lines drawn by it—a pressure that prompts Tocqueville to worry about majoritarian tyranny and to question democracy's ability to foster freedom of opinion. Further, like every form of collective identity, nationhood is based on distinctions that contrast our shared "we" with a "they" of other peoples or polities. It includes a negative moment: the equality substantiated by "We the People" implies the inequality of those who do not belong. As a result, the civic benefits of a strong collective self-definition are often bought at the price of cultural and racial bias and of excluding or exploiting populations that are viewed as different.

Tocqueville's psychological analysis of American identity and its racial underpinnings shines a bright light on these moral conundrums. His core insight is that the civic virtue and the attitudes and motivations that characterize engaged democratic citizens are difficult to disentangle from deeply held, exclusive attachments to a certain group and its way of life. As the example of the Anglo-Americans makes manifest, a robust civic life and extraordinary dedication to a shared democratic project is undergirded by a sense of ownership and prideful exceptionalism. Seeing their polity as the incarnation of universal political and moral principles, Americans understand themselves as a God-chosen, providential people endowed with a special destiny and historical mission.[24] Neither are Americans alone in seeing themselves this way: Tocqueville's critique of English national pride reveals similar patterns. And, as I show, his political oratory frequently appeals to, and seeks to awaken, his countrymen's own sense of national honor and global mission in an effort to reinforce their commitment to a liberal future.

For Tocqueville, then, the civic spirit and solidarity a free society vitally needs are closely intertwined with national pride. More often than not, civic action and sacrifice, as well as the social trust democracy depends on, are nurtured by prideful affirmation of the exceptional status of one's country and national belonging. Just as individual flourishing requires a positive self-image and confidence in one's faculties and strength, so too to be proud of itself is (as Tocqueville remarks in a notebook) "the first need of a people."[25] Break that pride, debunk the exceptionalism, and what you are likely to get is not warm and inclusive cosmopolitans but cold and selfish individuals, shut up, as Tocqueville suggestively put it, in the solitude of their own heart; or else fervent radicals quick to sacrifice civic fellowship on the altar of ideological faith.

In a recent book seeking to explain the global resurgence of nationalist movements, Yael Tamir asks: "Is nationalism a dormant evil force, waiting to pop out whenever there is a crisis, a force that must be repressed at all costs; or is it a constructive power, a worthwhile ideology that could and should be harnessed to make the world a better place?"[26] Although Tocqueville does not use Tamir's moral and political categories, his answer like hers would be: both. Rooted in unreflective attitudes and mechanisms of identification, democratic patriotism and loyalty to the nation are as politically indispensable as they are morally suspect and potentially destructive. This Janus-faced character of patriotic allegiance flows from the nature of human pride. As the locus of individual dignity and social identity, pride for Tocqueville (and for the French moralist tradition on which he drew) is the common spring of both virtue and cardinal vice: of the sense of dignity and devotion that sustain civic life and enable self-government, and of the desire to surpass and lord over others. This anthropological insight that virtue and vice share the same source is the fundamental dilemma and moral core of Tocqueville's liberalism.[27]

Tocqueville's psychological analysis thus suggests that there is no risk-proof form of democratic allegiance—a purely civic, and genuinely constitutional patriotism—that does not rest on exclusive categories or imply limits to political membership. Just as no constitution is simply good or immune to the erosion of democratic norms, so too there is no psychological mindset or civic attitude that is unencumbered by moral complexity or illiberal potential. Love of country, Tocqueville would agree with George Kateb, is selfishness writ large and, in this sense, a moral error. Yet, *pace* Kateb, this is not a reason to reject it, for no democratic polity can exist without it. A form of nationalism is a necessary though insufficient condition for a free society.[28]

Liberalism's dilemma, then, is not how to combat or suppress national sentiments and pride, but how to channel and construe them in desirable ways: how to mobilize patriotic support for institutions, while eschewing or moderating the psychological dynamics that endanger democratic norms and stimulate illiberal tendencies. This, moreover, is an ongoing task. While peoplehood, as Tocqueville claims, is conventional—the product of time and agreement rather than of genes or physical force—it is also a work in progress, whose meaning is never quite settled and may have to be revised with every new generation. This periodic necessity to reimagine national belonging and to foster and adjust the pride that underpins it is another consequence of the tensions between popular sovereignty and equality. In striving to reconcile these principles, democratic nationhood rests on what Tamir calls an "untidy compromise" between its particular and universal elements.[29] This very untidiness ensures that the boundaries of membership, if not always in question, are often liable to be called into question and become the substance of political contestation.

Chantal Mouffe has suggested that the contestation of peoplehood, and of a prevailing or "hegemonic" vision of who belongs to the demos, is the very definition of populism. In her view, far from pathological, populism is the heartbeat that periodically reinvigorates democratic politics. By giving voice to marginalized groups and bringing to light suppressed issues, populist movements don't simply endanger the institutional status quo. They also serve a democratic purpose. So if populism, as Jan-Werner Müller has argued, "is always a form of identity politics," for Mouffe this definition should be extended to democracy tout court. In like spirit, Rogers Smith contends that populist movements are successful because they resonate more readily with cultural anxieties and grasp better than established parties the need to manage the identitarian dimension of democratic life. Along with an outlet for grievances, what these movements offer are compelling stories of popular identity and rule that affirm the dignity of the people in order to mobilize and guide popular action. Not simply rejecting such stories but telling better—more complex and liberal—ones is the way to combat illiberal populism. As Mouffe and Smith contend, and Tocqueville would agree, our "populist moment" is not only a crisis of liberal democracy, but also an opportunity for its renewal.[30]

To remain liberal, then, democracy requires the ongoing construction of shared popular identity and the conciliation of national pride. Yet, as Tocqueville's analysis suggests, this construction and conciliation cannot happen simply from within. Just as individual identity vitally depends on the presence of a social mirror, so too a people must reflect itself "in the eyes of the world." Alongside institutional checks and balances and a vibrant democratic public, Tocqueville postulates active foreign policy and international engagement as integral to this end.

Globalization and Democracy

In one of *Democracy in America*'s most striking statements, Tocqueville claims that the people rule God-like over the political universe. The analogy brings home both the people's role as the centerpiece of democratic politics and the danger of idolatry that inheres in it: turning allegiance to the people into a nation-worship that takes on the intensity of religious passions. To guard against nationalism's becoming its own religion, Tocqueville argues that democracies must cultivate dimensions of transcendence and universality most readily found in religion and allow these to flourish in diverse forms that broaden the people's self-understanding and elevate the meaning of self-rule. As Alan S. Kahan has pointed out, Tocqueville's solution to the problem of national pride and political passions is eminently Madisonian. Rather than suppressing certain kinds of psychological and spiritual investments, Tocqueville proposes to multiply and let them check and balance each other. Tocqueville's analysis suggests, moreover, that democratic freedom requires that counterpoises be set to all terms of the democratic equation: equality and peoplehood, unity and diversity, particularity as well as universality, and to the different meanings and dimensions of sovereignty as well.[31]

In chapter three I argued that for Tocqueville robust international engagement is a necessary element of democracy's balancing act and a crucial means of sustaining its freedom. In the international context, a nation acts as one unit and it is there that the plurality that makes up a modern people can most readily conceive of itself as forming a single whole and see its diverse interests as interdependent. At the same time, by acting in the world a democratic polity can come to view its national life as forming a part of a larger picture that includes other peoples and comprehends all of humanity. For Tocqueville, in other words, the nation's involvement in the affairs of the world, and engaging in projects that transcend its particular needs or immediate interests, is essential to enlighten its self-understanding and moderate national pride. Needed to temper particularism, the experience of foreign politics also checks the ardor of dogmatic universalism—the all-too-human temptation to see the world in one's own image, and one's way of life as the only congruent with human dignity. In the context of international relations, national identity and political sovereignty are negotiated against alternative understandings of what it means to live a flourishing life and against competing visions of how the world should be governed. International politics, then, is a necessary reminder both of common humanity and of irreducible differences. It is the stage where the meaning of peoplehood and the know-how and limits of sovereignty are tested and refined in the "rough school" of political practice.

As Tocqueville's foreign policy writings remind us, no modern society can exist in splendid isolation from the rest of the world. Even an isolationist regime, which the early American republic exemplified, depends on foreign resources and international recognition. It can neither fully provide for itself, nor justify its own *Weltanschauung* without engaging in exchange and emulation, and in a tangled web of substantive and symbolic relations with other peoples or political systems. Yet, if international relations are necessary for each nation's thriving and self-definition, this also means that a society's manner of engaging abroad necessarily informs its political culture at home, and vice versa. Our ways of acting in the world help define who we are not only in the eyes of others, but also in our own. For Tocqueville, the keen awareness of this interdependence constitutes the specificity of democratic foreign policy and modern politics in general.

As chapter three argued, Tocqueville viewed democratization and globalization as correlative phenomena and the two faces of the complex process called modernity. The modern democratic world is an increasingly interconnected one in which mutual dependence is not a choice but a recognized fact. Along with the meaning of sovereignty, this fact calls into question time-honored distinctions between foreign and domestic, national and humanitarian, and "realist" and "idealist" approaches to international affairs. Tocqueville would thus disagree with contemporary theorists who draw a sharp boundary between rule-bound and pragmatic orientations, or between liberal universalism and nationalism.[32]

However, just as acknowledging the social dimensions of individual identity does not invalidate the aspiration to personal autonomy, so too recognizing the interdependence between cultures and peoples does not automatically rob self-government of its normative value and practical significance, as both globalization's critics and proponents often seem to suggest. In Tocqueville's view, active involvement in the world is a crucial precondition for national sovereignty rather than its antithesis. Vital for securing material resources and the global power balance, engagement abroad is no less critical for cultural and ideological self-understanding. Indeed, these aspects—external and internal, material and moral—are interrelated and necessarily inform each other. For a political community–*a* people—to exist, hence for democracy and popular rule to be feasible, there must be *many* peoples.[33]

For Tocqueville, then, a reliably liberal global order would in many ways mirror a liberal national one. Both necessitate a plurality and balance of powers, as well as robust participation guided by self-interest well understood. Both require a form of universality or appreciation for common humanity and also a form of particularism and pride in the excellence and unique contribution of one's own people. Both need to deal with the diversity of ethical perspectives and to manage human pride.

And yet, should not the fact of global interdependence suggest that, as on a national level so too on an international one, modernity is essentially a process of convergence? Would the democratic imperative to engage abroad and partake in efforts to solve global problems in common with other political and institutional actors inevitably lead to global integration: that is, to the dissolution of political identities and the creation of one unified humanity leaving peoplehood and sovereignty behind?[34] Put differently, if humankind's division into separate peoples, each aspiring to self-determination, is made rather than born and hence socially constructed, could humanity deconstruct this division and, by agreeing to agree, come together as "one equal civilization," in which all would view human life in the same light?[35]

As chapter three aimed to show, while in *Democracy in America* Tocqueville entertains the possibility of overcoming "the dissimilarities and the inequalities of men," his policy writings call into question both the feasibility of global unity and its desirability as well. Tocqueville's foreign policy interventions and his position on colonization reflect his understanding of the modern world as increasingly interconnected. Tocqueville charged France, and Western nations in general, with the responsibility to disseminate liberal democratic principles and urged that making these principles the emblem of their actions abroad was indispensable for sustaining them at home. At the same time, his colonial writings canvass the profound challenges inherent in the efforts to spread freedom and democracy—or one culture's definition of them—and thus to elaborate universally accepted norms. As I have argued, Tocqueville's analysis of European expansionism suggests that colonial empires were unlikely to long endure—not only because of bad faith or the incapacity of the imperial powers, but above all because of the structural contradictions of modern imperialism. The liberal empires of Britain and France strove to incorporate diverse populations and different peoples into a single institutional framework legitimized by the "new politics" of freedom and equality. As Tocqueville was among the first to perceive, this framework and the principle of popular sovereignty that underpinned it would sooner rather than later delegitimize the colonizers' efforts—a dynamic of which the rise and fall of the Soviet "empire of nations" and, more recently, "the war on terror" offer instructive reprises.[36]

Laying bare the necessarily violent character of modern imperialism and its political and moral conundrums, Tocqueville shows that the intensified contact between different parts of the world brought about by modern colonial empires is at least as likely to deepen and consolidate distinct political identities as it is to efface them. While the coming together of diverse political cultures and ethical perspectives results in imitation and learning from each other, different societies use these common lessons to pursue diverging visions of human dignity and modern life. Globalization, then, is both the coming together and coming apart of humanity, a making and breaking of a common world, and the continuous refashioning of the world's order.

Nor is this a bad thing. As Tocqueville's foreign policy writings evince, the push for global integration and the claim to universality that underpins it have an ugly synonym: empire. Nothing illustrates its unsettling features better than France's own colonial politics conducted in the name of a *mission civilisatrice* to spread equality and human brotherhood. Though regarding this mission with clear-eyed skepticism, Tocqueville's colonial stance was rooted in the belief that freedom and democracy are universal values and that France's "permanent interest" was to "replace despotic institutions with liberal ones everywhere." This belief is part and parcel of his imperialist legacy that has come under sustained scrutiny in recent decades.[37]

Tocqueville's colonial analysis makes clear that the dynamic of globalization is not self-sustaining. It requires political and military power to establish common rules and to guarantee their validity, with forceful means if necessary. Global norms, in other words, imply a global hegemon and an ongoing contest over hegemony.[38] As Tocqueville's critique of British abolitionism shows, hegemonic power even if well-intentioned is inevitably experienced as hypocritical and oppressive. To uphold its principles and achieve its moral purpose in a diverse and often hostile world, an aspiring superpower needs to negotiate an idealism about ends with flexibility about political priorities. Yet the pragmatic means of ensuring domination inevitably compromise the hegemon's professed humanitarian rationale, which in the end appears as little more than "an alibi of empire."[39]

While arising from specific historical circumstances, Tocqueville's critique of French colonial rule and Britain's attempted global supremacy extends to any sustained efforts to integrate peoples and populations with profoundly different self-understandings under a single system of governance. No matter how able or idealistic, such an effort is likely to meet with resistance and break on the rock of human diversity. This diversity, however, is not simply a negation of human equality, or a fact to be deplored. For the right to pursue "our own good in our own way" is, in J. S. Mill words, "the only freedom worthy of the name. Mankind are greater gainers by suffering each other to live as seems good to themselves, than by compelling each to live as seems good to the rest."[40] Diversity, in other words, is the inevitable corollary of an equal right to freedom. It is also a source and precondition of human dignity. To achieve a substantive integration on a global scale would entail a significant encroachment on, or the abolition of, this dignity.

And so, if one form of democratic tyranny consists in the apotheosis of peoplehood and an essentializing view of national differences, the other, darker vision depicted in *Democracy in America*'s final chapters is premised on losing sight of meaningful differences and with them political agency and freedom. No longer bound by collective categories and civic membership, the citizens are reduced to an indiscriminate "crowd of similar and equal men," each a stranger to the destiny of the others and to the idea of directing one's own life. As political identities lose their meaning and legitimacy, so too do existential alternatives. The space for choice and action radically shrinks and self-government gives way to technocratic governance laboring for the happiness of all by relieving each from "the trouble of thinking and the care of living."[41]

Thinking through modernity's dialectic of equality and difference, and its evolution further down the egalitarian road, Tocqueville worried that if globalism were to prevail in the end, it would succeed not in achieving actual universality, but in effectively suppressing the contestation of universality and the quest for new ways to be human. Paradoxically this would come about through ever-greater homogenization at home that erodes civic identities and political passions on local and national levels, and with them vibrant political cultures quickened by the desire for self-rule. The great threat Tocqueville points to is not only the tyranny of this or that particular formation, or local outbreaks of illiberalism, but a global discrediting of the sovereignty of peoples and of democratic politics as such.

Globalism, then, no less than nationalism, is a source of moral and political danger. While democracies, driven by the vital need for social harmony and consensus, might be tempted to stifle dissent and tyrannize over minorities in the name of national sovereignty, the globalist project of imposing a single normative perspective on the entire world poses no lesser risks. If nationalism and the exclusive fixation on national differences can be murderous, atrocities as great if not in fact greater have been committed under the banner of universalizing ideals: be they a "civilizing mission," "the socialist new man," or Allah's "Lordship throughout the world."[42] Democratic freedom and a humane order are imperiled from both sides: chauvinist particularism and imperial universalism. How to navigate the twin dangers of a nationalism that worships differences to the point of conflict and a cosmopolitan ideology nudging its way toward global empire? How to steer between Scylla and Charybdis, that eternal liberal metaphor, in our globalizing world?

For Liberal Moderation

At a turning point in Plato's *Republic*, Socrates is prompted by his interlocutors to discuss the relationship between philosophy and politics: why, for all the benefits that philosophy is said to bestow on its devotees, are philosophers considered useless to and destructive of political life? In response, Socrates introduces a striking metaphor that inspired centuries of political thought. Comparing statesmanship to steering a ship, Socrates claims that skilled navigation calls for more than the capacity to address immediate circumstances or chart one's way through political storms. Along with the poise and ability to act in inclement weather, statesmanship requires knowledge of the stars and the causes of weather: that is, a deeper insight into the nature of things.

Commenting on the virtues and shortcomings of the United States Constitution, Tocqueville makes his own use of the Socratic image:

> The law-maker resembles a man who plots his route in the middle of the sea. He too can navigate the ship that carries him, but he cannot change its structure, raise the wind, or prevent the ocean from heaving under his feet.[43]

If the Socratic image exalts philosophers as true pilots and insists that knowledge of causes and of fundamental laws is indispensable for virtuous politics, Tocqueville's reprise seems deflationary. It calls attention to the limitations of what even the most knowledgeable lawgivers can do in their effort to steer the ship of state.

Lawgiving, Tocqueville suggests, is not about building or manning a new ship from scratch, but about reorienting the course of an equipped vessel already afloat. Legislators, in other words, must rely on structures they cannot control and strive to give them a direction. Nor is this effort impregnable to changes in the weather or to history's storms. For all their skill, the lawgivers' influence on the "destiny of nations" is at most "indirect," and their genius largely consists in correctly diagnosing the materials and conditions they are working with: in short, in making virtue out of cultural and historical necessity.[44]

Constitutionalism, in this Tocquevillean image, is an art more than a science. And Tocqueville celebrates the American founders for excelling in this architectonic art. Rather than revealing transcendental truth, its purpose is to lay down the parameters of consent: to articulate "the self-evident truths" a particular community can agree on and devise shared procedures for settling disagreement. The knowledge the art of legislation requires is first and foremost self-knowledge: an appreciation of the particular people and the collective self for whom one legislates. If Plato's Socrates aimed to raise the bar for politics and elevate the view of what a wise statesmanship could accomplish, Tocqueville pulls in the opposite direction: that of moderating ideological hopes and dampening expectations of politics and philosophy alike.

To be sure, while Tocqueville may differ with Plato on the extent to which human affairs can be governed, he nonetheless agrees about the possibility of governing and foregrounds the central importance of knowledge for political life. Heralding the advance of a soon-to-be-global democratic revolution, the opening pages of his first and most famous work called for "a new political science" to illuminate and guide its course. And yet, while affirming the human capacity for knowledge, on which self-government is premised, Tocqueville also recognizes its limitations and points to such recognition as the precondition of liberal politics. As this book aimed to show, though sanguine about our ability for self-direction, Tocqueville-style liberalism is programmatically cautious and given to ambivalence. Striving "to see, not differently, but farther than parties," it seeks to acknowledge—not transcend—their partial truths and the legitimacy of partisan perspectives, thus opening space for peaceful compromise.[45]

Drawing on Tocqueville, I have suggested that, alongside circumstantial challenges or the usual cycle of political weather, democratic modernity is in the grip of enduring tensions that trigger populist cyclones. I proposed that the drama of democracy is powered by the conflict—and the synergies—between universalist values and cultural particularity, the ideal of equality and the practices of self-rule. Modern societies differ in how they understand and institutionalize these dimensions of democratic sovereignty and how they navigate the tensions between them, but all have to grapple with these tensions.

Liberalism, in this understanding, is one approach to addressing the dilemmas inherent in modern democracy. Affirming both the irreducible value of individuals and every society's right to govern itself, liberalism seeks ways to reconcile the frictions that arise from these twin aspirations to individual and collective autonomy. What distinguishes a liberal approach is the recognition that these frictions are as much a precondition for, as they are a threat to, democratic freedom. Not only problems to be solved, they are sources of energy that can be harnessed into a movement that is "regular and progressive."[46] A liberal politics, then, should not seek to resolve modern society's underlying tensions—not only because such a resolution would be difficult, but because it would be in many ways undesirable and inevitably inhumane.

To be liberal, in other words, democracy needs to be moderate and to steer clear of two kinds of extremes: being torn asunder by its social contradictions, and seeking to resolve these contradictions at the price of political and civil freedoms. If it is to maintain its freedoms, a democratic citizenry must learn, each generation anew, how to live with tensions and refuse to choose between often contradictory yet indispensable demands. This learning includes a respectful regard for the historical experience of particular nations and for the bonds of affection that hold them together, as much as an affirmation of universal norms and the regulative ideal of human fellowship. A viable liberal order necessitates both: a form of universalization and a form of particularism.

Crucially, in Tocqueville's view, such a civic education requires civic practice. Though theoretical insight is needed to guide it, to resist ideological simplifications liberal democracy vitally depends on the citizens' capacity to recognize the complexity of politics as practiced and life as actually lived, and hence the impossibility of a perfect solution and the undesirability of striving for it at any price. Surely, Tocqueville would agree with Levitzky and Ziblatt that political and intellectual elites carry a moral and civic responsibility to teach these liberal lessons. And his work (like theirs) offers an example as much as a theory of what such an elite-driven pedagogy could look like. Yet, as Tocqueville incisively argued, democracy's health and self-understanding does not depend on the quality of leadership alone. While crucially important, moralists and statesmen, judicious gatekeepers, and far-seeing party leaders are not sovereign any more than constitutions are. Nor can their message be effective and its quality sustained without engaged and informed publics, whose self-understanding is shaped and enlightened through participation in civic life.

If Tocqueville is right, the commitment to and trust in liberal democracy has to be built and rebuilt both from below and from above: in institutional practice and grassroots endeavors, through laws and policymaking, and through informal undertakings and everyday habits. The vitality of liberal democracy draws on the citizens' constant practice and experience, as much as on the elite's willingness to engage in civic dialogue and to interpret this experience through meaningful narratives that help bridge the distance between individuals and institutions, majority and minorities, the common people and the elites. To be free, democracy requires broad-based, ongoing efforts to sustain the sense of common fellowship and to reimagine "We the People."

NOTES

Introduction

1. *What is Democracy?*, directed by Astra Taylor (New York: Zeitgeist Films, 2018), DVD, 1:33:34 to 1:40:40.

2. See Frantz Fanon, *The Wretched of the Earth* (London: Penguin Modern Classics, 2001).

3. Astra Taylor's film adjusts Plato's original text, see Plato, *The Republic of Plato*, trans. Allan Bloom (New York: Basic Books, 1991), 472d. As Cornel West exclaims at an earlier juncture in the film, Plato's "challenge will never go away," Taylor, *What is Democracy?*, 0:11:20 to 0:11:30.

4. Throughout this volume, I follow Tocqueville's usage in referring to the United States as both America and the United States. I also occasionally follow his usage of Indians and Blacks to refer to the native and African American populations of the United States.

5. See Boris Vormann and Michael Weinman, eds., *The Emergence of Illiberalism* (New York: Routledge 2020); Ivan Krastev and Stephen Holmes, *The Light that Failed: A Reckoning* (London: Penguin, 2020); Anne Applebaum, *Twilight of Democracy: The Seductive Lure of Authoritarianism* (New York: Doubleday, 2020) and "Illiberal Democracy Comes to Poland," *Washington Post*, December 16, 2016; Fareed Zakaria, *The Future of Freedom: Illiberal Democracy at Home and Abroad* (New York: W. W. Norton, 2003).

6. See Patrick Deneen, *Why Liberalism Failed* (New Haven, CT: Yale University Press, 2018); Yoram Hazony, *The Virtue of Nationalism* (New York: Basic Books, 2018); Ryszard Legutko, *The Demon in Democracy: Totalitarian Temptations in Free Societies* (New York: Encounter Books, 2018); Charles Murray, *By the People: Rebuilding Liberty without Permission* (New York: Crown Forum, 2015). See also John Sides, Michael Tesler, and Lynn Vareck, *Identity Crisis: The 2016 Presidential Election Campaign and the Battle for the Meaning of America* (Princeton, NJ: Princeton University Press, 2018); John B. Judis, *The Nationalist Revival: Trade, Immigration and the Revolt against Globalization* (New York: Columbia Global Reports, 2018).

7. See Samuel Moyn, *Not Enough: Human Rights in an Unequal World* (Cambridge, MA: Harvard University Press, 2019); Jennifer Pitts, *Boundaries of the International: Law and Empire* (Cambridge, MA: Harvard University Press, 2018); Wendy Brown, *Undoing the Demos* (Cambridge MA: MIT Press, 2015); Partha Chatterjee, "Empire, Nations, Peoples: The Imperial Prerogative and Colonial Exceptions," *Thesis Eleven* 139, no. 1 (April 2017): 84–96. See also Pankaj Mishra, *Age of Anger: A History of the Present* (Farrar, Straus and Giroux, 2017); Saskia Sassen, *Losing Control?: Sovereignty in the Age of Globalization* (New York: Columbia University Press, 2015).

8. See Marc Plattner, "Illiberal Democracy and the Struggle on the Right," *Journal of Democracy* 30, no. 1 (January 2019): 5–19; Yascha Mounk, *The People vs. Democracy: Why Our Freedom Is in Danger and How to Save It* (Cambridge, MA: Harvard University Press, 2018); and "America is not a Democracy," *Atlantic*, March 2018; Jan Roger Eatwell and Matthew Goodwin, *National Populism: The Revolt Against Liberal Democracy* (London: Penguin Random House, 2018); Jan-Werner Müller, *What is Populism?* (London: Penguin Books, 2017); Jonathan Haidt, "When and Why Nationalism Beats Globalism," *American Interest* 12, no. 1 (July 2016), https://www.the-american-interest.com/2016/07/10/when-and-why-nationalism-beats-globalism.

9. For a compelling antecedent that has informed modern critiques both from the Left and the Right, see Carl Schmitt, *The Crisis of Parliamentary Democracy*, trans. Ellen Kennedy (Cambridge, MA: MIT Press, 1988); also Ewa Atanassow, "Popular Sovereignty on Trial: Tocqueville vs. Schmitt," in *When the People Rule: Popular Sovereignty in Theory and Practice*, ed. Ewa Atanassow, Thomas Bartscherer, and David Bateman (Cambridge: Cambridge University Press, forthcoming).

10. Alexis de Tocqueville, *The Tocqueville Reader: A Life in Letters and Politics*, ed. Alan. S. Kahan and Oliver Zunz (Oxford: Wiley-Blackwell, 2002), 153. See also Roger Boesche, *The Strange Liberalism of Alexis de Tocqueville* (Ithaca, NY: Cornell University Press, 1987).

11. See Alexis de Tocqueville, *Democracy in America: Historical-Critical Edition of De la démocratie en Amérique*, ed. Eduardo Nolla, trans. James T. Schleifer, 4 vols. (Indianapolis, IN: Liberty Fund, 2010) [henceforth *DA*], introduction, 6. This 4-volume bilingual edition departs from the original division of *DA* into 2 volumes. To facilitate referencing, I refer in square brackets to the conventional 2-volume division of *DA* by volume, part, and chapter.

12. Tocqueville, *DA*, introduction, 6; [1.1.3], 74–90; [2.2.1], 878. See also, Harvey Mansfield and Delba Winthrop, "Tocqueville's New Political Science," in *The Cambridge Companion to Tocqueville*, ed. Cheryl B. Welch (Cambridge, MA: Cambridge University Press, 2006), 81–107.

13. Tocqueville, *DA* [1.1.3], 89–90; [1.2.10], 655–66, 878.

14. Tocqueville, *DA* [2.4.1], 1193. Cf. Francis Fukuyama, "The March of Equality," *Journal of Democracy* 11, no. 1 (2000): 11–17. See also Melvin Richter, "Tocqueville on Threats to Liberty in Democracy," in *Cambridge Companion to Tocqueville*, 245–75.

15. See Petar Stankov, *The Political Economy of Populism: An Introduction* (Abingdon: Routledge, 2020); Shalini Randeria et. al, *Wenn Demokratien demokratisch untergehen* (Vienna: Passagen Verlag, 2019); Nadia Urbinati, *Me, the People: How Populism Transforms Democracy* (Cambridge, MA: Harvard University Press, 2019); Timothy Snyder, *The Road to Unfreedom: Russia, Europe, America* (New York: Penguin, 2018); P. C. Schmitter and T. L. Karl, "What Democracy Is . . . and Is Not." *Journal of Democracy* 2, no. 3 (1991): 75–88.

16. For a Tocqueville-inspired account of these deeper things see Joshua Mitchell, *American Awakening: Identity Politics and Other Afflictions of Our Time* (New York: Encounter Books, 2020).

17. I have drawn inspiration from Dani Rodrik's analysis and his much-debated trilemma, *The Globalization Paradox: Democracy and the Future of the World Economy* (New York: W. W. Norton, 2012).

18. See Bryan Garsten, "From Popular Sovereignty to Civil Society in Postrevolutionary France," in *Popular Sovereignty in Historical Perspective*, ed. Richard Bourke and Quentin Skinner (Cambridge: Cambridge University Press, 2017), 236–69; and Richard Bourke's introduction to the same volume. See also Dieter Grimm, *Sovereignty: The Origin and Future of a Political and Legal Concept*, trans. Belinda Cooper (New York: Columbia University Press, 2017), 52–60; Lucien Jaume, *Tocqueville: Aristocratic Sources of Liberty*, chap 1. Philip Knee, "Religion et souveraineté du peuple: de Rousseau à Tocqueville," *Canadian Journal of Political Science* 23 no. 2 (1990): 211–32; François Furet, "The Conceptual System of *Democracy in America*," in *The Workshop of History* (Chicago: University of Chicago Press, 1984), 167–96.

19. See Alan B. Spitzer, "Tocqueville's Modern Nationalism," *French History* 19, no. 1 (2005): 48–66; Françoise Mélonio, "L'idée de nation et idée de démocratie chez Tocqueville," *Littérature et nation* 7 (1991): 5–24; Stéphane Dion, "La conciliation du libéralisme et du nationalisme chez Tocqueville," *Tocqueville Review / La Revue Tocqueville* 16, no. 1 (Winter, 1995): 219–27; Tzvetan Todorov, "Tocqueville's Nationalism," *History and Anthropology* 4 (1990): 357–71.

20. See Jon Elster, *Alexis de Tocqueville: The First Social Scientist* (Cambridge: Cambridge University Press, 2009); and Aurelian Craiutu, "The Social Science of Democracy?," *Perspectives on Politics* 9, no. 2 (2011): 363–81. See also Heinz-Dieter Meyer, "'Tocqueville's Cultural Institutionalism Reconciling Collective Culture and Methodological Individualism," *Journal of Classical Sociology*, 3 no. 2 (2003): 197–220.

21. Alan S. Kahan, "Aristocracy in Tocqueville," *Tocqueville Review / La Revue Tocqueville* 27, no. 2 (Winter 2006): 323–48; Ran Halévi, "The Frontier between Aristocracy and Democracy," in *Tocqueville and the Frontiers of Democracy*, ed. Ewa Atanassow and Richard Boyd (Cambridge: Cambridge University Press, 2013), 53–73.

22. See Karl Marx, "The Eighteenth Brumaire of Louis Napoleon," in *Karl Marx and Friedrich Engels, The Marx-Engels Reader*, ed. Robert C. Tucker (New York: W. W. Norton, 1978), 594–617; Francis Fukuyama, *The End of History and the Last*

Man (New York: Free Press, 1992); Czeslaw Milosz, *The Captive Mind*, trans. Jane Zielonko (London: Penguin Modern Classics, 2001).

23. *DA* [2.1.20], 853–60.

24. Tocqueville, *DA* [2.4.8], 1285, my italics.

25. Tocqueville to Mme. Swetchine, February 26, 1857 in Zunz and Kahan, *Tocqueville Reader*, 336. For a further discussion see Alan S. Kahan, *Tocqueville, Democracy, and Religion: Checks and Balances for Democratic Souls* (Oxford: Oxford University Press, 2015), 7–8, 16–18; Doris S. Goldstein, *Trial of Faith: Religion and Politics in Tocqueville's Thought* (New York: Elsevier, 1975), chap. 1; Marvin Zetterbaum, *Tocqueville and the Problem of Democracy* (Stanford, CA: Stanford University Press, 1967), 15–17.

26. See Harvey Mansfield, "Providence and Democracy: Tocqueville's Alliance of Religion and Liberty," *Claremont Review of Books* 11, nos. 1–2 (Winter/Spring, 2010–11): 74–78; Kahan, *Tocqueville, Democracy, and Religion*, chap. 1; Aristide Tessitore, "Tocqueville's American Thesis and the New Science of Politics," in *The Spirit of Religion and the Spirit of Freedom: The Tocqueville Thesis Revisited*, ed. Michael Zuckert (Chicago: University of Chicago Press, 2017), 19–48; Michael Locke McLendon, "Tocqueville, Jansenism, and the Psychology of Freedom," *American Journal of Political Science* 50, no. 3 (July 2006): 664–75; David A. Selby, *Tocqueville, Jansenism, and the Necessity of the Political in a Democratic Age* (Amsterdam: Amsterdam University Press, 2015), chap. 7.

27. *DA*, introduction, 6, 10; [1.2.6], 389; [2.4.7], 1276–77L. See Joseph Hebert Jr., *More Than Kings and Less Than Men: Tocqueville on the Promise and Perils of Democratic Individualism* (Lanham, MD: Lexington Books, 2010); Aurelian Craiutu, "Tocqueville's Paradoxical Moderation," *Review of Politics* 67, no. 4 (2005): 599–630; Paul O. Carrese, *Democracy in Moderation: Montesquieu, Tocqueville, and Sustainable Liberalism* (New York: Cambridge University Press, 2018), chap. 3.

28. *DA*, introduction, 32; I echo here John Rawls, *Political Liberalism* (New York: Columbia University Press, 2004); Pierre Manent, "Tocqueville, Political Philosopher," in *The Cambridge Companion to Tocqueville*, ed. Cheryl B. Welch (Cambridge: Cambridge University Press, 2006), 108–20. Tracy B. Strong, "Seeing Differently and Seeing Further: Rousseau and Tocqueville," in *Friends and Citizens*, ed. Peter Denis Bathory and Nancy L. Schwartz (Lanham, MD: Rowman & Littlefield, 2001), 104–5.

29. See Tocqueville's fragment on, "How Patriotism Is Justified in the Eyes of Reason and Appears to It Not Only a Great Virtue but the Most Important," in Zunz and Kahan, *Tocqueville Reader*, 332–33.

30. *DA*, introduction, 27–28; [2.1.3–4], 726–41. For Tocqueville's account of the dangers of theory see Alexis de Tocqueville, *The Old Regime and the Revolution*, ed. Françoise Mélonio, trans. Alan S. Kahan (Chicago: University of Chicago Press, 1998), 1:195–201.

31. *DA*, introduction, 27; [1.2.6], 375–76; [1.2.9], 505–14. See Ivan Krastev and Stephen Holmes, "Explaining Eastern Europe: Imitation and Its Discontents," *Journal of Democracy* 29, no.3 (July 2018): 117–128, and Krastev and Holmes, *Light that Failed*, chap. 1. John Torpey, "The Problem of 'American Exceptionalism' Revisited," *Journal of Classical Sociology* 9, no. 1 (2009): 143–68.

32. *DA* [1.1.1], 44. Ewa Atanassow and Alan S. Kahan, eds., *Liberal Moments: Reading Liberal Texts* (London: Bloomsbury Academic: 2018), 1–12.

33. See Johann N. Neem, "Taking Modernity's Wager: Tocqueville, Social Capital, and the American Civil War," *Journal of Interdisciplinary History* 41, no. 4 (2011), 591–618; Nestor Capdevila, *Tocqueville ou Marx: Démocratie, Capitalisme, Révolution* (Paris: Presses universitaires de France, 2012), 7. A younger acquaintance and for a time a protégé, Arthur de Gobineau was Tocqueville's political ally, despite their heated and ultimately unbridgeable disagreement on the issue of race. Alexis de Tocqueville, *The European Revolution and Correspondence with Gobineau*, trans. and ed. John Lukacs (Garden City, NY: Doubleday, 1959); Roger Boesche, "Why Could Tocqueville Predict so Well?," *Political Theory* 11, no. 1 (February 1983): 79–103.

34. I echo Bonnie Honig, *Public Things: Democracy in Disrepair* (New York: Fordham University Press, 2017).

Chapter 1

1. *DA*, introduction, 4, my emphasis.

2. *DA*, introduction, 3–32; [1.1.3], 74–90; [2.1.3], 733; [2.2.1], 872–879. James T. Schleifer, *The Chicago Companion to Tocqueville's Democracy in America* (Chicago: University of Chicago Press, 2012), 56–60; Michael P. Zuckert, "On Social State," in *Tocqueville's Defense of Human Liberty*, ed. Peter Lawler and Joseph Alulis (New York: Garland Publishers, 1993), 3–19.

3. *DA* [1.2.5], 316; [2.2.1], 878; [2.3.5], 1007–19. Steven B. Smith, *Modernity and Its Discontents* (New Haven, CT: Yale University Press, 2016), 200. See also Nestor Capdevila, "Democracy and Revolution in Tocqueville," in *Tocqueville and the Frontiers of Democracy*, ed. Ewa Atanassow and Richard Boyd (Cambridge: Cambridge University Press, 2013), 33–52.

4. *DA* [2.2.2], 882.

5. *DA* [1.1.5], 142–166, and [2.4.6], 1245–1261. Ewa Atanassow, "Tocqueville's New Liberalism," in Atanassow and Kahan, *Liberal Moments*, 51–57. In *The Old Regime and the Revolution*, Tocqueville studies the historic rise of state centralization in France and its role in shaping the character of the French Revolution. Paul Rahe, *Soft Despotism, Democracy's Drift: Montesquieu, Rousseau, Tocqueville, and the Modern Prospect* (New Haven, CT: Yale University Press, 2009), chaps. 3 and 4.

6. *DA* [1.1.3], 90, my emphasis.

7. Among these sources, as the word "dogma" suggests, the imbrication of theology and politics looms large. David Selby, "Towards a Political Theology of Republicanism: The Contours of a Natural Contrast between Carl Schmitt and Alexis de Tocqueville," *History of Political Thought* 39, no. 4 (Winter 2018): 749–74; see also Selby, *Tocqueville, Jansenism, and the Necessity of the Political in a Democratic Age*, chap. 4.

8. Tocqueville, *DA* [1.1.4], 90, my emphasis, translation amended.

9. Tocqueville, *DA* [2.3.6], 1022–23 and [1.1.3], 90nM. Far from original, Tocqueville's claim is something of a philosophical commonplace that grounded seventeenth- and eighteenth-century conceptions of the social contract, e.g. Thomas Hobbes, *On the Citizen (De Cive)*, ed. Richard Tuck and Michael Silverthorne (Cambridge: Cambridge University Press, 1998), chap. 12, ¶8, 137 and David Hume's "Of the First Principles of Government," in *Political Essays*, ed. Knud Haakonssen (Cambridge: Cambridge University Press, 1994), 16.

10. Or, in Edmund Morgan's words, on fictions: i.e., principles and values that need not accurately describe but have the power to prescribe—to orient and govern—political life: Edmund Morgan, *Inventing the People: The Rise of Popular Sovereignty in England and America* (New York: W. W. Norton, 1989), 13–15. For an illuminating discussion, see Ioannis Evrigenis, "The Fact of Fiction: Popular Sovereignty as Belief and Reality," in *When the People Rule: Popular Sovereignty in Theory and Practice*, ed. Ewa Atanassow, Thomas Bartscherer, and David Bateman (Cambridge: Cambridge University Press, forthcoming).

11. Jean-Jacques Rousseau, *Of the Social Contract*, in *Rousseau: The Social Contract and Other Later Political Writings*, ed. and trans. Victor Gourevich (Cambridge: Cambridge University Press, 1997), bk. 1, chap. 5, 49 and bk. 2, chap. 6. For a comprehensive study of Tocqueville's attitudes to republicanism, see Jean-Patrice Lacam, *Tocqueville et la République* (Paris: L'Harmattan, 2020).

12. *DA* [1.1.4], 91; and [1.2.10], 631. Morgan, *Inventing the People*, 12–13.

13. *DA* [1.1.4], 92. Also *DA*, introduction, 3–4; and [1.1.2], 48–49.

14. *DA* [1.1.2], 49–50 and 65; [1.1.4], 92. Morgan, *Inventing the People*, chap. 6.

15. *DA* [1.1.4], 93; also [1.1.4], 77–78. Thomas Paine, "Common Sense," in *Rights of Man, Common Sense and Other Political Writings*, ed. Mark Philp (New York: Library of America, 1995), 1–60.

16. *DA*, 92–95; Morgan, *Inventing the People*, chaps. 6–8. As Amar puts the matter, the post-independence constitutional efforts were "dress rehearsals" for the framing of the Union, Akhil Reed Amar, "Of Sovereignty and Federalism," *Yale Law Journal*, 96 no. 7 (1987): 1439.

17. Thomas G. West, "Misunderstanding the American Founding," in *Interpreting Tocqueville's Democracy in America*, ed. Ken Masugi (Lanham, MD: Rowman & Littlefield, 1991), 155–77; Barbara Allen, "Racial Equality and Social Equality," in

Conversations with Tocqueville: The Global Democratic Revolution in the Twenty-first Century, ed. Aurelian Craiutu and Sheldon Gellar (Lanham, MD: Lexington Books, 2009), 85–115.

18. "The Declaration of Independence," in Alexander Hamilton, John Jay, and James Madison, *The Federalist*, ed. George W. Carey and James McClellan (Carmel, IN: Liberty Fund: 2001), 495–99, esp. 495, 497 [subsequent references to *The Federalist* refer to this volume]. Danielle Allen, *Our Declaration: A Reading of the Declaration of Independence in Defense of Equality* (London: Liveright, 2015), 116–17.

19. Jill Lepore, *These Truths: A History of the United States* (New York: W. W. Norton, 2018), chap. 3, esp. 96–100. See in this connection Jacques Derrida, "Declarations of Independence," *New Political Science* 7 (1986): 7–15. According to Derrida, the American Declaration of Independence at once created the people and spoke in the name of a preexisting people, an irreducible paradox.

20. Tocqueville, *DA*, introduction, 4; [1.1.2], 49–50; [1.1.4], 92; [1.2.10], 633; [2.2.1], 872–80. Pierre Manent, *Tocqueville and the Nature of Democracy* (Lanham, MD: Rowman & Littlefield, 1996), chap. 1.

21. Harvey C. Mansfield, "Tocqueville on Religion and Liberty," in *The Spirit of Religion and the Spirit of Freedom: The Tocqueville Thesis Revisited*, ed. Michael Zuckert (Chicago: University of Chicago Press, 2017), chap. 8, 190–94. Cf. James Caesar, "Tocqueville's Second Founding," in *Designing a Polity: American Constitution in Theory and Practice* (Lanham, MD: Rowman & Littlefield, 2011), 23–44. Joshua Mitchell, "Tocqueville's Puritans," in *The Cambridge Companion to Democracy in America*, ed. Richard Boyd (Cambridge: Cambridge University Press, 2022), 347–66.

22. *DA* [1.1.4], 96, my italics.

23. This is not to suggest that Tocqueville denies the necessity of political myths. As I argue in chapter 2, his analysis of national pride as a crucial psychological resource for democratic liberty shows its inevitable tensions with objectivity. In this sense, for Tocqueville as for Morgan, political life does not—and in important ways cannot—rest on factual truth. At best it is a contest of partial truths that vie for popular recognition.

24. *DA* [1.1.5], 104.

25. *DA* [1.1.2], 66; [1.1.4], 96; [1.2.1], 278. See also Tocqueville's rumination "Of the Different Ways that You Can Imagine the Republic," *DA* [1.2.10], 628–9nZ.

26. *Federalist*, no. 63 (James Madison), 329, emphasis in the original.

27. David Ciepley, "Is the U.S. Government a Corporation?: The Corporate Origins of Modern Constitutionalism," *American Political Science Review* 111, no. 2 (2017): 418–35, esp. 430. Akhil Reed Amar concurs: "By thus relocating true sovereignty in the People themselves . . . Americans domesticated government power and decisively repudiated British notions of 'sovereign' governmental omnipotence," Amar, "Of Sovereignty and Federalism," 1436.

28. Martin Loughlin and Neil Walker, *The Paradox of Constitutionalism: Constituent Power and Constitutional Form* (Oxford: Oxford University Press, 2007), 1.

29. Rousseau, *Social Contract*, bk. 2, chap. 6, 66–67; and chap. 12, 80. The distinction between sovereign and government, though not fully spelled out, informs the Declaration and its main source: John Locke, "Second Treatise on Government," in *Two Treatises on Government*, ed. Peter Laslett (Cambridge: Cambridge University Press, 1996), §§ 149, 155, 168, 207–10, 220–31, 240–43. It also underpins Montesquieu's claim that in a democratic republic the people, while competent to choose their ministers, should not themselves govern, see Montesquieu, *The Spirit of the Laws*, trans. Anne M. Cohler, Basia C. Miller, and Harold S. Stone (Cambridge: Cambridge University Press, 1989), bk. 2, chap. 2, 11–12. Consider in this connection abbé Sieyès's differentiation between constituent and constituted power (*pouvoir constituent* vs. *constitué*): Emanuel Joseph Sieyès, "What is the Third Estate?," in *Political Writings: Including the Debate between Sieyès and Tom Paine in 1781*, ed. and trans. Michael Sonenscher (Indianapolis, IN: Hackett, 2003), 92–162; Dieter Grimm, *Sovereignty: The Origin and Future of a Political and Legal Concept* (New York: Columbia University Press, 2015), chap. 2.

30. Morgan, *Inventing the People*, 83, 153; Istvan Hont, "The Permanent Crisis of a Divided Mankind: 'Contemporary Crisis of the Nation State' in Historical Perspective," *Political Studies* 42, no. 1 (1994): 166–231. "This idea of the people as imaginary body and constituent sovereigns (vs. actual rulers) is now accepted in all constitutional systems . . . It may even appear obvious," Julian H. Franklin, *John Locke and the Theory of Sovereignty* (Cambridge: Cambridge University Press, 1981), 124.

31. *DA*, 186nA. Rory Schacter, "Tocqueville's 'New Political Science' as a Correction of *The Federalist*," in *Exploring the Social and Political Economy of Alexis de Tocqueville*, ed. Peter Boettke and Adam Martin (London: Palgrave Macmillan, 2020), 9–35; Joseph Allulis, "The Price of Freedom: Tocqueville, the Framers, and the Antifederalists," *Perspectives on Political Science* 27, no. 2 (1998): 85–91.

32. See Richard Tuck, "Democratic Sovereignty and Democratic Government: The Sleeping Sovereign," in *Popular Sovereignty in Historical Perspective*, ed. Richard Bourke and Quentin Skinner (Cambridge: Cambridge University Press, 2017), 115–40; and Richard Tuck, *The Sleeping Sovereign: The Invention of Modern Democracy* (Cambridge: Cambridge University Press, 2016), chap. 4.

33. Rousseau, *Social Contract*, bk. 3, chap. 4, 91; Bryan Garsten, "Representative Government and Popular Sovereignty," in *Political Representation*, ed. Alexander S. Kirshner et al. (Cambridge: Cambridge University Press, 2009), 90–110.

34. See Jason Frank, *Constituent Moments: Enacting the People in Post-revolutionary America* (Durham, NC: Duke University Press, 2010). Though Morgan insists that presenting popular sovereignty as fiction need not imply "mere fiction," his choice of language seems guilty of blurring the difference. Dilip Gaonkar, "After the Fictions: Notes Towards a Phenomenology of the Multitude," *e-flux Journal*, no. 58, (October 2014): 1–15.

35. This distinction is central to the political vision of Carl Schmitt, one of liberalism's most implacable critics. Joel Isaac, "Constitutional Dictatorship in Twentieth Century American Political Thought," in *States of Exception in American History*, ed. Gary Gerstle and Joel Isaac (Chicago: University of Chicago Press, 2020), 225–53, esp. 227–28.

36. Peter Breiner, "The Dynamics of Political Equality in Rousseau, Tocqueville, and Beyond," in *The Anthem Companion to Alexis De Tocqueville*, ed. Daniel Gordon (New York: Anthem Press, 2019) 169–86.

37. *DA* [1.1.8], 245; [1.2.6], 375ff; [1.1.5], 142–66. See also *DA* 142nC for one reader's complaint about the emotional temperature of Tocqueville's arguments. Compare with *The Federalist*'s invocation of "parchment provisions" in *Federalist* no. 25 (Alexander Hamilton), 126; and especially in no. 48 (James Maddison), 260 and no. 73 (Alexander Hamilton), 380.

38. *DA* [2.2.4–9], 887–929. For a critical rethinking of these arguments, see *Beyond Tocqueville: Civil Society and Social Capital Debate in Comparative Perspective*, ed. Bob Edwards, Michael Folley, and Mario Diani (Hanover, NH: University Press of New England, 2001).

39. Abraham Lincoln, "The Gettysburg Address," November 19, 1863, Gettysburg, Pennsylvania, US, Abraham Lincoln Online, transcript, http://www.abrahamlincolnonline.org/lincoln/speeches/gettysburg.htm. For Tocqueville's anticipation of this formula see *DA* [1.2.5], 364.

40. Written for the purpose of informing public opinion and swaying it in favor of the Constitution, the *Federalist Papers* were as much an appeal to as they were an exercise of popular sovereignty. See also Bryan Garsten, "From Popular Sovereignty to Civil Society in Post-revolutionary France," in Bourke and Skinner, *Popular Sovereignty in Historical Perspective*, 236–69.

41. This is true of every branch including the judiciary and the Supreme Court. *DA* [1.1.8], 245. For a discussion of Tocqueville's approach to constitutional interpretation, see Philip C. Kissam, "Alexis de Tocqueville and American Constitutional Law: On Democracy, the Majority Will, Individual Rights, Federalism, Religion, Civic Associations, and Originalist Constitutional Theory," *Maine Law Review* 59, no.1 (2007): 54–56.

42. Consider Tocqueville's famous description of the American juries as an example of a virtuous circle between direct and representative forms. The interplay between a jury randomly drawn from the body of the people, and the judge, whose authority is based on expertise, reveals the need for the synergy of direct and representative elements to legitimate the court's ruling, *DA* [1.2.7], 449–50.

43. On this point see Hannah Arendt, *On Revolution* (New York: Penguin Books, 2006), 166–67. By repudiating sovereignty, Arendt takes Tocqueville's argument in a non-Tocquevillean direction. Roger Berkowitz, "Hannah Arendt: Power, Action, and the Foundation of Freedom," in Atanassow and Kahan, *Liberal Moments*, 152–59.

44. See Benjamin Constant, "The Liberty of the Ancients Compared with that of the Moderns," in *Political Writings*, ed. Biancamaria Fontana (Cambridge: Cambridge University Press, 1988), 308–28. Isaiah Berlin, "Two Concepts of Liberty," in *Liberty*, ed. Henry Hardy (Oxford: Oxford University Press, 2002), 166–217. For a contemporary reappraisal, see Annelien de Dijn, *Freedom: An Unruly History* (Cambridge, MA: Harvard University Press, 2020), chap. 5.

45. Constant, "Liberty of the Ancients," 326–28. Jessica L. Campbell argues that, unlike contemporary proponents of neo-republicanism, both Constant and Tocqueville had a more realistic—and resolutely modern—understanding of the challenges of making a republic for the moderns, see Jessica L. Campbell, "Machiavelli's Solutions for Tocqueville's Republic," *European Political Science Review* 1, no. 3 (2009): 375–400. Also Andreas Kalyvas and Ira Katznelson, *Liberal Beginnings: Making a Republic for the Moderns* (Cambridge: Cambridge University Press, 2008), 146–75.

46. These challenges, and "the history of the evils" they gave rise to, prompted Constant and the nineteenth-century French liberal mainstream to redefine modern liberty, hence to advocate limited suffrage and representative institutions that would channel as much as prevent broad-based participation: Constant, "Liberty of the Ancients," 317; Alan S. Kahan, *Liberalism in Nineteenth-Century Europe: The Political Culture of Limited Suffrage* (Hampshire: Palgrave Macmillan, 2003).

47. *DA* [1.1.3], 90; [1.2.9], 466–67; see also 666nF. Donald J. Maletz, "Tocqueville on Mores and the Preservation of Republics," *American Journal of Political Science* 49, no. 1 (2005): 1–15. The critical importance of mores is a point Tocqueville hears again and again from his American informants. Decades later, while writing the *Old Regime*, he claims that it is "the principal and, as it were, unique goal" of his work. See Alexis de Tocqueville, *Journey to America*, trans. George Lawrence, ed. J. P. Mayer (New Haven, CT: Yale University Press, 1959), 55, 85, 287n; and *Selected Letters on Politics and Society*, ed. Roger Boesche, trans. James Toupin (Berkeley, CA: University of California Press, 1986), 294.

48. *DA* [1.2.10], 633. "Providence," the passage continues, "has given to each individual . . . the degree of reason necessary for him to be able to direct himself in the things that interest him exclusively. Such is the great maxim on which in the United States civil and political society rests . . . Extended to the whole of the nation, it becomes the dogma of the sovereignty of the people," (633).

49. *DA* [1.2.9], 467–72. Kahan, *Tocqueville, Democracy, and Religion*, chap. 4. See in this connection Tocqueville's conversation with Francis Lieber in Tocqueville, *Journey to America*, 54–55.

50. *DA* [1.1.5], 98. For the implications of this claim for constitutional interpretation, see Bruce P. Frohnen, "Constitution-Reading through Tocqueville's Eyes," *Capital University Law Review* 42 (2014): 1–30.

51. *DA* [1.2.10], 633.

52. *DA* [1.2.10], 634. George Wilson Pierson, *Tocqueville and Beaumont in America* (Baltimore, MD: Johns Hopkins University Press 1996), 129–30. Robert Kraynak, "Tocqueville's Constitutionalism," *American Political Science Review* 81, no. 4 (1987): 1175–95.

53. During his American travels, Tocqueville jots down: "[i]n America free morals have made free political institutions. In France it is for free political institutions to mould morals. That is the end toward which we must strive but without forgetting the point of departure." Tocqueville, *Journey to America*, 150. For a further discussion see Dana Villa, "Religion, Civic Education, and Conformity," in Zuckert, *Spirit of Religion*, 217–37.

54. *DA* [1.1.2], 46 and [1.2.9], 456.

55. Harvey Mansfield, "Providence and Democracy," *Claremont Review of Books* 11, nos. 1–2 (Winter/Spring 2010/11): 75. Surveying colonial records, Tocqueville is astonished how quickly the original fervor of the Puritan founders gave way to toleration and pragmatism. Believers in experience, the Puritans were fast to learn from it, Tocqueville, *Journey to America*, 256–57; Tocqueville, *Selected Letters*, 48, 193. Edmund Morgan, *The Puritan Dilemma: The Story of John Winthrop* (London: Pierson, 2006), chap. 13.

56. *DA* [1.1.2], 48–49 and [1.2.9], 494–505.

57. *Federalist* no. 1 (Hamilton); Maletz, "Tocqueville on Mores and the Preservation of Republics," 1–15. See also Heinz-Dieter Meyer, "Tocqueville's Cultural Institutionalism: Reconciling Collective Culture and Methodological Individualism," *Journal of Classical Sociology* 2, no. 3 (2003): 197–220. In this volume see "Approaching Tocqueville" in the introduction.

58. Harvey Mitchell, *America after Tocqueville: Democracy Against Difference* (Cambridge: Cambridge University Press, 2004); Barbara Allen, "An Undertow of Race Prejudice in the Current of Democratic Transformation," in *Tocqueville's Voyages: The Evolution of His Ideas and Their Journey Beyond His Time*, ed. Christine Dunn Henderson (Indianapolis, IN: Liberty Fund, 2014), 242–75.

59. *DA* [1.2.10], 552.

60. In a footnote to this passage Tocqueville claims: "If the English of the Antilles had governed themselves, you can count on the fact that they would not have granted the act of emancipation that the mother country has just imposed." *DA* [1.2.10], 572 and [1.1.2], 61n13. For a discussion of Tocqueville's analysis of British abolitionism, see chap. 3.

61. *DA* [1.2.10], 630. Jennie C. Ikuta and Trevor Latimer, "Aristocracy in America: Tocqueville on White Supremacy," *Journal of Politics* 83, no. 2 (2021): 547–59.

62. *DA* [1.2.10], 583. Abraham Lincoln, "House Divided Speech," June 16, 1858, Springfield, Illinois, US, Abraham Lincoln Online, transcript, http://www.abrahamlincolnonline.org/lincoln/speeches/house.htm.

63. Sean Wilentz, "Many Democracies: On Tocqueville and Jacksonian America," in *Reconsidering Tocqueville's Democracy in America*, ed. Abraham S. Eisenstadt (New Brunswick, NJ: Rutgers University Press, 1988), 207–28; James L. Crouthamel, "Tocqueville's South," *Journal of the Early Republic* 2, no. 4 (Winter, 1982): 381–401; Kissam, "Alexis de Tocqueville and American Constitutional Law," 42–51; H. G. Nicholas, "Tocqueville and the Dissolution of the Union," *Revue Internationale de Philosophie* 13, no. 49 (1959): 320–29; Allen, "Racial Equality and Social Equality," 85–115; Sean Beienburg, "States' Rights Gone Wrong?: Secession, Nullification, and Reverse-Nullification in Contemporary America," *Tulsa Law Review* 53 (2018): 191; Garry Wills, "Did Tocqueville 'Get' America?" *New York Review of Books* 1.1, no. 7 (April 29, 2004); Daniel Choi, "Unprophetic Tocqueville: How Democracy in America Got the Modern World Completely Wrong," *Independent Review* 12, no. 2, (Fall 2007): 165–78; Rogers Smith, "Beyond Tocqueville, Myrdal, and Hartz: The Multiple Traditions in America," *American Political Science Review* 87, no. 3 (1993): 549–66.

64. Jennifer Pitts, introduction to *Tocqueville on Empire and Slavery*, ed. Jennifer Pitts (Baltimore, MD: Johns Hopkins University Press, 2001), xvi. For a critical overview of Tocqueville scholarship see B. Tillery Jr., "Reading Tocqueville Behind the Veil: African American Receptions of Democracy in America, 1835–1900," *American Political Thought* 7, no. 1 (2018), 1–25, esp. 1–3; and Alvin B. Tillery Jr., "Tocqueville as Critical Race Theorist: Whiteness as Property, Interest Convergence, and the Limits of Jacksonian Democracy," *Political Research Quarterly* 62, no. 4 (2009): 639–52. See also, Alison McQueen and Burke A. Hendrix, "Tocqueville in Jacksonian Context: American Expansionism and Discourses of American Indian Nomadism in Democracy in America," *Perspective on Politics* 15, no. 3 (2017): 663–77.

65. Roger Boesche, "Why Could Tocqueville Predict so Well?," *Political Theory* 11, no. 1 (February 1983): 79–103. Harvey C. Mansfield, "Tocqueville and the Future of American Constitutionalism," in *The Normative Constitution: Essays For the Third Century*, ed. Charles W. Johnson, Kent E. Robson, and Richard Sherlock (Lanham, MD: Rowman & Littlefield, 1995).

66. *DA* [1.2.10], 583, 591–92, 646–47. One reason for Tocqueville's skepticism was the war of 1812, *DA* [1.1.8], 274–5, 591, and 591n53. For detailed accounts of Tocqueville's American travels see Pierson, *Tocqueville and Beaumont in America*; and Leo Damrosch, *Tocqueville's Discovery of America* (New York: Farrar, Straus and Giroux, 2011).

67. *DA* [1.2.10], 582–626; Ralph C. Hancock, "Tocqueville on the Good of American Federalism," *Publius* 20, no. 2 (1990): 89–91. Andrew G. I. Kilberg argues that, far from being merely historical, "the debate over the identity of the people still rages," in "We the People: The Original Meaning of Popular Sovereignty," *Virginia Law Review* 100, no. 5 (September 2014): 1061–109.

68. *DA* [1.1.8], 252. The language of innovation was part of the framers' own pitch. As James Madison put it before the Virginia ratifying convention, the federal Constitution "is in a manner unprecedented ... We cannot find one express example in the experience of the world," quoted in Kilberg, 1109.

69. *DA* [1.1.8], 251, 254, 262. In this section Tocqueville closely follows the view and the language of the *Federalist*, no. 39 (James Madison). In a note he acknowledges his frequent reliance on the *Federalist Papers* commending them as a "complete treatise," which "though special to America, ought to be familiar to statesmen of every country," *DA* [1.1.8], 192n8.

70. *DA* [1.1.8], 253–55. See also Montesquieu, *Spirit of the Laws*, bk. 9, chap. 1.

71. *DA* [1.1.8], 271–72. Kissam, "Tocqueville and American Constitutional Law," 47–48.

72. On a closer look, even the initial celebration is much qualified: "The Union is an ideal nation that exists only in the mind so to speak; intelligence alone reveals its extent and its limits. Once the general theory is well understood, the difficulties of application remain; they are innumerable," *DA* [1.1.8], 265.

73. *DA* [1.2.10], 531–42. As I argue in chapter 3, the fate of racial minorities in the United States is one reason Tocqueville's colonial policy endorses a strong central authority with extensive administrative competences.

74. *DA* [1.2.10], 590. Keith E. Whittington, "The Political Constitution of Federalism in Antebellum America: The Nullification Debate as an Illustration of Informal Mechanisms of Constitutional Change," *Publius* 26, no. 2 (Spring 1996): 1–24. Whittington on p. 20 argues that the nullification crisis was a watershed moment for the ascendance of a "new attitude" to federalism: a turn from the nationalist construction of the Federalist Party and the Marshall court to a localist one elaborated by the Taney court, which maintained that the interests of the states were not merely different but mutually "hostile."

75. Calhoun's position harkens back to the Virginia and Kentucky resolutions of 1799, in part drafted by Madison himself. Both resolutions claimed that the Constitution is a "compact" among the states, which have the right and duty to interpret and enforce its terms. See Whittington, "Political Constitution of Federalism," 4. For an account of the controversy and its reception in German federal jurisprudence, see Grimm, *Sovereignty*, 51–67.

76. "Experience has proven until now that when a state stubbornly wanted something and demanded it resolutely, the state never failed to obtain it; and that when it clearly refused to act, it was left free to do so," *DA* [1.2.10], 591 and 622.

77. McCulloch v. Maryland 17 U.S. (4 Wheat.) 316 (1819), cited in Kissam, "Alexis de Tocqueville and American Constitutional Law," 54; Whittington, "Political Constitution of Federalism," 6, 23.

78. *DA* [1.2.10], 584–85.

79. *DA* [1.1.5], 142–66; see also [1.1.5], 163nE.

80. *DA* [1.1.5], 147.

81. "It is at the very same time necessary and desirable that the central power that directs a democratic people be active and powerful," *DA* [2.4.7], 1265; Atanassow, "Tocqueville's New Liberalism," 54–55.

82. Delba Winthrop, "Tocqueville on Federalism," *Publius* 6, no. 3 (1976): 97. See also Martin Diamond, "The Ends of Federalism," in *Tocqueville's Political Science: Classic Essays*, ed. Peter A. Lawler (New York: Garland Publishing, 1992), 116–22. Kissam, "Alexis de Tocqueville and American Constitutional Law," 60. As Koritansky points out, for Tocqueville there is no purely institutional way to reconcile the simultaneous need for active self-government and strong central power. Hence the crucial importance he attaches to mores and religion, John Koritansky, *Alexis de Tocqueville and the New Science of Politics* (Durham, NC: Carolina Academic Press, 1986), 87. See also John Koritansky, "Decentralization and Civic Virtue in Tocqueville's 'New Science of Politics,'" *Publius* 5, no. 3 (1975): 63–81.

83. *DA* [1.2.10], 584nO; also 586nP. "Sovereignty can have a multitude of agents, but there is always only one sovereign power, just as in one man there is always only one will applied to different objects and served by different organs" (82–84). For a related view—what Amar calls "agency theory"—see *Federalist*, no. 46 (James Madison); Amar, "Of Sovereignty and Federalism," 1424–25. See also Rousseau, *Social Contract*, bk. 2 chap. 2.

84. *DA* [1.2.10], 586 and 587nQ.

85. *DA* [1.2.10], 583. *Federalist* nos. 27 and 33 (Alexander Hamilton). Joshua Miller, "The Ghostly Body Politic: The Federalist Papers and Popular Sovereignty," *Political Theory*, 16, no. 1 (1988): 106.

86. Ralph C. Hancock notes that these are precisely the rights that the American Civil War amendments transfer to the federal government: see Hancock, "Tocqueville on the Good of American Federalism," 91. Cf. Kilberg, "We the People," 1083–4.

87. *DA* [1.2.10], 588, translation amended.

88. *DA* [1.1.8] 265; [1.2.10], 588.

89. *DA* [1.1.5], 158; [1.1.8], 269; [1.2.10], 584 and 584nN.

90. *DA* [1.2.10], 589; [1.1.8], 265. "The sovereignty of the Union is an abstract thing connected to only a small number of external matters. The sovereignty of the states is felt by all the senses; it is understood without difficulty; every moment, it is seen in action. One is new; the other was born with the people themselves. The sovereignty of the Union is a work of art. The sovereignty of the states is natural; it exists by itself, without effort, like the authority of the father of a family," *DA* [1.1.8], 269.

91. *DA* [1.2.10], 590. For an emphatic agreement see Keith Whittington, "Revisiting Tocqueville's America," in Edwards, Foley, and Diani, *Beyond Tocqueville*, 23–25. For alternative views, see William J. Novak, "The Myth of the Weak American State,"

American Historical Review 113, no. 3 (2008): 752–72; also Ira Katznelson, "Flexible Capacity: The Military in Early American Statebuilding," in *Shaped by War and Trade: International Influences on American Political Development*, ed. Ira Katznelson and Martin Shefter (Princeton, NJ: Princeton University Press, 2001), esp. chap. 4.

92. DA [1.2.10], 605. Winthrop, "Tocqueville on Federalism," 105–6.

93. DA [1.1.8], 269. See in this connection, Mark. E. Graber, *Dred Scott and the Problem of Constitutional Evil* (Cambridge: Cambridge University Press, 2010).

94. DA [1.2.2], 283–84. The quoted phrase refers to the Federalist Party, which disappeared from the American political landscape shortly after the war of 1812. Tocqueville's analysis of the prospects for the Union reads as an elegy for the Federalist vision.

95. "The Constitution had not destroyed the individuality of the states and all bodies, whatever they may be, have a secret instinct that carries them toward independence. This instinct is more pronounced in a country like America, where each village forms a kind of republic accustomed to governing itself," DA [1.2.10], 615. Ironically, it is the American people's republican mores that stand in the way of a more perfect union.

96. In Whittington's account, the nullification debate was a clash between three different visions of federalism: Calhoun's "radical federalism," Webster's trenchant nationalism, and Jackson's "centrist federalism," all three plausibly claiming Madisonian credentials, Whittington, "The Political Constitution of Federalism," 14–15. See also Adam Tate, "James Madison and State Sovereignty, 1780–1781," *American Political Thought* 2, no. 2 (Fall 2013): 174–97.

97. DA [1.2.10], 610, 572; [1.1.8], 186–190; [1.2.5], 318–19. For a related argument see Sveinn Jóhannesson, "'Securing the State': James Madison, Federal Emergency Powers, and the Rise of the Liberal State in Post-Revolutionary America," *Journal of American History* 104 (September 2017): 363–85. See also Tocqueville's account of the faltering German confederation of 1849, *Recollections: The French Revolution of 1848*, ed. J. P. Mayer and A. P. Kerr, trans. George Lawrence (New Brunswick, NJ: Transaction Publishers, 1995), 244–48.

98. DA [1.2.10], 611.

99. DA [1.2.10], 615–16.

100. Helmut Anheier, "Democracy Challenged," in *Governance Report 2017*, ed. The Hertie School of Governance (Oxford: Oxford University Press), 14. Julia Azari, "It's the Institutions, Stupid: The Real Roots of America's Political Crisis," *Foreign Affairs*, June 11 (2009), https://www.foreignaffairs.com/articles/united-states/2019-06-11/its-institutions-stupid. Cf. Vivien A. Schmidt, "Democracy and Legitimacy in the European Union Revisited: Input, Output and 'Throughput,'" *Political Studies* 61, no. 1 (2013): 2–22.

101. DA [1.2.10], 597–98. For a discussion of this statement in light of Tocqueville's distinction between instinctive and reflective public spirit, see chapter 2 and Ewa

Atanassow, "Patriotism in Democracy: What We Can Learn from Tocqueville," in *Tocquevillean Ideas: Contemporary European Perspectives*, ed. Zbigniew Rau and Marek Tracz-Tryniecki (Lanham, MD: University Press of America, 2014), 39–58.

102. *DA* [1.2.10], 592.

103. *DA* [1.2.10], 599, 597. "Maine and Georgia," Tocqueville observes, "placed at two extremities of a vast empire, naturally find more real ease in forming a confederation than Normandy and Brittany, which are separated only by a stream," *DA* [1.1.8], 272.

104. *DA* [1.2.10], 600–601. In the drafts for this section Tocqueville writes: "The true bond of the Americans is this, much more than love of country and nationality. These two things are more apparent than real, but the others differentiate the Americans from all other peoples. What makes their common bond is what separates them from the others," *DA* [1.2.10], 598–99nZ.

105. Nothing illustrates this discrepancy more effectively than Tocqueville's famous description of Kentucky and Ohio: two states, one slave and one free, separated by a river, *DA* [1.2.10,] 557–61; see also Thomas Jefferson, *Notes on the State of Virginia* (New York: Norton Library, 1954), query 18. Crouthamel, "Tocqueville's South," 381–401.

106. *DA* [1.2.10], 601. Neem, "Taking Modernity's Wager," 591–618.

107. *DA* [1.2.10], 614; John Quincy Adams is Tocqueville's source for this view in *Journey to America*, 49–50.

108. Tocqueville's most sustained account of the America frontier can be found in his posthumously published travelogue "Fortnight in the Wilderness," in *DA*, appendix 2, 1303–59. For a discussion see Ewa Atanassow, "*Fortnight in the Wilderness*: Tocqueville on Nature and Civilization," *Perspectives on Political Science* 35, no. 1 (2006): 22–30.

109. *DA* [1.2.10], 614. Ralph Lerner, *The Thinking Revolutionary* (Ithaca, NY: Cornell University Press, 1988), 185.

110. *DA* [1.2.10], 614. Also [1.1.2], 52.

111. Kissam, "Alexis de Tocqueville and American Constitutional Law," 44. For an extended discussion of the integrative power of constitutions see Dieter Grimm, *Constitutionalism: Past, Present, and Future* (Oxford: Oxford University Press, 2019), chap. 6. While in pp. 150–51, Grimm takes the United States as an example of integration by constitution, he deliberately leaves the Civil War and the constitutional politics that led to it out of his purview.

112. *DA* [1.2.10], 598, my emphasis.

113. *DA*, 270. Rousseau, *Social Contract*, bk.1 chap. 5–7 and bk. 2 chap. 10.

114. Pierre Manent, "Democracy without Nations?," *Journal of Democracy* 8, no. 2 (1997): 95.

115. Rousseau, *Social Contract*, bk. 2, chap. 12, 81.

116. *DA* [1.1.4], 97, translation amended. While in English "people" can be either singular or plural, in French *peuple* is singular and connotes a corporate body rather than a multitude. For an account of Tocqueville's sources for this statement, see Selby, *Tocqueville, Jansenism, and the Necessity of the Political in a Democratic Age*, 122–128.

117. "Men put the grandeur of the idea of unity in the means; God, in the end; the result is that this idea of grandeur leads us to a thousand petty things. To force all men to march with the same step, toward the same purpose, that is a human idea. To introduce an infinite variety in actions, but to combine them so that all these actions lead by a thousand paths toward the accomplishment of a great design, that is a divine idea. The human idea of unity is almost always sterile; that of God, immensely fruitful. Men think to attest to their grandeur by simplifying the means. It is the purpose of God which is simple. His means vary infinitely," *DA* [2.4.3], 1200n1292. For a discussion see Kahan, *Tocqueville, Democracy, and Religion*, 59–67.

118. "I regard as impious and detestable the maxim that in matters of government the majority of a people has the right to do everything, and nonetheless I place the origin of all powers in the will of the majority. Am I in contradiction with myself?," *DA* [1.2.7], 410. Adduced in Kissam, "Tocqueville and American Constitutional Law," 53.

Chapter 2

1. Dieter Grimm, *Sovereignty: The Origin and Future of a Political and Legal Concept*, trans. Belinda Cooper. (New York: Columbia University Press, 2015), 43–44. Also Olga Bashkina, "Nations against the People," in *Sovereignty in Action*, ed. Bas Leijssenaar and Neil Walker (Cambridge: Cambridge University Press, 2019), 159–76.

2. Rogers Brubaker, "Populism and Nationalism," *Nations and Nationalism* 26, no. 1, (2020): 44–66, esp. 45–46. Brubaker's critical review of these debates argues against strict conceptual separation. For an overview of the vast literature that questions its modernist bias, see Steven Grosby, *Nationalism: A Very Short Introduction* (Oxford: Oxford University Press, 2005). See also Rogers Smith, introduction to *Political Peoplehood* (Chicago: University of Chicago Press, 2015), 1–15.

3. See Bruno Bosteels, "Introduction: The People Which Is Not One," in Alain Badiou, et al., *What Is a People?*, trans. Jody Gladding (New York: Columbia University Press, 2016), 2–20, esp. 2–3.

4. *DA* [1.1.4], 97nM. For the problem of the people in Jacksonian America, see "Peoplehood" in chap. 1.

5. *DA* [2.1.15], 815.

6. For a full discussion see Paul A. Rahe's 3-volume study, *Republics Ancient and Modern* (Chapel Hill: University of North Carolina Press, 1994), and specifically vol. 1, chap. 7 for his characterization of Athens as an illiberal democracy.

7. For a more nuanced view, see Kostas Vlassopoulos, "Free Spaces: Identity, Experience and Democracy in Classical Athens," *Classical Quarterly New Series* 57, no. 1 (May 2007): 33–52. See also Demetra Kasimis, *The Perpetual Immigrant and the Limits of Athenian Democracy* (Cambridge: Cambridge University Press, 2018).

8. Around the time Tocqueville's passage is written only about 2 percent of adult males could vote in French national elections. In local ones the suffrage was considerably broader, reaching 40 to 60 percent. Alan S. Kahan, *Liberalism in Nineteenth Century Europe: The Political Culture of Limited Suffrage* (Hampshire: Palgrave McMillan, 2003).

9. *DA* [1.2.6], 380, my emphasis.

10. Tocqueville analyzes local and partisan divisions in similar terms, *DA* [1.2.7], 411n3; [1.2.2], 279–88; [1.2.9], 508.

11. Rogers Brubaker, *Grounds for Difference* (Cambridge, MA: Harvard University Press, 2015).

12. *DA* [1.1.4], 95–96. For Tocqueville's own politics of suffrage see Robert Gannett, "Tocqueville and the Politics of Suffrage," *Tocqueville Review / La Revue Tocqueville* 27 (2006): 209–26. Gianna Englert, "'The Idea of Rights': Tocqueville on The Social Question," *Review of Politics* 79 (2017): 649–74; Cf. Smith, *Political Peoplehood*, chap. 6; Johann N. Neem "Who Are 'The People'?: Locating Popular Authority In Postrevolutionary America," *Reviews in American History*, 39, no. 2 (June 2011): 267–73.

13. E.g. *DA* [1.2.4], 307; [2.1.2], 719; [2.1.21], 863; [2.2.15], 956; [2.3.8], 1035; [2.4.4], 1214.

14. *DA* [2.3.5], 1009; [2.3.17], 1089; Pierre Manent, *Tocqueville and the Nature of Democracy*, trans. John Waggoner (Latham, MD: Rowman & Littlefield, 1996), 10; Kahan, "Aristocracy in Tocqueville," 328–29. Halévi, "The Frontier between Aristocracy and Democracy," 53–73. For a similar account, see Liah Greenfeld, *Nationalism: A Short History* (Washington, DC: Brookings Institution, 2019), 1–11.

15. As Tocqueville points out, its political unity too was imperfect, *DA* [1.1.5], 147–8; [1.2.10], 636.

16. *DA* [2.3.1], 990; [2.3.5], 1011; [2.2.2], 884.

17. *DA* [1.2.3], 293; [1.2.6], 380; [2.3.21], 1141.

18. *DA*, introduction, 6; [1.1.3], 74–90; [1.1.4], 96–97; [1.2.10], 633, 636. As Tocqueville recaps, "[w]hat is understood by republic in the United States is the slow and tranquil action of society on itself. It is an ordered state actually based on the enlightened will of the people. It is a conciliatory government, where resolutions mature over a long time, are debated slowly and are executed with maturity," *DA* [1.2.10], 630.

19. Rogers Brubaker, *Citizenship and Nationhood in France and Germany* (Cambridge, MA: Harvard University Press, 1992), 44–45. Though in America

revolutionary violence was for the most part directed outward, it too featured elements of civil war: e.g., the forced exile and persecution of loyalists. Maya Jasanoff, *Liberty's Exiles: American Loyalists in the Revolutionary World* (New York: Alfred A. Knopf, 2012); Thomas B. Allen. *Tories: Fighting for the King in America's First Civil War* (New York: HarperCollins, 2011).

20. *DA* [1.2.7], 405; [2.3.1], 993. "In America," Tocqueville comments, "men who are so removed from the majority by their opinion can do nothing against the power of the majority; all others hope to win it over."

DA [1.1.4], 309–10. Whittington, "Revisiting Tocqueville's America," 21–22.

21. *DA* [1.2.10], 599; [1.2.9], 467–87; [2.1.5], 742–53. Tocqueville notes: "Unbelievers are found in America, but unbelief finds, so to speak, no organ there," *DA* [1.2.7], 419. Kahan, *Tocqueville, Democracy, and Religion*, chap. 4. For a critique of Tocqueville's account of religious harmony in America, see Phillip C. Kissam, "Alexis de Tocqueville and American Constitutional Law: On Democracy, the Majority Will, Individual Rights, Federalism, Religion, Civic Associations, and Originalist Constitutional Theory," *Maine Law Review* 59, no. 1 (2007): 47–48; and Catherine Zuckert, "The Saving Minimum?: Tocqueville on the Role of Religion in America—Then and Now," in *The Spirit of Religion and the Spirit of Liberty: The Tocqueville Thesis Revisited*, ed. Michael Zuckert (Chicago: University of Chicago Press, 2017), 242–65.

22. *DA* [1.2.1], 278–79; Manent, *Tocqueville and the Nature of Democracy*, chap. 1.

23. *DA* [2.2.2], 883; [2.3.18], 1100.

24. Tocqueville dates its beginnings to the Reformation, *DA* [2.1.1], 704; [2.3.18], 1093–115. As discussed, although ancient republics were significantly different from the feudal polity, they were similar in this respect: there too the greater part of society—including slaves and metics—lay outside the boundaries of the demos and beyond the purview of patriotism.

25. Bernard Yack, "Popular Sovereignty and Nationalism," *Political Theory* 29, no. 4 (2001). See also, John Breuilly, ed., *The Oxford Handbook of the History of Nationalism* (Oxford: Oxford University Press, 2013); Liah Greenfeld, *Nationalism: Five Roads to Modernity* (New Haven, CT: Harvard University Press, 1992); Ernest Gellner, *Nations and Nationalism* (Ithaca, NY: Cornell University Press, 1983). For a dissenting view, see Steven Grosby, "The Nation of the United States and the Vision of Ancient Israel," in *Biblical Ideas of Nationality: Ancient and Modern* (Winona Lake, IN: Eisenbrauns, 2002), 213–33.

26. While historians conventionally date modern manifestations of nationalism to the Atlantic Revolutions, as a concept nationalism only gained currency in the late nineteenth century. Pauli Kettunen, "The Concept of Nationalism in Discussions on a European Society," *Journal of Political Ideologies* 23, no. 3 (2018), 342–69; Hans Kohn, *The Idea of Nationalism: A Study of Its Origins and Background* (London: Routledge, 2005).

27. *DA* [1.2.6], 384–86.

28. The literature on nationalism abounds in such dichotomies: ethnos/demos; civic/ethnic nationalism; nationalism vs. patriotism. See e.g., Emerich K. Francis, *Ethnos und Demos: Soziologische Beitraege zur Volkstheorie* (Berlin: Duncker & Humblot, 1965); Roger Brubaker, "In the Name of the Nation: Reflections on Nationalism and Patriotism," in *Citizenship Studies*, 8 no. 2 (2004): 115–27. For a sustained discussion see, Bernard Yack, *Nationalism and the Moral Psychology of Community* (Chicago: University of Chicago Press, 2012), chap. 1. Also Yael Tamir, "Not So Civic: Is There a Difference between Ethnic and Civic Nationalism?," *Annual Review of Political Science* 22 (May 2019): 419–34.

29. *DA* [1.1.5,] 159 and Rousseau, *Social Contract*, bk. 3, chap. 4; Ewa Atanassow, "Patriotism in Democracy: What We Can Learn from Tocqueville," in *Tocquevillean Ideas: Contemporary European Perspectives*, ed. Zbigniew Rau and Marek Tracz-Tryniecki (Lanham, MD: University Press of America, 2014), 39–58.

30. *DA* [1.2.6], 385, 387. See also "The Principle of Popular Sovereignty" in chap. 1.

31. Ringo Ossewaarde, *Tocqueville's Moral and Political Thought: New Liberalism* (London: Routlege, 2004), 159–59. Maurizio Viroli, *For Love of Country: An Essay on Patriotism and Nationalism* (Oxford: Clarendon Press, 1997), 181–82. For a nuanced account, see Kahan, *Tocqueville, Democracy, and Religion*, 102–14.

32. *DA* [1.2.10], 597–98. See also "Forging Allegiance" in chap. 1. For the allegation of incoherence and its subsequent retraction, see Jon Elster, *Political Psychology* (Cambridge: Cambridge University Press, 1993), 112; and Elster, *Alexis de Tocqueville: The First Social Scientist*, 4.

33. *DA* [1.2.6], 385.

34. *DA* [1.2.6], 387, my emphasis.

35. Empirical studies point to patriotic joy (or being *froh*) as a non-discriminatory sentiment that affirms one's country without devaluing others. While partly supportive of these findings, Tocqueville's analysis raises questions about their constitutional implications. Horst-Alfred Heinrich, "Emotions toward the Nation," in *Methods, Theories, and Empirical Applications in the Social Sciences*, ed. Samuel Salzborn, Eldad Davidov, and Jorst Reinecke (Wiesbaden: Springer VS, 2012), 227–34; see also Horst-Alfred Heinrich, "Dimensional Differences between Nationalism and Patriotism" in *Dynamics of National Identity*, ed. Jürgen Grimm et al. (New York: Routledge, 2016), 44–63.

36. *DA* [1.2.6], 387.

37. I echo here Benedict Anderson, *Imagined Communities: Reflections on the Origin and Spread of Nationalism* (London: Verso, 2006).

38. "The inhabitant [of the United States] applies himself to the interest of his country as to his own. He glories in the glory of the nation; in the success that it obtains he *believes to recognize* his own work, and he is uplifted by it . . . He has for his country a sentiment analogous to that for his family," *DA* [1.1.5], 160.

39. *DA* [1.2.6], 388.
40. *DA* [1.2.10], 598.
41. *DA* [2.2.4], 893, my emphasis.
42. *DA* [2.2.7], 914; [1.1.5], 142, 166; also Robert T. Gannett, "Tocqueville and Local Government," *Review of Politics* 67, no. 4 (2005): 724–25.
43. *DA* [1.2.6], 389–92; Dale T. Miller, "The Norm of Self-Interest," *American Psychologist* 54, no. 12 (1999): 1054; cited in Elster, *Alexis de Tocqueville: The First Social Scientist*, 9. Miller's study shows that self-interest is a widely shared cultural norm that influences both how individuals behave and how they account for their behavior. Like Tocqueville, Miller finds that "people often act and speak in accordance with their perceived self-interest solely because they believe to do otherwise is to violate a powerful descriptive and prescriptive expectation." Miller, "Norm of Self-Interest," 1054 and *DA*, [2.2.8], 920–21.
44. *DA*, introduction, 20; [1.1.4], 91nA; [1.1.5], 108; [1.2.5], 316; [1.2.6], 391; [2.2.1], 878; [2.2.8], 918–25; [2.3.5], 1007–19. Tocqueville observes that "American legislation appeals to individual interest; that is the great principle found constantly when you study the laws of the United States," *DA* [1.1.5], 128.
45. *DA* [1.2.6], 387; [1.1.5], 160; [2.1.13], 808; [2.2.8], 926–29; [2.3.5], 1017. Delba Winthrop, "Rights, Interests, and Honor," in *Tocqueville's Defense of Human Liberty*, ed. Peter A. Lawler and Joseph Alulis (New York: Garland Publisher, 1993), 203–22; Harvey Mansfield, "Self-Interest Rightly Understood," *Political Theory* 23, no. 1 (1995): 48–66.
46. *DA* [1.2.5], 142–66, esp. 160; [2.2.5], 885–902. For a discussion see Atanassow, "Tocqueville's New Liberalism," 53–56.
47. *DA* [1.1.5], 102. Tocqueville's notes on the government of India credit municipal institutions both for the survival of Hindu culture and for lack of interest in general politics: "The entire political life of the Indians withdrew into the town; the entire administration was concentrated there. As long as the town still existed, who controlled the empire was of little importance to the inhabitants. They hardly noticed the change of masters," cited in *DA*, 102nG.
48. As Tocqueville notes while analyzing the old regime clergy, such a threat inheres in "all groups, political as well as religious, that are strongly united and well-constituted," in Tocqueville, *The Old Regime*, 175.
49. *DA* [1.2.4], 304. M. I. Finley, *Democracy Ancient and Modern* (New Brunswick, NJ: Rutgers University Press, 2018), chap. 3. Harvey C. Mansfield, "On the Difference between Party and Faction," in *Philosophy, Politics, and the Conversation of Mankind*, ed. Todd Breyfogle, Paul Franco, and Eric Kos (Colorado Springs: Colorado College, 2016), 211–26.
50. *Federalist* no. 10 (James Madison); Edmund S. Morgan, *Inventing the People: The Rise of Popular Sovereignty in England and America* (New York: W. W. Norton, 1988), 273; Michael Zuckert, "James Madison," in Atanassow and Kahan, *Liberal Moments*, 43–50.

51. Recognizing the need for such an agreement is one reason, perhaps, for the inclusion of *Federalist* no. 2 (John Jay). Donald J. Maletz, "Tocqueville on Mores and the Preservation of Republics," *American Journal of Political Science* 49, no. 1 (2005): 1–15; Neem, "Taking Modernity's Wager," 605–16; Gannett, "Tocqueville and Local Government," 724, 726–31; John C. Koritansky, "Decentralization and Civic Virtue in Tocqueville's 'New Science of Politics,'" *Publius* 5, no. 3 (1975): 63–81.

52. *DA* [1.2.10], 646.

53. *DA* [1.2.10], 598–99nZ.

54. Peter Lawler, "The Human Condition: Tocqueville's Debt to Rousseau and Pascal," in *Liberty, Equality, Democracy*, ed. Eduardo Nolla (New York: New York University Press, 1992), 1–20. An aphoristic fragment first published in Beaumont's edition of Tocqueville's works reads: "Give me flesh and pride and I will make you a man," Alexis de Tocqueville, *Œuvres complètes*, 18 vols. ed. Françoise Mélonio (Paris: Gallimard, 1989); my translation [henceforth *OC*], 16:572.

55. *DA* [2.3.3], 1070; see also *DA* [2.3.13] and *OC* 16:230.

56. In volume two of *Democracy in America* Tocqueville depicts with anecdotal flourish the cruelty of class relations in aristocratic society, which he attributes to institutionalized disparities that stimulate pride and preclude sympathy between classes and peoples, *DA* [2.3.1], 988–94. Compare with Blaise Pascal, *Pensées and Other Writings* (Oxford: Oxford Classics, 1995), 240, 74, and 190; Montesquieu, *The Persian Letters*, trans. C. J. Betts (London: Penguin Books, 1993), letter LXXVIII.

57. *DA* [2.3.19], 1126. This insight is well attested by both developmental psychology and many civil rights movements. D. Hart and M. K. Matsuba, "The Development of Pride and Moral Life," in *The Self-Conscious Emotions: Theory and Research*, ed. J. L. Tracy, R. W. Robins, and J. P. Tangney (New York: Guilford Press, 2007), 114–33. Syin Haynes, "What's Changed—and What Hasn't—in 50 Years of Pride Parades," *Time Magazine*, June 26, 2020, https://time.com/5858086/pride-parades-history/.

58. Peter Augustine Lawler, *The Restless Mind: Alexis de Tocqueville on the Origin and Perpetuation of Human Liberty* (Lanham, MD: Rowman & Littlefield, 1993), chap. 4; Harvey C. Mansfield and Delba Winthrop, "Tocqueville's New Political Science," in *The Cambridge Companion to Tocqueville*, ed. Cheryl Welch (Cambridge: Cambridge University Press, 2006), 84; Mitchell, *Fragility of Freedom*, 3–5; Zuckert, "On Social State," 16–17.

59. Tocqueville's very first letter home of April 26, 1831 observes: "[The Americans] believe themselves to be quite different. People here seem to me reeking of national pride; it pierces through all their politeness," *OC* 14: 83, my translation; also *OC* 5:1:293.

60. *DA* [1.1.5.], 160. Ralph C. Hancock, "Tocqueville on the Good of American Federalism," *Publius* 20, no. 2 (1990): 103; see also in this volume "From Interest to Instinct" in chap. 2.

61. *DA* [1.2.10], 601; see also *Journey to America*, 329–30, 351. Tocqueville's discussion of the Anglo-American point of departure probes the primary sources of that confidence, *DA* [1.1.2].

62. *DA* [1.2.10], 573, 581, 600. Alvin B. Tillery Jr., "Tocqueville as Critical Race Theorist: Whiteness as Property, Interest Convergence, and the Limits of Jacksonian Democracy," *Political Research Quarterly*, 62, no. 4 (December, 2009): 639–52. Tocqueville does not only critique American national pride but also points to its legitimate object. Commenting on the Constitutional convention of 1787, he writes: "If ever America was capable of rising for a few moments to the high level of glory that the proud imagination of its inhabitants would like constantly to show us, it was at this supreme moment when the national power had, in a way, just abdicated authority," *DA* [1.1.8], 189. Not military or commercial prowess, let alone racial origins, but the American people's peaceful and voluntarily submission to the wisdom of its leading citizens is, in his view, its true claim to glory and national pride.

63. On Tocqueville's debt to La Bruyère, see Lucien Jaume, *Tocqueville: The Aristocratic Sources of Liberty*, trans. Arthur Goldhammer (Princeton NJ: Princeton University Press, 2013), 145–46, 238–41; and Kahan, *Tocqueville, Democracy, and Religion*, 18–23.

64. *DA* [2.3.16], 1086–87. As Tocqueville remarks in an endnote, England is in fact a country in transition: while ruled by an aristocratic class, it is an "aristocracy of money" whose ranks are to some extent mobile, *DA* [2.2.19], 975–76n1286; Tocqueville, *Old Regime*, 1, 17, 105, 240. If, on the other hand, the English of Tocqueville's time enjoyed uncontested preeminence, it was with regard to their empire, which made England the world's superpower *OC* 3:1:478 and 3:2:425–27.

65. *DA* [2.3.16], 1086–87.

66. *DA*, introduction, 20. As Tocqueville indicates, aristocratic pride too depends on social recognition: the tacit recognition of the legitimacy of birthright. Yet aristocratic institutions conceal this fact, which time and usage have consecrated as a "sort of natural right" (1087). Tocqueville calls this ignorance.

67. *DA* [2.3.16], 1086.

68. Mitchell, *Fragility of Freedom*, 79. Though vanity thrives in the fertile soil of egalitarian *moeurs*, it is not an exclusively democratic phenomenon. In the *Old Regime* Tocqueville points to vanity as a "natural" characteristic of the French, moreover the secret source of much of their history's evil, see Tocqueville, *Old Regime*, 1:164, 162–71.

69. *DA* [1.2.6], 395–401; [1.2.10] 557–61; [2.2.15], 956–57; [2.3.1], 987–95.

70. *DA* [2.3.19], 1126nR.

71. André Jardin, *Tocqueville: A Biography* (New York: Farrar, Straus and Giroux, 1988), 290. Robert T. Gannett, "Tocqueville as Politician: Revisiting the Revolution of 1789," in *Enlightening Revolutions*, ed. Svetozar Minkov (Lanham, MD: Lexington Books, 2006), 235–58. For an appraisal of Tocqueville's theory and practice of

democratic leadership, see Brian Danoff, "Lincoln and Tocqueville," *Review of Politics* 67, no. 4 (2005): 685–719 and Brian Danoff and L. Joseph Hebert Jr., *Alexis de Tocqueville and the Art of Democratic Statesmanship* (Lanham, MD: Lexington Books, 2010).

72. Richard Boyd, *Uncivil Society: The Perils of Pluralism and the Making of Modern Liberalism* (Lanham, MD: Lexington Books, 2004), chaps. 5–6.

73. François Furet, *Revolutionary France* (Oxford: Wiley-Blackwell, 1995), 358–59; M. S. Anderson, *The Eastern Question: A Study in International Relations* (New York: Macmillan, 1966), chap. 4. As Jardin notes, with the affair of Egypt "France was caught up in the most intense international crisis that the July monarchy had yet experienced," *Tocqueville*, 316.

74. *OC* 3:2:288–301. Tocqueville's first speech in the Chamber, delivered on July 2, 1839, also concerned foreign policy and Near Eastern affairs. Articulating his vision of France's role in the world, it spelled out the principles that would guide, almost a decade later, Tocqueville's brief tenure as a foreign minister of the Second Republic. *OC* 3.2, 255–68 and *Recollections*, 240–41n. For a detailed discussion of the context of that speech and Tocqueville's involvement in the Eastern question see Mary Lawlor, *Alexis de Tocqueville in the Chamber of Deputies: His Views on Foreign and Colonial Policy* (Washington, DC: Catholic University of America Press, 1959), chap. 3.

75. *OC* 3:2:291, 321. As discussed in the next chapter, Tocqueville uses similar tropes in his speeches on colonial policy and foreign affairs, *OC* 3:2:326, 398, 426, 750–51.

76. *OC* 3:2:285–87, 298–301, 271–72. See also Tocqueville's letters to Henry Reeve, François Corcelle, and Pierre Paul Royer-Collard, which voice misgivings about the dangers of a possible war and France's support for the aging autocrat of Egypt, *OC* 6:1:62–3, 335–36; and 11, 91, 108; 15, 149; and 8:1:420–21.

77. *OC* 3:2:299–301. Cf. *OC* 6:1:61–63, 334–35, *OC* 3:2:287, 307; Jean-Louis Benoît, "Relectures de Tocqueville," *Le Banquet*, no. 16 (2001): 2–20.

78. See e.g., Kahan, *Tocqueville, Democracy and Religion*, 110. Roger Boesche, "The Dark Side of Tocqueville," *Review of Politics* 67, no. 4 (2005): 738; Tzvetan Todorov, *On Human Diversity: Nationalism, Racism, and Exoticism in French Thought*, trans. Catherine Porter (Cambridge, MA: Harvard University Press, 1998), 194–97.

79. *OC* 3:2:287, 307. In his Swiss notebooks, Tocqueville notes: "The first need of a people is to impose respect on its neighbors and to be proud of itself," *OC* 5:2:184; cited in Kahan, *Tocqueville, Democracy and Religion*, 111n46. See his letter to Gustave de Beaumont, in Alexis de Tocqueville, *Selected Letters on Politics and Society*, ed. Roger Boesche. trans, James Toupin (Berkeley, CA: University of California Press), 143. Alan B. Spitzer, "Tocqueville's Modern Nationalism," *French History* 19, no. 1 (March 2005): 48–66.

80. *OC* 6:1:324–44 and Byong-Hoon Suh, "Mill and Tocqueville: A Friendship Bruised," *History of Political Ideas* 42, no. 1 (2016): 55–72. As Jennifer Pitts has argued,

on the question of national pride, which so dangerously divided their countries, Tocqueville and Mill were much closer than has been recognized, *A Turn to Empire* (Princeton NJ: Princeton University Press, 2005), 195–96.

81. Alexis de Tocqueville, *Recollections: The French Revolution of 1848*, ed. J. P. Mayer and A. P. Kerr, trans. George Lawrence (New Brunswick, NJ: Transaction Publishers, 1995), 233n3; Roger Boesche, "Why Could Tocqueville Predict so Well?," *Political Theory* 11, no. 1 (February 1983): 79–103.

82. In 1829 to 1830 Tocqueville attended Guizot's lectures on the "History of the Civilization in France" which, in a letter, he described as "prodigious" and "truly extraordinary," *OC* 8:1:80, 91. *Democracy in America* reflects this admiration, *DA* 18nA. For discussions of Guizot's formative influence, see: Jaume, *Tocqueville*, chap. 12; Nicholas Toloudis, "Tocqueville's Guizot Moment," *French Politics, Culture & Society* 28, no. 3 (Winter 2010): 1–22; Melvin Richter, "Tocqueville and Guizot on Democracy," *History of European Ideas* 30 (2004): 61–82. See also Pierre Rosanvallon's magisterial *Le moment Guizot* (Paris: Gallimard, 1985), parts 1 and 2.

83. *OC* 3:2:380, 383–35, 433. As Craiutu notes, Guizot's appeal. *Enrichissez-vous* became emblematic of the policies and general orientation of the July regime, Aurelian Craiutu, "Tocqueville's Paradoxical Moderation," *Review of Politics* 67, no. 4 (2005), 610 and 610n31. Furet, *Revolutionary France*, 359–60. Pierre Manent, "Guizot et Tocqueville devant l'ancien et le nouveau," in *François Guizot et la culture politique de son temps*, ed. Marina Valensise (Paris: Gallimard, 1991), 26–34.

84. Aurelian Craiutu, "Tocqueville and the Political Thought of the French Doctrinaires," *History of Political Thought* 20, no. 3 (1999): 456–493; also William Selinger, "*Le grand mal de l'époque*: Tocqueville on French Political Corruption," *History of European Ideas*, 42, no. 1 (2016): 73–94.

85. *OC* 3:2:258–59, my emphasis. Unless otherwise noted, all translations of the speeches are mine.

86. *OC* 3:2:299; also 304–5, 317, 345, 376–7; see also the preface to volume 1 of Tocqueville's *Old Regime*.

87. *OC* 3:2:301, 304–5, 346–47, 351, 398–99, 425. Tocqueville's warning gained striking plausibility during the events of 1848, *OC* 6:1:61–2, *OC* 11, 90; Tocqueville, *Recollections*, 11–17, also 240–41.

88. *OC* 3:2:265, 299, 433, 200n, 301n; cf. Tocqueville, *Journey to America*, 366; *OC* 3:1:36–37; Tocqueville, *Old Regime*, 1.246–47. Cf. Tocqueville, *Recollections*, 240. *OC* 6:1:61–3, *OC* 11, 90; *OC* 5:1:197.

89. *OC* 3:2:300 and 265, 340, 381. Also *DA* [1.1.5], 158.

90. *OC* 3:2:433. Spitzer, "Tocqueville's Modern Nationalism," 55.

91. *DA* [1.2.5], 371 and 371n17; [1.2.10], 624–25; [1.2.9], 453; Herbert Dittigen, "Tocqueville Reconsidered: Foreign Policy and the American Democracy," in *Liberty, Equality, Democracy*, ed. Eduardo Nolla (New York: New York University Press, 1992), 79. See also "Honor, Nationhood, Globalization" in chap. 3.

92. *OC* 6:1:330, my translation and emphasis. The language here is reminiscent of the chapter on democratic ambition *DA* [2.3.19], 1116–27. See also J. S. Mill's letter of December 23, 1840 to Robert Barclay Fox, referred to in Pitts, *A Turn to Empire*, 196.

93. Starting in 1840 this debate stretches over the course of three years and another Anglo-French embroilment over the right of search, which I discuss in chapter 3 of this volume. *OC* 6:1:329–47.

94. *OC* 6:1:331, see also *OC* 11, 90. Around the same time Tocqueville writes to Reeve: "A misfortune, an immense misfortune is brewing, not only for our two countries but for the general cause of liberty and for the independence of Europe," *OC* 6:1:61.

95. *OC* 6:1:331, 333–37, 341. See also *OC* 15, 149. Note Tocqueville's untiring denunciation of Napoleonic yearnings. For a critical appraisal see Richard Boyd, "Tocqueville and the Napoleonic Legend," in *Tocqueville and the Frontiers of Democracy*, ed. Ewa Atanassow and Richard Boyd, (Cambridge: Cambridge University Press, 2013), 264–90.

96. *OC* 6:1:336–37 and *DA* [2.3.16], 1086–87, ampersands in original.

97. Pitts, *A Turn to Empire*, 195–96. Georgios Varouxakis, *Mill on Nationality* (London: Routledge, 2002), chap. 7, esp. 122–23. See also Abram L. Harris, "John Stuart Mill: Servant of the East India Company," *Canadian Journal of Economics and Political Science / Revue canadienne d'Economique et de Science politique* 30, no. 2 (May 1964): 185–202.

98. *OC* 6:1:341, my translation. The quote is from a letter Mill wrote in French. See also *OC* 6:1:337, *OC* 3:2: 201; *OC* 11, 157; Seymour Drescher, *Tocqueville and England* (Cambridge, MA: Harvard University Press, 1964), 161. For a comprehensive discussion of Mill's approach to foreign affairs, see Georgios Varouxakis, *Liberty Abroad: J. S. Mill on International Relations* (Cambridge: Cambridge University Press, 2013).

99. J. S. Mill, *Considerations on Representative Government*, in *On Liberty, Utilitarianism and Other Essays* ed. Mark Philp and Frederick Rosen (Oxford: Oxford University Press, 2015), 388–407; and *Collected Works of John Stuart Mill*, vol. 30, ed. J. M. Robson (Toronto: University of Toronto Press, 1990), esp. 77–89; Quentin Taylor, "Radical Son: The Apprenticeship of John Stuart Mill," *Humanitas* 26, nos. 1–2 (2013): 129–52, esp. 139; Alan Ryan, "Bureaucracy, Democracy, Liberty: Some Unanswered Questions in Mill's Politics," in *J. S. Mill's Political Thought: A Bicentennial Reassessment*, ed. Nadia Urbinati and Alex Zakaras (Cambridge: Cambridge University Press, 2007), 147–165; and Karuna Mantena "Mill and the Imperial Predicament," in Urbinati and Zakaras, *J. S. Mill's Political Thought*, 298–318. Varouxakis, *Liberty Abroad*, chap. 5.

100. William Selinger, *Parliamentarism: From Burke to Weber* (Cambridge: Cambridge University Press, 2019), chap. 6. By contrast, in an 1857 letter to Lord Hatherton occasioned by the Sepoy uprising, Tocqueville urges the abolition of the

company and blames the mishandling of Indian affairs on the lack of parliamentary oversight. *OC* 7, 281–82 and 3:1:494; Suh, "Mill and Tocqueville," 67–69.

101. *OC* 6:1:332, my italics.

102. *OC* 6:1:331, 333. Varouxakis, *Mill on Nationality*, 122.

103. *OC* 6:1:335. Jardin, "Tocqueville, homme politique," in *Alexis de Tocqueville: Zur Politik in der Demokratie*, ed. Michael Hereth and Jutta Höffken (Berlin: Nomos Verlagsgesellschaft, 1981), 105. Spitzer "Tocqueville's Modern Nationalism," 59–66. On the importance of infrastructure for Mill's view of progress, see Ryan, "Bureaucracy, Democracy, Liberty," 154–55.

104. *OC* 6:1:336; Tocqueville, *Selected Letters*, 151–52.

105. See Tocqueville, *Recollections*, 241n. *OC* 3:2:20, 290, 294, 296–97, 302, 332, 316n, 291n; 3:2:126, 109; 6:1:335; *OC* 11, 107–9; Ralph Lerner, *Revolutions Revisited: Two Faces of the Politics of the Enlightenment* (Chapel Hill: University of North Carolina Press, 1994), chap. 7.

106. *DA* [1.2.10], 587; see also *OC* 3;2:205–7.

107. *OC* 3:2:382. "Foreward to the Twelfth Edition," *DA*, 13/3 77. Tocqueville's analysis of national pride points to the interrelation of domestic and foreign affairs under democratic conditions, Drescher, *Tocqueville and England*, 156; also David Clinton, "Tocqueville's Challenge," in *Tocqueville's Political Science: Classic Essays*, ed. Peter A. Lawler (New York: Garland Publishing, 1992), 295.

108. *DA* [2.4.7], 1264. Cheryl B. Welch, "Tocqueville on Fraternity and Fratricide," in *The Cambridge Companion to Tocqueville*, ed. Cheryl B. Welch (Cambridge University Press, 2006): 305–10.

109. Jean-Jacques Rousseau, "Considerations on the Government of Poland," in Gourevitch, *Social Contract and Other Later Political Writings*, 179–93. See also Marc F. Plattner, "Rousseau and the Origins of Nationalism," and Pierre Hassner, "Rousseau and the Theory and Practice of International Relations," in *The Legacy of Rousseau*, ed. Clifford Orwin and Nathan Tarcov (Chicago: University of Chicago Press, 1997), 183–99, and 200–203.

110. *OC* 3:1:213. On the rhetoric of visibility and performance in Tocqueville see Richard Boyd, "Imperial Fathers and Favorite Sons: J. S. Mill, Alexis de Tocqueville, and Nineteenth-Century Justifications of Empire," in *Feminist Reinterpretations of Alexis de Tocqueville*, ed. Eileen Hunt Botting, and Jill Locke (University Park, PA: Penn State University Press, 2008), 225–52.

111. Jan-Werner Müller, *Constitutional Patriotism* (Princeton, NJ: Princeton University Press, 2008). For a sustained critique, see Yack, *Nationalism and the Moral Psychology*, chap. 1.

112. Rogers Smith, *Stories of Peoplehood: The Politics and Morals of Political Membership* (Cambridge: Cambridge University Press, 2003); and "Popular Sovereignty, Populism, and Stories of Peoplehood," in *When the People Rule: Popular Sovereignty*

in Theory and Practice, ed. Ewa Atanassow, Thomas Bartscherer, and David Bateman (Cambridge: Cambridge University Press, forthcoming).

113. Mounk, *The People vs. Democracy*, 3; Chantal Mouffe, *For a Left Populism* (London: Verso 2018), 1.

114. *DA* [1.1.2], 27; [2.3.21], 1142–43.

Chapter 3

1. *DA*, introduction, 16. Dani Rodrik, *The Globalization Paradox: Democracy and the Future of the World Economy* (New York: W. W. Norton, 2011), chap. 2; also Keegan Callanan, *Montesquieu's Liberalism and the Problem of Universal Politics* (Cambridge: Cambridge University Press, 2018); See also Liah Greenfeld, *Nationalism: A Short History* (Washington, DC: Brookings Institution, 2019), chap. 5.

2. *DA* [2.3.18], 1093–115.

3. *DA* [2.3.18], 1093–94; Tocqueville's definition claims to broaden the understanding of honor in feudal society, and in its leading theorist Montesquieu. As a draft note states: "Montesquieu spoke about *our* honor and not about honor," *DA* [2.3.18], 1110nV, my emphasis. Céline Spector, "Commerce, Glory, and Empire: Montesquieu's Legacy," trans. Patrick Camiller, in *Tocqueville and the Frontiers of Democracy*, ed. Ewa Atanassow and Richard Boyd (Cambridge: Cambridge University Press, 2013), 202. Ran Halévi, "La pensée politique de l'honneur," in *Penser et vivre l'honneur à l'époque moderne*, ed. Hervé Drévillon and Diego Venturino (Rennes: Presses Universitaires de Rennes, 2011), 109–26.

4. *DA* [2.3.18], 1114, my emphasis. In this section I draw on my "Nationhood: Democracy's Final Frontier?," in Atanassow and Boyd, *Tocqueville and the Frontiers of Democracy*, 178–201.

5. *DA* [2.3.17], 1089.

6. *DA* [2.3.6], 1022. In the *Old Regime*, Tocqueville studies the drawn-out democratizing process, and its political driver: absolutism and state centralization. Ran Halévi, "Louis XIV: The Originator of the French Nation," (lecture, Ben-Gurion University of the Negev, Beersheba, Israel, June 12, 2019). Also Jay M. Smith, *Nobility Reimagined: The Patriotic Nation in Eighteenth-Century France* (Ithaca, NY: Cornell University Press, 2005), esp. chap. 4.

7. For a related analysis see Greenfeld, *Nationalism*, esp. 118–20. Dani Rodrik's analysis of economic globalization highlights a similarly paradoxical dynamic. Arguing that a developed economy rests on a set of moral and institutional prerequisites that require a strong government to sustain them, Rodrik notes: "Governments help reduce transaction costs within national boundaries, but they are a source of friction in trade *between* nations." Rodrik, *Globalization's Paradox*, 20.

8. Karl Marx and Friedrich Engels, "Manifesto of the Communist Party," in *The Marx-Engels Reader*, ed. Robert C. Tucker (New York: W. W. Norton, 1978),

469–500, esp. 474–77 and 488–89n8. See also in the same volume Marx's most virulent repudiation of national and religious particularity in Karl Marx, "On the Jewish Question," 26–52.

9. For a sustained account of Tocqueville's economic thought, see Richard Swedberg, *Tocqueville's Political Economy* (Princeton, NJ: Princeton University Press, 2009). See also Tocqueville's *Memoirs on Pauperism and Other Writings: Poverty, Public Welfare, and Inequality*, ed. and trans. Christine Dunn Henderson (Notre Dame, IN: University of Notre Dame Press, 2021).

10. Marx and Engels, "Manifesto," 475–76; *DA* [1.2.10], 275, 395; [2.1.17], 838; [2.3.17], 1090–92; [2.4.8], 1275; also *OC* 5:1:190–91. For a sustained comparison between Tocqueville and Marx, see Nestor Capdevila, *Tocqueville ou Marx: Démocratie, Capitalisme, Révolution* (Paris: Presses universitaires de France, 2012).

11. *DA* [1.2.5], 135; [1.2.9], 452–54. Stephen A. Garrett, "Foreign Policy and the Democracies: De Tocqueville Revisited," *Virginia Quarterly Review* 48, no. 4 (Autumn 1972), 483. In what follows, I also draw on David Clinton, "Tocqueville's Challenge," in *Tocqueville's Political Science: Classic Essays*, ed. Peter A. Lawler (New York: Garland Publishing, 1992), 291–312 and David Clinton, *Tocqueville, Lieber, and Bagehot* (New York: Palgrave McMillan, 2003); Zbigniew Brzezinski, "War and Foreign Policy, American Style," *Journal of Democracy* 11, no. 1 (2000): 172–78. Paul Carrese, "Tocqueville's Foreign Policy of Moderation and Democracy Expansion," in *Alexis de Tocqueville and the Art of Democratic Statesmanship*, ed. Brian Danoff and L. Joseph Herbert Jr. (Lanham, MD: Lexington Books, 2011), 299–322.

12. In his memoirs Tocqueville concludes "[D]emocracies . . . generally have only very confused and mistaken ideas about foreign affairs and invariably decide questions of foreign policy for reasons of internal convenience," Alexis de Tocqueville, *Recollections: The French Revolution of 1848*, ed. J. P. Mayer and A. P. Kerr, trans. George Lawrence (New Brunswick, NJ: Transaction Publishers, 1995), 244. For a sustained discussion of this claim see Garrett, "Foreign Policy and the Democracies," 483.

13. *DA* [1.2.5], 363, 370; [2.1.2], 724.

14. *DA* [1.2.5], 371, and 317n17. For a discussion see Carrese, "Tocqueville's Foreign Policy," 307 and in this volume see "Case Study 2" in chap. 2.

15. *DA* [1.2.5], 369–70; [2.3.1], 993; [2.1.17], 838.

16. *DA* [2.3.1], 993 94.

17. *DA* [2.3.1], 993; [2.1.3], 731–32; Strong, "Seeing Differently and Seeing Further: Rousseau and Tocqueville," 104–5. Clifford Orwin, "Compassion and the Softening of Mores," *Journal of Democracy* 11, no. 1 (2000): 142–48. For a sustained discussion of Cicero and the politics of triumph, see Mary Beard, *Roman Triumph* (Cambridge, MA: Harvard University Press, 2009), chaps. 4 and 6.

18. *DA* [2.3.1], 993; and [2.1.3]; *DA* [1.1.8], 225; Clinton, "Tocqueville's Challenge," 292. J. S. Mill develops a similar point in chapter 18 of "Considerations on

Representative Government," in *On Liberty, Utilitarianism and Other Essays* (Oxford: Oxford University Press, 2015), 388–407.

19. *DA* [1.2.5], 371n17; *OC* 6.1, 335–36. See also Tocqueville's letter to Gustave de Beaumont, April 8, 1853, *OC* 8:3:101–2, cited in Clinton "Tocqueville on Democracy, Obligation, and the International System," *Review of International Studies* 19 (1993): 227–43, esp. 230. Cf. Garrett, "Foreign Policy and the Democracies," 487.

20. Tocqueville's foreign policy writings are collected in volume 3 parts 1 and 2 of the *Oeuvres Complètes*. Only a handful of these have been translated into English. A selection of the colonial and antislavery writings are available in Alexis de Tocqueville, *Writings on Empire and Slavery*, ed. Jennifer Pitts (Baltimore, MD: Johns Hopkins University Press, 2001), henceforth *WES*. When available, I refer to the English editions. All other translations are my own.

21. *OC* 3:2:256, 273–85; 3:1:254, 271, 299–300, 305, 355, 413. A draft note for his second speech in parliament reads: "Pour moi la question extérieure domine toutes les autres; si le ministère la traite bien, je ne le chicanerai aisément pour le reste," *OC* 3:2:309.

22. *WES*, 122.

23. Carrese, "Tocqueville's Foreign Policy of Moderation and Democracy Expansion," 311. For a critical appraisal of the concept of grand strategy see, Alexander Kirss, "Does Grand Strategy Matter?," *Strategic Studies Quarterly* 12, no. 4 (2018): 116–32. Also John Lewis Gaddis, *On Grand Strategy* (London: Penguin Books, 2018), esp. 17–27.

24. *OC* 3:2:289n, 255–408; 6:1:355; *OC* 11, 91, 108–9; As a foreign minister Tocqueville contemplated "mak[ing] good some of the damage done in 1815," Tocqueville, *Recollections*, 246. Yet the geopolitical conjuncture and the brevity of his time in office issued in a cautious if not timid foreign policy, Clinton, "Tocqueville's Challenge," 296; Sharon Watkins, *Alexis de Tocqueville and the Second Republic* (Lanham, MD: University Press of America, 2003), chap. 7, esp. 368–79; A. J. P. Taylor, *The Struggle for Mastery in Europe 1848–1918* (Oxford: Clarendon Press, 1954), 34.

25. *DA* [2.2.2–3]. For related discussions see "Equality of Conditions?" in chap. 1 and "From Interest to Instinct" in chap. 2.

26. *OC* 3:2:326; 3:1:88, 111, 125, 213–14; Seymour Drescher, *Tocqueville and England* (Cambridge: Harvard University Press, 1964), 151–54.

27. *OC* 3:2:280, also 291; 3:1:88–89. Compare with *DA*, 152, 487, 490, 492, 661–66.

28. For instances of the analogy between individual and nation see *DA*, 27–8, 186, 190, 226, 320, 361, 390, 539, 676; and *OC* 6:1:143 cited in Clinton, "Tocqueville on Democracy," 239. Analyzing group behavior through the lens of individual psychology dates back to antiquity. For an overview, see Janice Stein, "Psychology and Foreign Policy," in *Oxford Bibliographies*, ed. Patrick James (Oxford: Oxford University Press), last reviewed September 2020, https://www.oxfordbibliographies.com/view/document/obo-9780199743292/obo-9780199743292-0252.xml.

29. *DA* [1.1.8], 255–63; [2.2.2–3], 881–86; and *OC* 3:2:280, 291, 325–33.

30. *DA* [2.2.4], 894; [1.2.6], 393; and *OC* 3:2:280, 291; 3:1:88–89; 3:2:256–65; 288–301, 323–33, 376–87, 433–51.

31. Garrett, "Foreign Policy and the Democracies," 486–87.

32. Marx and Engels, "Manifesto," 474–5 and 474n. *OC* 3:2:279–80, also 282, 284, 290, 270–71; Drescher, *Tocqueville and England*, 156. *DA* [1.2.10], 878; Tocqueville, *Recollections*, chap. 4.

33. *OC* 3:2:271, 289–301, 345, 430; *DA*, appendix, 1347; Barbara Allen, *Tocqueville, Covenant, and the Democratic Revolution* (Lanham MD: Lexington Books, 2005), 239–40; Roger Boesche, "The Dark Side of Tocqueville," *Review of Politics* 67, no. 4 (2005), 737–52; Drescher, *Tocqueville and England*, 152–69.

34. *OC* 3:2:271, 345, 430. Demin Duan, "Reconsidering Tocqueville's Imperialism," *Ethical Perspectives* 17, no. 3 (2010), 415–47.

35. *DA* [1.2.10], 647–48, my italics. See also Tocqueville's 1841 letter to Secretary of War John C. Spencer and his impromptu speech on the strategic importance of Cherbourg, in A. Craiutu and J. Jennings, *Tocqueville on America after 1840* (Cambridge: Cambridge University Press), 59–60, 373–74.

36. *OC* 3:2:345.

37. Compare Tocqueville's account of the New England township, *DA* [1.1.5], 63–65; [2.4.1] 1n. On Tocqueville's borrowings from Montesquieu and Washington see Carrese, "Tocqueville's Foreign Policy of Moderation and Democracy Expansion," 303–6.

38. Clinton, "Tocqueville on Democracy, Obligation, and the International System," 233. Cf. Kenneth Waltz, *Man, the State, and War: A Theoretical Analysis* (New York: Columbia University Press, 2001).

39. Ironically, France and the United States, the two modern constitutional states founded on a declared commitment to human rights, were among those who resisted Britain's abolitionist efforts the longest. While France signed an agreement to a mutual right of visitation in 1831 in exchange for Britain's support for the July regime, the wave of anti-British sentiments following the controversy over the Eastern question prompted the revision of existing conventions. Matthew Mason, "Keeping up Appearances: The International Politics of Slave Trade Abolition in the Nineteenth-Century Atlantic World," *William and Mary Quarterly* 66, no. 4 (2009), 809–32; Paul Michael Kielstra, *The Politics of Slave Trade Suppression* (London: Palgrave Macmillan, 2000), esp. 156–57, 207–60. Seymour Drescher, "History's Engines: British Mobilization in the Age of Revolution," *William and Mary Quarterly* 66, no. 4 (October 2009): 737–56.

40. A. Craiutu and J. Jennings, *Tocqueville on America After 1840*, 59; *OC* 3:2:325–55, *WES*, 207. For a discussion of Tocqueville's works on abolition, see Cheryl Welch, "Tocqueville on Democracy After Abolition," *Tocqueville Review / La Revue Tocqueville* 27, no. 2 (2006): 227–54.

41. *OC* 3:2:421–33, also 403–20; 3:1:79–111, Drescher, *Tocqueville and England*, 164. Compare with Mason, "Keeping up Appearances," 831. Also Charles H. Fairbanks Jr., "The British Campaign Against the Slave Trade: An Example of a Successful Human Rights Policy," in *Human Rights and American Foreign Policy*, ed. Fred E. Baumann (Gambier, OH: Public Affairs Conference Center Kenyon College, 1982), 87–135.

42. Mason shows how by mid-nineteenth century the profound change in moral opinion pushed statesmen to join moralists and humanitarians "in their need to be (or at least to be perceived as being) on the right side" of history in Mason "Keeping up Appearances," 832. For related critiques of the twentieth-century human rights regime and its legal politics see Samuel Moyn, *Not Enough: Human Rights in an Unequal World* (Cambridge, MA: Harvard University Press, 2018); Posner, *The Twilight of Human Rights Law* (Oxford: Oxford University Press, 2014).

43. See a letter to N. W. Senior on November 15, 1857 in *OC* 6:2:206; also 3:2:341, 3:1:88–9, 505; Jennifer Pitts, *A Turn to Empire* (Princeton, NJ: Princeton University Press, 2005), 226. For a concise overview of the 1857 rebellion and its consequences, see John Keay, *India: A History* (London: Harper Press, 2010), 436–47.

44. Tocqueville describes in similar terms the liberal side effects of aristocratic orders and predicates democratic freedom on the possibility of replicating these effects with democratic means. *DA* [2.3.26], 1182–83; [2.4.7], 1167; see Tocqueville, *The Old Regime*, preface and bk. 2, chap. 11, 171–79.

45. Christopher Brown, *Moral Capital: Foundations of British Abolitionism* (Chapel Hill: University of North Carolina Press, 2012). As Brown argues, the drive behind Britain's abolitionist movement was the "profound yearning for moral worth" that arose in the aftermath of American independence.

46. *OC* 3:2:326.

47. *OC* 3:2:271, 289–301, 345, 43.

48. For a discussion of Tocqueville's "grand strategy for France" see Carrese, "Tocqueville's Foreign Policy," 311–13; also Robert T. Gannett, "Tocqueville as Politician: Revisiting the Revolution of 1789," in *Enlightening Revolutions*, ed. Svetozar Minkov (Lanham, MD: Lexington Books, 2006), 235–58.

49. *OC* 3:2:426, my translation; also 291, 319; Tocqueville, *Recollections*, 240 and 240n. For Tocqueville's frustrated efforts to apply these principles in practice during his time in office see Clinton, *Tocqueville, Lieber, and Bagehot*, chap. 1.

50. *WES*, 207.

51. Gianna Englert, "Tocqueville's Politics of Grandeur," *Political Theory* (September, 2021): 649–74. Englert argues that Tocqueville's politics of greatness was neither Bonapartist nor limited to the international realm. *OC* 3:1:88, 111, 125–26; 3:2:326; 6:3:275. *WES*, 206–7. Delba Winthrop, "Writings on Empire and Slavery," *Society* 1 (2002): 110–13.

52. Welch, "Tocqueville on Democracy After Abolition," 228; also Kahan, *Tocqueville, Democracy, and Religion*, chap. 3; Winthrop, "Writings on Empire and

Slavery," 113. Alan B. Spitzer, "Tocqueville's Modern Nationalism," *French History* 19, no. 1 (March 2005): 49–53.

53. *OC* 3:2:326, 291; 3:1:88, 110–11, 125–26, 329–30; 1985a, 291, 326–27, 421–28. For the most ringing of these appeals, see the speech of January 27, 1848. Calling the principles of the French Revolution his "intellectual fatherland," Tocqueville declared them to be greater than his physical country, *OC* 3:2:745–58.

54. *OC* 3:1:48, 75, 110, 124, 226, 300, 323, 329–30, 355, 423; 3:1:326–9, 332; Winthrop, "Writings on Empire and Slavery," 110–13.

55. Mason notes that appeal to rivalry and national honor to promote abolition was a well-established practice in European affairs in the nineteenth century. It is by becoming an object of global competition between the great powers that, from a utopian ideal, the abolitionist movement grew into a social and political force, Mason, "Keeping up Appearances," 809, 832.

56. For an overview of the idealism vs. realism debate in the study of international relations, see Víctor Ramon Fernandes, "Idealism and Realism in International Relations: An Ontological Debate," *JANUS.NET, e-journal of International Relations* 7, no. 2 (November 2016–April 2017): 14–25. Robert M. A. Crawford, *Idealism and Realism in International Relations* (New York: Routledge, 2000).

57. *DA* [1.1.8], 259; *OC* 3:2:279–80 and "Sovereignty and Peoplehood" in chap. 1. As Stephan A. Garrett observes, the American people are reluctant to go to war for containment or a purely pragmatic reason but expect a "righteous/altruistic cause," Garrett, "Foreign Policy and the Democracies," 488.

58. See Ewa Atanassow, "Colonization and Democracy: Tocqueville Reconsidered," *American Political Science Review* 111, no. 1 (2017): 83–96. For a discussion of Tocqueville's time in office see Drescher, *Tocqueville and England*, chap. 8; Mary Lawlor, *Alexis de Tocqueville in the Chamber of Deputies: His Views on Foreign and Colonial Policy* (Washington, DC: Catholic University of America Press, 1959), chaps. 3 and 4; André Jardin, "Tocqueville, homme politique," in *Alexis de Tocqueville: Zur Politik in der Demokratie*, ed. Michael Hereth and Jutta Höffken (Berlin: Nomos Verlagsgesellschaft, 1981): 93–114. For a comprehensive account of Tocqueville's statesmanship during the Second Republic, see Edward T. Gargan, *Alexis de Tocqueville: The Critical Years 1848–1851* (Washington, DC: Catholic University of America Press, 1955), and Watkins, *Tocqueville and the Second Republic*.

59. *OC* 3:1:298, 254, 271, 300, 305, 355, 413; *WES*, 122, 127.

60. All colonial works are included in *OC* 3:1. A selection of Tocqueville's colonial works is included in *WES*. For a comparison between Tocqueville's accounts of Ireland and Algeria, see Alan S. Kahan, "Tocqueville: Liberalism and Imperialism," in *French Liberalism from Montesquieu to the Present Day*, ed. R. Geenens and H. Rosenblatt (Cambridge: Cambridge University Press, 2012), 152–66.

61. *DA* [1.2.10], 515–52, esp. 519, 541, 569. Pitts, *A Turn to Empire*, 197. As Lerner points out, the last chapter of the first volume of *Democracy* suggests "some large

generalizations about the world rivalry among colonial powers and its possible outcome," Lerner, *The Thinking Revolutionary* (Ithaca, NY: Cornell University Press, 1988), 185–86.

62. *DA* [1.2.10], 516–17, 539 and 539n19; for the exceptional character see the comparative account of ancient and modern slavery *DA* [1.2.10], 549–55.

63. Tocqueville first studies this encounter in *A Fortnight in the Wilderness*, a posthumously published record of his 1831 journey to the American frontier in *DA* 1303–59, see esp. 1338 and 1351. As I have argued, the travelogue is also Tocqueville's earliest exploration of the meaning of civilization and democracy's ultimate limits, *OC* 5:1:342–87; Ewa Atanassow, "*Fortnight in the Wilderness*: Tocqueville on Nature and Civilization," *Perspectives on Political Science* 35, no. 1 (2006): 22–30.

64. For a sustained discussion see Spector, "Commerce, Glory, and Empire," 204–11. Also, Callanan, *Montesquieu's Liberalism*, chap. 6; Vickie Sullivan, *Montesquieu and the Despotic Ideas of Europe* (Chicago: University of Chicago Press, 2017), esp. 176–79; Anthony Pagden, *Peoples and Empires* (New York: Modern Library, 2001), chap. 7.

65. *DA* [1.2.10], 542, 527–28n7. Spector, "Commerce, Glory, and Empire," 212.

66. *DA* [1.2.10], 533–46. Cf. Sean Wilentz, *The Rise of American Democracy: Jefferson to Lincoln* (New York: W. W. Norton, 2005), 427–28.

67. *DA* [1.2.10], 547. Swedberg, *Tocqueville's Political Economy*, 43–72; James Walvin, *The Slave Trade* (New York: W. W. Norton, 2012). See also Andrés Reséndez, *The Other Slavery: The Uncovered Story of Indian Enslavement in America* (Boston: Houghton Mifflin Harcourt, 2016).

68. Compare *DA* [1.2.10], 538, 547 with Montesquieu, *The Spirit of the Laws*, bk. 21, chap. 21; Nathaniel Wolloch, "Barbarian Tribes, American Indians and Cultural Transmission: Changing Perspectives from the Enlightenment to Tocqueville," *History of Political Thought* 34, no. 3 (Autumn 2013): 507–23. For a contemporary reappraisal see Matthew Lange, James Mahoney, and Matthias vom Hau, "Colonialism and Development: A Comparative Analysis of Spanish and British Colonies," *American Journal of Sociology* 111, no. 5 (2006): 1412–62.

69. Ann Thomson, "Arguments for the Conquest of Algiers in the Late Eighteenth and Early Nineteenth Centuries," *Maghreb Review* 14, nos. 1–2 (1989): 108; also Ann Thomson, *Barbary and Enlightenment: European Attitudes Towards the Maghreb in the 18th Century* (Leiden: E. J. Brill, 1987). Charles-Robert Ageron, *Modern Algeria: A History from 1830 to the Present* (Trenton, NJ: African World Press, 1991), chap. 1. James McDougall, *A History of Algeria* (Cambridge: Cambridge University Press, 2017), chap. 1, esp. 31–36.

70. Gillian Weiss, "Imagining Europe through Barbary Captivity," *Taiwan Journal of East Asian Studies* 4, no. 1 (2007): 49–67. Also McDougall, *History of Algeria*, 45–47; Frank Lambert, *The Barbary Wars: American Independence in the Atlantic World* (New York: Hill and Wang, 2007).

71. Jennifer E. Sessions, *By Sword and by Plow: France and the Conquest of Algeria* (Ithaca, NJ: Cornell University Press, 2011), 19–66; Vincent Confer, *France and Algeria* (New York: Syracuse University Press, 1966), chap. 1. For critical surveys of the disputed beginning of the conquest and its prehistory, see Amar Hamdani, *La vérité sur l'expédition d'Alger* (Paris: Balland 1985).

72. *OC* 3:1:39–40, 140, 180, 239, 315–8, 356–61; 5:2:197, 212; 13:2:85; 3:2:270–71. Christian Bégin, "Tocqueville et l'Algérie," *Tocqueville Review / La Revue Tocqueville* 30, no. 2 (2009): 179–203.

73. *WES*, 5, 92; also 20, 59–61, 124–6, 134–37, 168–73. As a newly published letter to Louis Juchault de Lamoricière shows, amid the Eastern crisis of 1840, Tocqueville acknowledged that France might be forced to abandon Algeria but insisted that she should not withdraw from Northern Africa unless compelled to do so, *OC* 17:2:112–13.

74. For a detailed discussion of the pervasive influence of Saint-Simonian ideology on the early decades of Algerian colonization onward see Osama Abi-Mershed, *Apostles of Modernity: Saint-Simonians and the Civilizing Mission in Algeria* (Stanford, CA: Stanford University Press, 2010); and Emma Deputy, "Ideologies of Development in French Algeria: Saint-Simonians, Manifest Destiny, and Globalization," in *African Culture and Global Politics*, ed. Toyin Falola and Danielle Sanchez (New York: Routledge, 2014), 17–36.

75. The two pillars of Tocqueville's colonial policy—the rejection of territorial aggrandizement, epitomized in his opposition to what he saw as pointless and impolitic expeditions in Kabylia; and the demand for securing participatory civil government, individual rights and the conditions of individual entrepreneurship that would help jumpstart the economic and political life—amounted to a complete repudiation of the colonial vision of Thomas Robert Bugeaud, Algeria's first governor general, whom Tocqueville helped oust from power. For a full discussion see Cheryl Welch, "Out of Africa: Tocqueville's Imperial Voyages," in *Tocqueville's Voyages: The Evolution of His Ideas and Their Journey Beyond His Time*, ed. Christine Dunn Henderson (Indianapolis, IN: Liberty Fund, 2014), 304–34; and Swedberg, *Tocqueville's Political Economy*, chap. 7.

76. *WES*, 5–26, 144–46.

77. *WES*, 23, 62, 65. Letter to Corcelle, December 1, 1846, in Alexis de Tocqueville, *Lettres choisies: Souvenirs, 1814–1859* (Paris: Gallimard, 2003), 571, my translation.

78. Timothy Mason Roberts "The Role of French Algeria in American Expansion during the Early Republic," *Journal of the Western Society for French History* 43 (2015): 153–64.

79. *WES*, 70. This much quoted phrase occurs in Tocqueville's posthumously published "Essay on Algeria," in *OC* 8:1:449–51; 3:1:215 n1.

80. *WES*, 62, 52; italics in the original.

81. *OC* 3:1:197.

82. *WES*, 36–58. Reconstructing this complexity, Osama Abi-Mershed recommends moving away from the monolithic categories of 'colonizer' and 'colonized' that "accommodate poorly the social and cultural variations within French Algeria," Abi-Mershed, *Apostles of Modernity*, 10.

83. *WES*, 70. With equal vehemence, Tocqueville castigated practices of expropriation (*WES*, 71). Opposed to despoliation and lawless violence, throughout his Algerian involvement Tocqueville struggled to chart a policy that would contain within legal limits both land redistribution and unconventional war. See Margaret Kohn, "Empire's Law: Alexis de Tocqueville on Colonialism and the State of Exception," *Canadian Journal of Political Science* 41, no. 2 (2008): 255–78.

84. *OC* 5:2:216–7; 3:1:197, 323, 421–2. Recognizing Tocqueville's call for containing violence, Welch remains skeptical of its sincerity and interprets his search for a moderate position on Algeria as a sign of self-delusion, Cheryl B. Welch "Colonial Violence and the Rhetoric of Evasion," *Political Theory* 31, no. 2 (2003): 247–56.

85. *WES*, 138, 251–52. *OC* 3:1:324. For an excellent account of the colonial dilemma, see McDougall, *A History of Algeria*, 120–28.

86. *WES*, 145–46.

87. *OC* 3:1:243, 319–23, 329, 340–41; also 88–9, 105, 113, 327–28. Tocqueville, *Lettres Choisies*, 565–6; *OC* 15:224; 3:1:142, 150, 177, 330–47; 5:2:201, 205. For an analysis of Tocqueville's call for "tutelage" that would "put a revolution in the hands of government," see Welch, "Democracy after Abolition," 240–47 and "Out of Africa," 325–28.

88. Jennifer Pitts, "Empire and Democracy: Tocqueville and the Algeria Question," *Journal of Political Philosophy* 8 (2002): 295–318; Roberts "The Role of French Algeria in American Expansion," 154–58, 164. Kevin Duan, "The Demands of Glory: Tocqueville and Terror in Algeria," *Review of Politics* 80 (2018): 31–55. Olivier Le Cour Grandmaison, "Quand Tocqueville légitimait les boucheries," *Le Monde* diplomatique, June 2001, https://www.monde-diplomatique.fr/2001/06/LE_COUR_GRANDMAISON/1706; Lina Benabdallah, "Tocqueville in Algeria and Epistemic Violence," *Al Jazeera Opinion* (blog), July 20, 2020, https://www.aljazeera.com/opinions/2020/7/7/on-tocqueville-in-algeria-and-epistemic-violence.

89. *WES*, 65. Welch notes the "brutal clarity" with which Tocqueville documents the failings of France, Welch, "Out of Africa," 311.

90. See the 1833 sketch titled "Some Ideas About What Prevents the French from Having Good Colonies," *WES*, 1–4. Also *OC* 3:2:271; *OC* 14:146. By the time Tocqueville writes the *Old Regime*, Algeria has come to epitomize ancien régime politics and spirit of government: see Tocqueville, *Old Regime*, 1:273, 281, 342; and 2:282, 310, 362, 482.

91. *WES*, 25, 111, 118, 145. How to account for this change of mind remains an unresolved question for Tocqueville scholars. For a discussion, see Atanassow, "Colonization and Democracy," 87.

92. *WES*, 144. Compare with *DA* [1:2:10], 544, 1349–51.

93. Ageron, *Modern Algeria*, 38–39, and notes. For a discussion of Napoleon III's reforms, and the Saint-Simonian roots of his Arab kingdom, see Abi-Mershed, *Apostles of Modernity*, chap. 6. Later in the century, "Algerian community leaders vigorously opposed proposals by radical reformers in France ... for the abolition of discriminatory 'personal status' and collective conferment of citizenship." McDougall, *History of Algeria*, 125.

94. WES, 142, 146, 19–20; Welch "Out of Africa," 314.

95. OC 3:1:243, 319–23, 329; Tocqueville, *Lettres Choisies*, 565. The ministry retorted that the pious foundations used their finances to support impious causes, such as terror and armed resistance: OC 3:1:167–79, 323, 420–25, 424.

96. OC 3:1:421–2, 169, my translation.

97. DA [2.1.5], 746–47; Kahan, *Tocqueville, Democracy, and Religion*, 183–88. Tocqueville studied the Koran, in what he knew to be a flawed translation. He also contemplated learning Arabic, OC 3:1:129–62; 5:2:206–7.

98. WES, 23–5, 138–9, 235n7; OC 3:1:174.

99. Kohn, "Empire's Law," 260–74; Abi Mershed shows how and why France's Algerian policy alternated between *assimilation* and *association*, each entailing a distinct set of contradictions for colonial practice. The classic account of colonial understanding of these terms remains Raymond Betts, *Assimilation and Association in French Colonial Theory, 1870–1914* (Lincoln: University of Nebraska Press, 2005).

100. Alexis de Tocqueville, *Selected Letters on Politics and Society*, ed. Roger Boesche trans. James Toupin. (Berkeley, CA: University of California Press, 1986), 360–65. Reviewing the historiographical debates about the causes of the rebellion, Keay concludes: "The evidence for any organized incitement is unconvincing. Shared distrust was sufficient to concert action. British arrogance sufficient to incite it." Keay, *India: A History*, 438.

101. For Tocqueville, we may recall, pride is the sentiment of one's dignity and worth, and as such a necessary (though insufficient) precondition for self-government. See chapter 2.

102. OC 18:486, my translation and emphasis. Jean-Louis Benoît, *Comprendre Tocqueville* (Paris: Armand Collin, 2004), 140.

103. DA [2.3.18], 1114–15.

104. DA, 1354. Also Tocqueville, *Old Regime*, 2:262, See also Tocqueville's letter to Gustave de Beaumont, November 3, 1853 in OC 8:3:163.

105. In *The Globalization Paradox*—from which I borrow the title of this section—Dani Rodrik shows the importance of imperialism for the first great wave of economic globalization in the long nineteenth century, Rodrik, *Globalization Paradox*, chap. 2.

106. DA, 27, 47, 49 and 566–78, 1134, 1141; Matthias Bohlender, "Demokratie und Imperium. Tocqueville in Amerika und Algerien," *Berliner Journal für Soziologie* 4 (2005): 523–40, 525–7. See also Wilentz, *Rise of American Democracy*, chap. 1.

107. DA, 28; WES, 60–61.

108. WES 65, 67, and 17–19. See also Amine Boukerche, *L'Algérie de Tocqueville: Chronique d'une colonisation ratée* (Rennes: Editions Apogée, 2018), chap. 7 For an account of the Emir's Islamic sovereignty see McDougall, *A History of Algeria*, 58–72; and John Kaiser, *Commander of the Faithful: The Life and Times of Emir Abd El-Kader* (Rheinbeck, NY: Monkfish Book Publishing, 2008). As Roberts observes, "Abdelkader's short-lived regime brought uniform taxation and representative tribal government to North Africa for the first time," Roberts, "Role of French Algeria in American Expansion," 165. The Emir's own political-philosophical vision can be found in Abd el-Kader, *Lettre aux Français* (Paris: Libella, 2011).

109. See in this connection Tocqueville's 1846 letter to General Lamoricière—an Algerian general made national hero by effecting Abd el-Kader's capitulation—which considers various 'methods' of revolutionizing Arabic society that would give "the people properly so called an importance it has not had," Tocqueville, *Lettres choisies*, 562–65, my translation.

110. WES, 19–23, 76–77, 122–123. The epitome of this learning is the relationship between Emir Abd-el-Kader and general Eugène Daumas while the latter was deployed in Algeria, and the book they coauthored after the Emir's capitulation, Eugène Daumas, and Abd el-Kader, *Dialogue sur l'hippologie arabe: Les chevaux du Sahara et les moeurs du désert* (Lonrai: Actes Sud, 2008). Another example is the Zouave regiments of the French infantry, originally composed of native soldiers from the eponymous Berber tribe, which became the envy of many a Western army, see Jean Joseph Gustave Cler, *The Zouave Officer: Reminiscences of an Officer of Zouaves; The 2nd Zouaves of the Second Empire on Campaign in North Africa and the Crimean War* (Leonaur, 2010).

111. *DA*, introduction, 16; Tocqueville, *Selected Letters*, 294. See Tzvetan Todorov, *The Inner Enemies of Democracy*, trans. Andrew Brown (Cambridge: Polity Press, 2014), chap. 3. As Todorov's critique of political messianism shows, in the twenty first century modern democracies are still learning these lessons.

112. As James McDougall observes, "Prosper Enfantin, the father of Saint-Simonian social reform argued in his 1843 brochure that Algeria could provide for a new 'association' of settler and indigenous interests that by regenerating society through communal labor, would ultimately re-civilize France itself, overcoming the social ills of industrial capitalism and urbanization, and ensuring a more peaceful future of progress for all," McDougall, *A History of Algeria*, 93. See also Atanassow, "Colonization and Democracy," 92–93.

113. WES, 168, 127, 23; Englert, "Tocqueville's Politics of Grandeur," 14–15. Welch, *Out of Africa*, 307–8, 315–6. Selinger, "*Le grand mal de l'époque*: Tocqueville on French Political Corruption," 73–94; Hugh Brogan, *Alexis de Tocqueville, A Life* (London: Profile Books, 2006), chap. 16.

114. Jennifer E. Sessions and Tod Shepard both show that neither modern Algerian history nor France's own can be understood independently of the historical experience that began in 1830: see Sessions, *By Sword and by Plow* and Tod Shepard,

The Invention of Decolonization: The Algerian War and the Remaking of France (Ithaca, NY: Cornell University Press, 2006).

115. *WES*, 145; *OC* 3:1:328, and 153; Welch, "Out of Africa," 311.

116. *DA*, introduction, 20; [1.2.10], 636. Ran Halévi, "Frontier between Aristocracy and Democracy," 53–73.

117. Richard Boyd, "Imperial Fathers and Favorite Sons: J. S. Mill, Alexis de Tocqueville, and Nineteenth-Century Visions of Empire," in *Feminist Reinterpretations of Alexis de Tocqueville*, ed. Eileen Hunt Botting, and Jill Locke (University Park, PA: Penn State University Press, 2008), 225–52. McDougall, *A History of Algeria*, chap. 2. In *The Paradox of Liberation*, Michael Walzer shows how the same paradox was inherited by the secular, Western-educated anti-colonial elites and the postcolonial orders they strove to put in place. Michael Walzer, *The Paradox of Liberation: Secular Revolutions and Religious Counterrevolutions* (New Haven, CT: Yale University Press, 2015), esp. chap 1. See also Karuna Mantena, "Popular Sovereignty and Anticolonialism," in Bourke and Skinner, *Popular Sovereignty in Historical Perspective*, 297–319; Sandipto Dasgupta, "Gandhi's Failure: Anticolonial Movements and Postcolonial Futures," *Perspectives on Politics* 15, no. 3 (2017): 647–62.

118. *WES*, 24. For a contemporary analysis of this dilemma, see Daniel Chirot, "Does Democracy Work in Deeply Divided Societies?," in Zoltan Barany and Robert G. Moser, *Is Democracy Exportable?* (Cambridge: Cambridge University Press, 2009), 85–109.

119. *OC* 3:1:481; *WES*, 18–22, 39, 63–80.

120. *DA* [2.3.18], 1114; and see "Honor, Nationhood, Globalization" in chap. 3.

121. *DA* 7, 491, 1280; Karl Marx, "Economic and Philosophic Manuscripts of 1844," in Marx and Engels, *Marx-Engels Reader*, 84; in the same volume see also pp. 34–35, 46, 52, 193–200. Following Kołakowski, Eric Hobsbawm notes that Marx's claim about the inevitable overthrow of bourgeois society and humanity's emancipation from its contradictions "represents a hope, read into his analysis of capitalism, but not a conclusion necessarily imposed by that analysis," Eric Hobsbawm, introduction to *The Communist Manifesto: A Modern Edition*, by Karl Marx and Frederick Engels (London: Verso, 1998), 25. Leszek Kołakowski, *Main Currents of Marxism* (New York: W. W. Norton, 2008), 1:130.

Conclusion

1. Steven Levitsky and Daniel Ziblatt, *How Democracies Die: What History Reveals about Our Future* (London: Penguin Books), 3, 5.

2. Levitsky and Ziblatt, *How Democracies Die*, 212.

3. Levitsky and Ziblatt, 19, my emphasis.

4. Levitsky and Ziblatt, 19. In the American context, this "unashamedly elitist" perspective, as Jan Werner Müller has called it, is hardly an outlier: from Alexander

Hamilton through Walter Lippmann, to J. Schumpeter and V. O. Key, leaders and scholars have questioned the reality of a coherent democratic public and its capacity to serve as guardian of constitutional norms. For an insightful discussion, see Adam Davis, "The Voices of the People," in *When the People Rule: Popular Sovereignty in Theory and Practice*, ed. Ewa Atanassow, Thomas Bartscherer, and David Bateman (Cambridge: Cambridge University Press, forthcoming). Jan Werner Müller, "Is This Really How It Ends?: Democracy's Midlife Crisis," review of *How Democracies Die*, by Steven Levitsky and Daniel Ziblatt and *How Democracy Ends*, by David Runciman, *Nation*, April 22, 2019, https://www.thenation.com/article/archive/how-democracies-dies-how-democracy-ends-book-review/.

5. Levitsky and Ziblatt do not cite Tocqueville even once, which is quite unusual for a book on American democracy.

6. Levitsky and Ziblatt, *How Democracies Die*, 205.

7. For an eloquent exception see Jason Brennan, *Against Democracy* (Princeton, NJ: Princeton University Press, 2017).

8. See Jan-Werner Müller, *Contesting Democracy: Political Ideas in Twentieth Century Europe* (Princeton, NJ: Princeton University Press, 2017); David Runciman, *The Confidence Trap: A History of Democracy in Crisis from World War I to the Present* (Princeton, NJ: Princeton University Press, 2015). See also Ivan Krastev, *After Europe* (Philadelphia: University of Pennsylvania Press, 2017); Philipp C. Schmitter and Terry L. Karl, "What Democracy Is . . . and Is Not," *Journal of Democracy* 2, no. 3 (1991): 75–88.

9. Francis Fukuyama, "Liberalism and Its Discontents: The Challenges from the Left and the Right," *American Purpose*, October 2020, https://www.americanpurpose.com/articles/liberalism-and-its-discontent/. Also Josiah Ober, *Demopolis: Democracy Before Liberalism in Theory and Practice* (Cambridge: Cambridge University Press, 2017).

10. For a related account Greenfeld, *Nationalism: A Short History*, 9–11.

11. I echo here the language of the French "Declaration of the Rights of Man and the Citizen." Dieter Grimm, "The Various Faces of Fundamental Rights," in *The Double-Facing Constitution*, ed. Jacco Bomhoff et al. (Cambridge: Cambridge University Press, 2020), 413–28; David Armitage, *The Declaration of Independence: Global History* (Cambridge, MA: Harvard University Press, 2008); Lynn Hunt, *Inventing Human Rights: A History* (New York: W. W. Norton, 2008).

12. As Ruth Bader Ginsburg observed: "The founding fathers rebelled against the patriarchal power of kings and the idea that political authority may legitimately rest on birth status. They . . . stated a commitment in the Declaration of Independence to equality and in the Declaration and Bill of Rights to individual liberty. Those commitments had growth potential. As historian Richard Morris wrote, a prime portion of the history of the U.S. Constitution, and a cause for celebration, is the story of the extension (through amendment, judicial interpretation, and practice) of

constitutional rights and protections to once excluded groups: to people who were once held in bondage, to men without property, to native Americans, and to women... I recognize that the equal stature under the law that women are achieving in this century is part of the U.S. constitutional legacy, part of the original understanding, in this vital sense," Ruth Bader Ginsburg, "Constitutional Adjudication as a Means of Realizing the Equal Stature of Men and Women Under the Law," *Tocqueville Review / La Revue Tocqueville* 14, no. 1 (Winter 1993): 125–37.

13. *DA* [2.2.13], 946; Aristotle, *Politics*, trans. Carnes Lord (Chicago: University of Chicago Press, 2013), bk. 3, 1276 b16–1277 b32. One of the most consequential modern analyses of this tension can be found in Karl Marx, "On the Jewish Question," in Marx and Engels, *The Marx-Engels Reader*, 26–52.

14. *DA* [2.2.2–7]; [2.3.17], 1089–91; [1.2.6], 380.

15. *DA* [1.1.5], 108.

16. *DA* [1.2.10], 633; [2.4.7], 1265.

17. *DA* [1.1.5], 135.

18. Jason Frank, *Constituent Moments: Enacting the People in Postrevolutionary America* (Durham, NC: Duke University Press, 2010), chap. 4.

19. Levitsky and Ziblatt, *How Democracies Die*, 231, 118ff, 9.

20. Robert Putnam, *Bowling Alone: The Collapse and Revival of American Community* (New York: Simon & Schuster, 2020); Timothy P. Carney, *Alienated America* (New York: HarperCollins, 2019); Charles Murray, *Coming Apart* (New York: Crown Forum, 2013); Peter Mair, *Ruling the Void: The Hollowing of Western Democracy* (London: Verso, 2013).

21. Béla Greskovits, "Rebuilding the Hungarian Right Through Conquering Civil Society: The Civic Circles Movement," *East European Politics*, 36, no. 2 (2020): 247–66. Gianpaolo Baiocchi and Ernesto Ganuza, *Popular Democracy: The Paradox of Participation* (Stanford, CA: Stanford University Press, 2017). See also Sheri Berman, "Civil Society and the Collapse of the Weimar Republic," *World Politics* 49, no. 3 (1997): 401–29.

22. See coverage on Joe Biden's post-election victory speech on November 5, 2020: Colby Itkowitz et al., "Joe Biden, in Victory Speech, Says, 'This is the Time to Heal in America,'" *Washington Post*, November 7, 2020, https://www.washingtonpost.com/elections/2020/11/07/trump-biden-election-live-updates/; and Elizabeth Dias, "Biden and Trump Say They're Fighting For America's 'Soul.' What Does that Mean?," *New York Times*, October 17, 2020, https://www.nytimes.com/2020/10/17/us/biden-trump-soul-nation-country.html. President Biden's inaugural further reinforced his conciliatory message by calling for the "most elusive of all things in a democracy: unity."

23. Abraham Lincoln, "First Inaugural Address," March 4, 1861, Washington, DC, US, The Avalon Project, transcript, https://avalon.law.yale.edu/19th_century/lincoln1.asp. See also Rogers Smith, *Stories of Peoplehood: The Politics and Morals of Political Membership* (Cambridge: Cambridge University Press, 2003).

24. For an exploration of the theological dimensions of nationhood, see Stevan Grosby, "The Nation of the United States and the Vision of Ancient Israel," in *Biblical Ideas of Nationality: Ancient and Modern* (Winona Lake, IN: Eisenbrauns, 2002), 213–33 and Anthony Smith, *Chosen Peoples: Sacred Sources of National Identity* (Oxford: Oxford University Press, 2004). For an account of providentialism Russian style, see Stephen Kotkin, "Russia's Perpetual Geopolitics: Putin Returns to the Historical Pattern," *Foreign Affairs* 95, no. 3 (2016): 2–9.

25. Tocqueville, *OC* 5:2:184; cited in Kahan, *Tocqueville, Democracy, and Religion*, 111n46.

26. Yael Tamir, *Why Nationalism* (Princeton, NJ: Princeton University Press, 2019), 5.

27. For a related argument, though without reference to Tocqueville, see Tzvetan Todorov, *The Inner Enemies of Democracy*, trans. Andrew Brown (Cambridge: Polity Press, 2014), chap. 4, esp. 100–103.

28. George Kateb, *Patriotism and Other Mistakes* (New Haven, CT: Yale University Press, 2006) and John Baskin, "Mistakes We've Made: A Conversation with George Kateb," *The Point* 22 (Summer 2020): 132–43. See also Stephen B. Smith, *Reclaiming Patriotism in an Age of Extremes* (New Haven, CT: Yale University Press, 2021).

29. Tamir, *Why Nationalism*, chap. 3; Pierre Manent, *La raison des nations* (Paris: Gallimard, 2006), 14.

30. Chantal Mouffe, *For a Left Populism* (London: Verso, 2018); Jan-Werner Müller, *What is Populism?* (London: Penguin, 2017), 3. Rogers Smith, *This Is Not Who We Are: Populism and Peoplehood* (New Haven, CT: Yale University Press, 2020) and "Popular Sovereignty, Populism, and Stories of Peoplehood," in Atanassow, Bartscherer, Bateman, *When the People Rule*.

31. Alan S. Kahan, "Checks and Balances for Democratic Souls: Alexis de Tocqueville on Religion in Democratic Societies," *American Political Thought* 4 (2015): 100–19. See also Heather Pangle Wilford, "Like a God on Earth: Popular Sovereignty in Tocqueville's *Democracy in America*," in *People Power: Popular Sovereignty from Machiavelli to Modernity*, ed. Robert G. Ingram and Christopher Barker (Manchester: Manchester University Press, 2022), 160–181.

32. For an insightful discussion, see Heather Pangle, "Liberalism and Nationalism," *National Affairs* (Fall 2019): 142–58. Also, see John J. Mearsheimer, *The Great Delusion: Liberal Dreams and International Realities* (New Haven, CT: Yale University Press, 2018).

33. For a related point see Rodrik, *The Globalization Paradox*, 253.

34. These questions motivate Adam Lupel's *Popular Sovereignty and Globalization* (London: Routledge, 2011). They also underpin the ongoing debates on the political nature of the EU, Jan Pieter Beetz, "Safeguarding, Shifting, Splitting or Sharing?:

Conflicting Conceptions of Popular Sovereignty in the EU-Polity," *Journal of European Integration* 41, no. 7 (2019): 937–53.

35. *DA* [2.3.18], 1114. As chapters 10 and 11 of the book of Genesis evidence, though newly urgent, these questions are hardly new.

36. *WES*, 207. Francine Hirsch, *Empire of Nations* (Ithaca, NY: Cornell University Press, 2005). For an insightful critique of the "war on terror" in comparison with the Soviet empire, see Todorov, *Inner Enemies*, chap. 3.

37. *OC* 3:1:426, my translation. For an overview of the scholarly debates see Ewa Atanassow, "Colonization and Democracy: Tocqueville Reconsidered," *American Political Science Review* 111, no. 1 (2017): 83–85.

38. In *The Globalization Paradox*, Rodrik shows the importance of imperialism for enabling the first great wave of economic globalization in the long nineteenth century. While different in approach, the Pax Americana erected after World War II likewise implied the presence of hegemonic power, Rodrik, *Globalization Paradox*, chap. 2. See also Stephen Hopgood, *The Endtimes for Human Rights* (Ithaca, NY: Cornell University Press, 2014), 96–118.

39. See Karuna Mantena, *Alibis of Empire* (Princeton, NJ: Princeton University Press, 2010); Michael Walzer, "Political Action: The Problem of Dirty Hands," *Philosophy & Public Affairs* 2, no. 2 (1973): 160–80.

40. J. S. Mill, *On Liberty, Utilitarianism and Other Essays* (Oxford: Oxford University Press, 2015), 15.

41. *DA* [2.4.6], 1251, 1249.

42. Michael Walzer "Spheres of Affection," in *For Love of Country?*, ed. Martha C. Nussbaum (Boston, MA: Beacon Press, 2002), 125–27; Sayyid Qutb, "Milestones," in *Sayyid Qutb Reader: Selected Writings on Politics, Religion, and Society*, ed. Albert J. Bergesen (London: Routledge, 2008); cited in A. Tugendhaft, *The Idols of Isis* (Chicago: University of Chicago Press, 2020), 27–28.

43. *DA* [1.1.8], 264.

44. *DA* [1.1.8], 263.

45. *DA*, introduction, 1:16, 32; Pierre Manent, "Tocqueville, Political Philosopher," in *The Cambridge Companion to Tocqueville*, ed. Cheryl Welch (Cambridge: Cambridge University Press, 2006), 108–20. Ira Katznelson, "On Liberal Ambivalence," *Political Theory* 40, no. 6 (December 2012): 779–88.

46. *DA*, introduction, 9.

BIBLIOGRAPHY

Abd el-Kader. *Lettre aux Français*. Paris: Libella, 2011.
Abi-Mershed, Osama. *Apostles of Modernity: Saint-Simonians and the Civilizing Mission in Algeria*. Stanford, CA: Stanford University Press, 2010.
Ageron, Charles-Robert. *Modern Algeria: A History from 1830 to the Present*. Trenton, NJ: African World Press, 1991.
Allen, Barbara. "Racial Equality and Social Equality." In *Conversations with Tocqueville: The Global Democratic Revolution in the Twenty-First Century*, edited by Aurelian Craiutu and Sheldon Gellar, 85–115. Lanham, MD: Lexington Books, 2009.
———. *Tocqueville, Covenant, and the Democratic Revolution*. Lanham, MD: Lexington Books, 2005.
———. "An Undertow of Race Prejudice in the Current of Democratic Transformation." In *Tocqueville's Voyages: The Evolution of His Ideas and Their Journey Beyond His Time*, edited by Christine Dunn Henderson, 242–75. Indianapolis, IN: Liberty Fund, 2014.
Allen, Danielle S. *Our Declaration: A Reading of the Declaration of Independence in Defense of Equality*. London: Liveright, 2015.
Allen, Thomas B. *Tories: Fighting for the King in America's First Civil War*. New York: HarperCollins, 2011.
Allulis, Joseph. "The Price of Freedom: Tocqueville, the Framers, and the Antifederalists." *Perspectives on Political Science* 27, no. 2 (1988): 85–91.
Amar, Akhil Reed. "Of Sovereignty and Federalism." *Yale Law Journal* 96, no. 7 (1987): 1425–1519.
Anderson, Benedict. *Imagined Communities: Reflections on the Origin and Spread of Nationalism*. London: Verso, 2006.
Anderson, Kevin B. *Marx at the Margins: On Nationalism, Ethnicity, and Non-Western Societies*. Chicago: University of Chicago Press, 2016.
Anderson, M. S. *The Eastern Question: A Study in International Relations*. New York: MacMillan, 1966.
Anheier, Helmut. "Democracy Challenged." In *Governance Report 2017*, edited by The Hertie School of Governance. 13–20. Oxford: Oxford University Press, 2017.

Applebaum, Anne. "Illiberal Democracy Comes to Poland." *Washington Post*, December 16, 2016. https://www.washingtonpost.com/news/global-opinions/wp/2016/12/22/illiberal-democracy-comes-to-poland/.

———. *Twilight of Democracy: The Seductive Lure of Authoritarianism*. New York: Doubleday, 2020.

Arendt, Hannah. *On Revolution*. New York: Penguin Books, 2006.

Aristotle. *Politics*. Translated by Carnes Lord. Chicago: University of Chicago Press, 2013.

Armitage, David. *The Declaration of Independence: Global History*. Cambridge, MA: Harvard University Press, 2008.

Atanassow, Ewa. "Colonization and Democracy: Tocqueville Reconsidered." *American Political Science Review* 111, no. 1 (2017): 83–96.

———. "*Fortnight in the Wilderness*: Tocqueville on Nature and Civilization." *Perspectives on Political Science* 35, no. 1 (2006): 22–30.

———. "Illiberal Democracy and Conceptual Clarity: Report from a Debate." *Global Policy Journal* (blog), July 31, 2017. http://www.globalpolicyjournal.com/blog/31/07/2017/illiberal-democracy-and-conceptual-clarity-report-debate.

———. "Nationhood: Democracy's Final Frontier?." In Atanassow and Boyd, *Tocqueville and the Frontiers of Democracy*, 178–201.

———. "Patriotism in Democracy: What We Can Learn from Tocqueville." In *Tocquevillean Ideas: Contemporary European Perspectives*, edited by Zbigniew Rau and Marek Tracz-Tryniecki, 39–58. Lanham, MD: University Press of America, 2014.

———. "Popular Sovereignty on Trial: Tocqueville vs. Schmitt." In Atanassow, Bartscherer, and Bateman, *When the People Rule*, forthcoming.

———. "Tocqueville's Frontiers." *Journal of Democracy* 20, no. 2 (April 2009): 167–75.

———. "Tocqueville's New Liberalism." In Atanassow and Kahan, *Liberal Moments*, 51–57.

Atanassow, Ewa, Thomas Bartscherer, and David Bateman, eds. *When the People Rule: Popular Sovereignty in Theory and Practice*. Cambridge: Cambridge University Press, forthcoming.

Atanassow, Ewa, and Richard Boyd, eds. *Tocqueville and the Frontiers of Democracy*. Cambridge: Cambridge University Press, 2013.

Atanassow, Ewa, and Alan S. Kahan, eds. *Liberal Moments: Reading Liberal Texts*. London: Bloomsbury Academic, 2018.

Azari, Julia. "It's the Institutions, Stupid: The Real Roots of America's Political Crisis." *Foreign Affairs*, June 11, 2009. https://www.foreignaffairs.com/articles/united-states/2019-06-11/its-institutions-stupid.

Baiocchi, Gianpaolo and Ernesto Ganuza. *Popular Democracy: The Paradox of Participation*. Stanford, CA: Stanford University Press, 2017.

Bashkina, Olga. "Nations against the People." In *Sovereignty in Action*, edited by Bas Leijssenaar and Neil Walker, 159–76. Cambridge: Cambridge University Press, 2019.

Baskin, John. "Mistakes We've Made: A Conversation with George Kateb." *The Point* 22 (Summer 2020): 132–43.

Beard, Mary. Roman Triumph. Cambridge, MA: Harvard University Press, 2009.

Beetz, Jan Pieter. "Safeguarding, Shifting, Splitting, or Sharing?: Conflicting Conceptions of Popular Sovereignty in the EU-Polity." *Journal of European Integration* 41, no. 7 (2019): 937–53.

Bégin, Christian. "Tocqueville et l'Algérie." *Tocqueville Review / La Revue Tocqueville* 30, no. 2 (2009): 179–203.

Beienburg, Sean. "States' Rights Gone Wrong? Secession, Nullification, and Reverse-Nullification in Contemporary America." *Tulsa Law Review* 53 (2018): 191.

Benabdallah, Lina. "On Tocqueville in Algeria and Epistemic Violence." *Al Jazeera Opinion* (blog), July 20, 2020. https://www.aljazeera.com/opinions/2020/7/7/on-tocqueville-in-algeria-and-epistemic violence.

Benoît, Jean-Louis. *Comprendre Tocqueville*. Paris: Armand Collin, 2004.

———. "Relectures de Tocqueville." *Le Banquet*, no. 16 (2001): 2–20.

Berkowitz, Roger. "Hannah Arendt: Power, Action, and the Foundation of Freedom." In Atanassow and Kahan, *Liberal Moments*, 152–59.

Berlin, Isaiah. "Two Concepts of Liberty." In *Liberty*, edited by Henry Hardy, 166–217. Oxford: Oxford University Press, 2002.

Berman, Sheri. "Civil Society and the Collapse of the Weimar Republic." *World Politics* 49, no. 3 (1997): 401–29.

Betts, Raymond. *Assimilation and Association in French Colonial Theory, 1870–1914*. Lincoln: Nebraska University Press, 2005.

Biden, Joseph. "Victory Speech." *Washington Post*. November 7, 2020, https://www.washingtonpost.com/elections/2020/11/07/trump-biden-election-live-updates/.

Boesche, Roger. "The Dark Side of Tocqueville." *Review of Politics* 67, no. 4 (2005): 737–52.

———. *The Strange Liberalism of Alexis de Tocqueville*. Ithaca, NY: Cornell University Press, 1987.

———. "Why Could Tocqueville Predict so Well?." *Political Theory* 11, no. 1 (February 1983): 79–103.

Bohlender, Matthias. "Demokratie Und Imperium. Tocqueville in Amerika Und Algerien." *Berliner Journal Für Soziologie* 3 (2005): 523–40.

Bosteels, Bruno. "Introduction: The People Which Is Not One." In *What Is a People?*, by Alain Badiou, Pierre Bourdieu, Judith Butler, Georges Didi-Huberman, Sadri Khiari, Jacques Rancière, translated by Jody Gladding, 2–20. New York: Columbia University Press, 2016.

Boukerche, Amine. *L'Algérie de Tocqueville: Chronique d'une colonization ratée*. Rennes: Editions Apogée, 2018.

Boyd, Richard. "Imperial Fathers and Favorite Sons: J. S. Mill, Alexis de Tocqueville, and Nineteenth-Century Justifications of Empire." In *Feminist Reinterpretations of Alexis de Tocqueville*, edited by Eileen Hunt Botting and Jill Locke, 225–52. University Park, PA: Penn State University Press, 2008.

———. *Uncivil Society: The Perils of Pluralism and the Making of Modern Liberalism*. Lanham, MD: Lexington Books, 2004.

Brennan, Jason. *Against Democracy*. Princeton, NJ: Princeton University Press, 2017.

Breiner, Peter. "The Dynamics of Political Equality in Rousseau, Tocqueville, and Beyond." In *The Anthem Companion to Alexis De Tocqueville*, edited by Daniel Gordon, 169–86. New York: Anthem Press, 2019.

Breuilly, John, ed. *The Oxford Handbook of the History of Nationalism*. Oxford: Oxford University Press, 2013.

Brogan, Hugh. *Alexis de Tocqueville: A Life*. London: Profile Books, 2006.

Brown, Christopher. *Moral Capital: Foundations of British Abolitionism*. Chapel Hill, NC: University of North Carolina Press, 2012.

Brown, Wendy. *Undoing the Demos*. Cambridge, MA: MIT Press, 2015.

Brubaker, Rogers. *Citizenship and Nationhood in France and Germany*. Cambridge, MA: Harvard University Press, 1992.

———. *Grounds for Difference*. Cambridge, MA: Harvard University Press, 2015.

———. "In the Name of the Nation: Reflections on Nationalism and Patriotism." *Citizenship Studies* 8, no. 2 (2004): 115–27.

———. "Populism and Nationalism." *Nations and Nationalism* 26, no. 1 (2020): 44–66.

Brzezinski, Zbigniew. "War and Foreign Policy, American Style." *Journal of Democracy* 11, no. 1 (2000): 172–78.

Caesar, James. "Tocqueville's Second Founding." In *Designing a Polity: American Constitution in Theory and Practice*, 23–44. Lanham, MD: Rowman & Littlefield, 2011.

Callanan, Keegan. *Montesquieu's Liberalism and the Problem of Universal Politics*. Cambridge: Cambridge University Press, 2018.

Campbell, Jessica L. "Machiavelli's Solutions for Tocqueville's Republic." *European Political Science Review* 1, no. 3 (2009): 375–400.

Capdevila, Nestor. "Democracy and Revolution in Tocqueville." In Atanassow and Boyd, *Tocqueville and the Frontiers of Democracy*, 33–52.

———. @rf:*Tocqueville et Les Frontières de La Démocratie*. Paris: Presses universitaires de France, 2007.

———. *Tocqueville ou Marx. Démocratie, Capitalisme, Révolution*. Paris: Presses universitaires de France, 2012.

Carney, Timothy P. *Alienated America*. New York: HarperCollins, 2019.

Carrese, Paul. *Democracy in Moderation: Montesquieu, Tocqueville, and Sustainable Liberalism*. New York: Cambridge University Press, 2018.

———. "Tocqueville's Foreign Policy of Moderation and Democracy Expansion." In *Alexis de Tocqueville and the Art of Democratic Statesmanship*, edited by Brian Danoff and L. Joseph Herbert Jr., 299–322. Lanham, MD: Lexington Books, 2011.

Chatterjee, Partha. "Empire, Nations, Peoples: The Imperial Perogative and Colonial Expections." *Thesis 11* 139, no. 1 (April 2017): 84–96.

Chirot, Daniel. "Does Democracy Work in Deeply Divided Societies?." In *Is Democracy Exportable?*, edited by Zoltan Barany and Robert G. Moser, 85–109. Cambridge: Cambridge University Press, 2009.

Choi, Daniel. "Unprophetic Tocqueville: How Democracy in America Got the Modern World Completely Wrong." *Independent Review* 12, no. 2 (Fall 2007): 165–78.

Ciepley, David. "Is the U.S. Government a Corporation?: The Corporate Origins of Modern Constitutionalism." *American Political Science Review* 111, no. 2 (2017): 418–35.

Cler, Jean J. G. *The Zouave Officer: Reminiscences of an Officer of Zouaves; The 2nd Zouaves of the Second Empire on Campaign in North Africa and the Crimean War*. Leonaur, 2010.

Clinton, David. "Tocqueville's Challenge." In *Tocqueville's Political Science: Classic Essays*, edited by Peter A. Lawler. New York: Garland Publishing, 1992.

———. *Tocqueville, Lieber, and Bagehot*. London: Palgrave Macmillan, 2003.

———. "Tocqueville on Democracy, Obligation, and the International System." *Review of International Studies* 19, no. 3 (July 1993): 227–43.

Confer, Vincent. *France and Algeria*. New York: Syracuse University Press, 1966.

Constant, Benjamin. "The Liberty of the Ancients Compared with that of the Moderns." In *Political Writings*, edited by Biancamaria Fontana, 308–28. Cambridge: Cambridge University Press, 1988.

Craiutu, Aurelian. "The Social Science of Democracy?." *Perspectives on Politics* 9, no. 2 (2011): 363–81.

———. "Tocqueville and the Political Thought of the French Doctrinaires." *History of Political Thought*, no. 3 (1999): 456–93.

———. "Tocqueville's Paradoxical Moderation." *Review of Politics* 67, no. 4 (2005): 599–630.

Craiutu, Aurelian, and Jennings, Jeremy. *Tocqueville on America after 1840*. Cambridge: Cambridge University Press, 2009.

Crawford, Robert M. A. *Idealism and Realism in International Relations*. London: Routledge, 2000.

Crouthamel, James L. "Tocqueville's South." *Journal of the Early Republic* 2, no. 4 (Winter 1982): 381–401.

Damrosch, Leo. *Tocqueville's Discovery of America*. New York: Farrar, Straus and Giroux, 2011.

Danoff, Brian. "Lincoln and Tocqueville." *Review of Politics* 67, no. 4 (2005): 685–719.

Danoff, Brian, and Hebert, L Joseph. *Alexis de Tocqueville and the Art of Democratic Statesmanship*. Lanham, MD: Lexington Books, 2010.

Dasgupta, Sandipto. "Gadhi's Failure: Anticolonial Movements and Postcolonial Futures." *Perspectives on Politics* 15, no. 3 (2017): 647–62.

Daumas, Eugène, and Abd el-Kader, *Dialogue sur l'hippologie arabe: Les chevaux du Sahara et les moeurs du desert*. Lonrai: Actes Sud, 2008.

Davis, Adam. "The Voices of the People." In Atanassow, Bartscherer, and Bateman, *When the People Rule*, forthcoming.

Day, Tom G. "Democratic Decay: Conceptualising an Emerging Research Field." *Hague Journal on the Rule of Law* 11, no. 1 (2019): 9–36.

Dias, Elizabeth. "Biden and Trump Say They're Fighting For America's 'Soul.' What Does that Mean?." *New York Times*, October 17, 2020, https://www.nytimes.com/2020/10/17/us/biden-trump-soul-nation-country.html.

Deneen, Patrick. *Why Liberalism Failed*. New Haven, CT: Yale University Press, 2018.

Deputy, Emma. "Ideologies of Development in French Algeria: Saint Simonians, Manifest Destiny, and Globalization." In *African Culture and Global Politics*, edited by Toyin Falola and Danielle Sanchez, 17–36. New York: Routledge, 2014.

Derrida, Jacques. "Declarations of Independence." *New Political Science* 7 (1986): 7–15.

Diamond, Martin. "The Ends of Federalism." In *Tocqueville's Political Science: Classic Essays*, edited by Peter Lawler, 116–22. New York: Garland Publishing, 1992.

Dijn, Annelien de. *Freedom: An Unruly History*. Cambridge, MA: Harvard University Press, 2020.

Dion, Stéphane. "La conciliation du libéralisme et du nationalisme chez Tocqueville." *Tocqueville Review / La Revue Tocqueville* 16, no. 1 (1995): 219–27.

Dittigen, Herbert. "Tocqueville Reconsidered: Foreign Policy and the American Democracy." In *Liberty, Equality, Democracy*, edited by Eduardo Nolla, 75–90. New York: New York University Press, 1992.

Drescher, Seymour. "History's Engines: British Mobilization in the Age of Revolution." *William and Mary Quarterly* 66, no. 4 (October 2009): 737–56.

———. *Tocqueville and England*. Cambridge, MA: Harvard University Press, 1964.

Duan, Demin. "Reconsidering Tocqueville's Imperialism." *Ethical Perspectives* 17, no. 3 (2010): 415–47.

Duan, Kevin. "The Demands of Glory: Tocqueville and Terror in Algeria." *Review of Politics* 80, no. 1 (Winter 2018): 31–55.

Eatwell, Jan Roger and Matthew Goodwin. *National Populism: The Revolt Against Liberal Democracy*. London: Penguin Random House, 2018.

Elster, Jon. *Alexis de Tocqueville: The First Social Scientist.* Cambridge: Cambridge University Press, 2009.

———. *Political Psychology.* Cambridge: Cambridge University Press, 1993.

Englert, Gianna. "'The Idea of Rights': Tocqueville on The Social Question." *Review of Politics* 79 (2017): 649–74.

———. "Tocqueville's Politics of Grandeur." *Political Theory* (September 22, 2021): 649–674.

Evrigenis, Ioannis. "The Fact of Fiction: Popular Sovereignty as Belief and Reality." Atanassow, Bartscherer, and Bateman, *When the People Rule,* forthcoming.

Fairbanks, Charles H. Jr. "The British Campaign against the Slave Trade: An Example of a Successful Human Rights Policy." In *Human Rights and American Foreign Policy,* edited by Fred E. Baumann, 87–135. Gambier, OH: Public Affairs Conference Center Kenyon College, 1982.

Fanon, Frantz. *The Wretched of the Earth.* London: Penguin Modern Classics, 2001.

Fernandes, Victor Ramon. "Idealism and Realism in International Relations: An Ontological Debate." *JANUS.NET: e-journal of International Relations* 7, no. 2 (November 2016-April 2017): 14–25.

Finley, M. I. *Democracy Ancient and Modern.* New Brunswick, NJ: Rutgers University Press, 2018.

Francis, Emerich K. *Ethnos und Demos: Soziologische Beitraege zur Volkstheorie.* Berlin: Duncker & Humboldt, 1965.

Frank, Jason. *Constituent Moments: Enacting the People in Postrevolutionary America.* Durham, NC: Duke University Press, 2010.

Franklin, Julian H. *John Locke and the Theory of Sovereignty.* Cambridge: Cambridge University Press, 1981.

Frohnen, Bruce P. "Constitution-Reading through Tocqueville's Eyes." *Capital University Law Review* 42 (2014): 1–30.

Fukuyama, Francis. *The End of History and the Last Man.* New York: Free Press, 1992.

———. "Liberalism and Its Discontents. The Challenges from the Left and the Right." *American Purpose,* October 2020. https://www.americanpurpose.com/articles/liberalism-and-its-discontent/.

———. "The March of Equality." *Journal of Democracy* 11, no. 1 (2000): 11–17.

Furet, François. "The Conceptual System of Democracy in America." In *The Workshop of History,* 167–96. Chicago: University of Chicago Press, 1984.

———. *Revolutionary France.* Oxford: Wiley-Blackwell, 1995.

Gaddis, John Lewis. *On Grand Strategy.* Penguin Books, 2018.

Gannett, Robert T. "Bowling Ninepins in Tocqueville's Township." *American Political Science Review* 97, no. 1 (2003): 1–16.

———. "Tocqueville and Local Government." *Review of Politics* 67, no. 4 (2005): 729–31.

———. "Tocqueville as Politician: Revisiting the Revolution of 1789." In *Enlightening Revolutions*, edited by Svetozar Minkov, 235–58. Lanham, MD: Lexington Books, 2006.

———. "Tocqueville and the Politics of Suffrage." *Tocqueville Review / La Revue Tocqueville* 27 (2006): 209–26.

Gaonkar, Dilip. "After the Fictions: Notes Towards a Phenomenology of the Multitude." *e-flux Journal* 58 (October 2014): 1–15.

Gargan, Edward T. *Alexis de Tocqueville: The Critical Years 1848–1851*. Washington, DC: Catholic University of America Press, 1955.

Garrett, Stephen A. "Foreign Policy and the Democracies: De Tocqueville Revisited." *Virginia Quarterly Review* 48, no. 4 (Autumn 1972): 481–500.

Garsten, Bryan. "From Popular Sovereignty to Civil Society in Post-revolutionary France." In *Popular Sovereignty in Historical Perspective*, edited by Richard Bourke and Quentin Skinner, 236–69. Cambridge: Cambridge University Press, 2017.

———. "Representative Government and Popular Sovereignty." In *Political Representation*. edited by Alexander S. Kirshner, Ian Shapiro, Susan C. Stokes, Elizabeth Jean Wood, and Alexander S. Kirshner, 90–110. Cambridge: Cambridge University Press, 2009.

Geenens, Raf, and Helena Rosenblatt, eds. *French Liberalism from Montesquieu to the Present Day*. Cambridge: Cambridge University Press, 2012.

Gellner, Ernest. "Constitutional Adjudication as a Means of Realizing the Equal Stature of Men and Women under the Law." *Tocqueville Review / La Revue Tocqueville* 14, no. 1 (1993): 125–37.

———. *Nations and Nationalism*. New Perspectives on the Past. Ithaca, NY: Cornell University Press, 1983.

———. Goldstein, Doris S. *Trial of Faith: Religion and Politics in Tocqueville's Thought*. New York: Elsevier, 1975.

Ginsburg, Ruth Bader. "Constitutional Adjudication as a Means of Realizing the Equal Stature of Men and Women under the Law." *Tocqueville Review / La Revue Tocqueville* 14, no. 1 (1993): 125–37.

Graber, Mark E. *Dred Scott and the Problem of Constitutional Evil*. Cambridge: Cambridge University Press, 2010.

Greenfeld, Liah. *Nationalism: A Short History*. Washington DC: Brookings Institution, 2019.

———. *Nationalism: Five Roads to Modernity*. Cambridge, MA: Harvard University Press, 1992.

Greskovits, Béla. "Rebuilding the Hungarian Right Through Conquering Civil Society: The Civic Circles Movement." *East European Politics* 36, no. 2 (2020): 247–66.

Grimm, Dieter. *Constitutionalism: Past, Present, and Future*. Oxford: Oxford Univeristy Press, 2019.

---. *Sovereignty: The Origin and Future of a Political and Legal Concept.* Translated by Belinda Cooper. New York: Columbia University Press, 2015.

---. "The Various Faces of Fundamental Rights." In *The Double-Facing Constitution*, edited by Jacco Bornhoff, David Dyzenhaus, and Thomas Poole, 413–28. Cambridge: Cambridge University Press, 2020.

Grosby, Steven. *Nationalism: A Very Short Introduction.* Oxford: Oxford University Press, 2005.

---. "The Nation of the United States and the Vision of Ancient Israel." In *Biblical Ideas of Nationality: Ancient and Modern*, 213–33. Winona Lake, IN: Eisenbrauns.

Haidt, Jonathan. "When and Why Nationalism Beats Globalism." *American Interest*, July 2016. https://www.the-american-interest.com/2016/07/10/when-and-why-nationalism-beats-globalism/.

Halévi, Ran. "La Pensée Politique de l'honneur." In *Penser et vivre l'honneur à l'époque*, edited by Hervé Drévillon and Diego Venturino, 109–26. Rennes: Presses Universitaires de Rennes, 2011.

---. "The Frontier between Aristocracy and Democracy," In Atanassow and Boyd, *Tocqueville and the Frontiers of Democracy*, 53–73.

---. "Louis XIV: The Originator of the French Nation." Lecture presented at Ben-Gurion University of Negev, Beersheba, Israel, June 12, 2019.

Hamdani, Amar. *La Vérité sur l'expédition d'Alger.* Paris: Balland, 1985.

Hamilton, Alexander, James Madison, and John Jay. *The Federalist.* Edited by George W. Carey and James McClellan. Indianapolis, IN: Liberty Fund, 2001.

Hancock, Ralph C. "Tocqueville on the Good of American Federalism." *Publius* 20, no. 2 (1990): 89–108.

Harris, Abram L., "John Stuart Mill: Servant of the East India Company." *Canadian Journal of Economics and Political Science / Revue canadienne d'Economique et de Science politique* 30, no. 2 (May 1964): 185–202.

Hart, D., and M. K. Matsuba. "The Development of Pride and Moral Life." In *The Self-Conscious Emotions: Theory and Research*, edited by R. W. Robins, J. P. Tangney, and J. L. Tracy. New York: Guilford Press, 2007.

Hasewend, Katharina, Ludger Hagedorn, and Shalini Randeria. *Wenn Demokratien Demokratisch Untergehen.* Vienna: Passen Verlag, 2019.

Hassner, Pierre. "Rousseau and the Theory and Practice of International Relations." In *The Legacy of Rousseau*, edited by Clifford Orwin and Nathan Tarcov, 200–203. Chicago: University of Chicago Press, 1997.

Hau, Matthias vom, Lange, Matthew, and Mahoney, James. "Colonialism and Development: A Comparative Analysis of Spanish and British Colonies." *American Journal of Sociology* 111, no. 5 (2006): 1412–62.

Haynes, Syin. "What's Changed—and What Hasn't—in 50 Years of Pride Parades." *Time Magazine*, June 26, 2020: https://time.com/5858086/pride-parades-history/.

Hazony, Yoram. *The Virtue of Nationalism.* New York: Basic Books, 2018.

Heinrich, Horst-Alfred. "Dimensional Differences between Nationalism and Patriotism." In *Dynamics of National Identity: Media and Societal Factors of What We Are,* edited by Jürgen Grimm, Leonie Huddy, Peter Schmidt, and Josef Seethaler, 44–63. New York: Routledge, 2016.

———. "Emotions toward the Nation." In *Methods, Theories, and Empirical Applications in the Social Sciences,* edited by Samuel Salzborn, Eldad Davidov, and Jost Reinecke, 227–34. Wiesbaden: Springer VS, 2012.

Hendrix, Burke A., and Alison McQueen. "Tocqueville in Jacksonian Context: American Expansionism and Discourses of American Indian Nomadism in Democracy in America." *Perspective on Politics* 15, no. 3 (2017): 663–77.

Hebert Jr., Joseph. *More than Kings and Less than Men: Tocqueville on the Promise and Perils of Democratic Individualism.* Lanham, MD: Lexington Books, 2010.

Hirsch, Francine. *Empire of Nations.* Ithaca, NY: Cornell University Press, 2005.

Hobsbawm, Eric. Introduction to *The Communist Manifesto: A Modern Edition,* by Karl Marx and Frederick Engels, 1–28. London: Verso, 1998.

Hobbes, *On the Citizen (De Cive).* Edited by Richard Tuck and Michael Silverthorne. Cambridge: Cambridge University Press, 1998.

Honig, Bonnie. *Public Things: Democracy in Disrepair.* New York: Fordham University Press, 2017.

Hont, Istvan. "The Permanent Crisis of a Divided Mankind: 'Contemporary Crisis of the Nation State' in Historical Perspective." *Political Studies* 42, no. 1 (1994): 116–231.

Hopgood, Stephen. *The Endtimes for Human Rights.* Ithaca, NY: Cornell University Press, 2014.

Hume, David. "Of the First Principles of Government." In *Political Essays,* edited by Knut Haakonssen, 16–19. Cambridge: Cambridge University Press, 1994.

Hunt, Lynn. *Inventing Human Rights: A History.* New York: W. W. Norton, 2008.

Ikuta, Jennie C., and Trevor Latimer. "Aristocracy in America: Tocqueville on White Supremacy." *Journal of Politics* 83, no. 2 (2021): 547–59.

Isaac, Jeffrey C. "Is There Illiberal Democracy?: A Problem with No Semantic Solution." *Public Seminar,* July 12, 2017. https://publicseminar.org/2017/07/is-there-illiberal-democracy/.

Isaac, Joel. "Constitutional Dictatorship in Twentieth Century American Political Thought." In *States of Exception in American History,* edited by Joel Isaac and Gary Gerstle, 225–56. Chicago: University of Chicago Press, 2020.

Colby Itkowitz, Amy B. Wang, Meryl Kornfield, Derek Hawkins, John Wagner and Kim Bellware, "Joe Biden, in Victory Speech, Says, 'This is the Time to Heal in America,'" *Washington Post,* November 7, 2020, https://www.washingtonpost.com/elections/2020/11/07/trump-biden-election-live-updates/.

Jardin, André. *Tocqueville: A Biography.* New York: Farrar, Straus and Giroux, 1989.

———. "Tocqueville, Homme Politique." In *Alexis de Tocqueville: Zur Politik in Der Demokratie*, edited by Michael Hereth and Jutta Höffken, 93–114. Baden-Baden: Nomos Verlagsgesellschaft, 1981.
Jasanoff, Maya. *Liberty's Exiles: American Loyalists in the Revolutionary World*. New York: Alfred A. Knopf, 2012.
Jaume, Lucien. *Tocqueville: The Aristocratic Sources of Liberty*. Translated by Arthur Goldhammer. Princeton, NJ: Princeton University Press, 2013.
Jefferson, Thomas. *Notes on the State of Virginia*. New York: Norton Library, 1954.
Jóhannesson, Sveinn. "'Securing the State': James Madison, Federal Emergency Powers, and the Rise of the Liberal State in Post-Revolutionary America." *Journal of American History* 104 (September 2017): 363–86.
Judis, John B. *The Nationalist Revival: Trade, Immigration and the Revolt against Globalization*. New York: Columbia Global Reports, 2018.
Kahan, Alan S. "Aristocracy in Tocqueville." *Tocqueville Review / La Revue Tocqueville* 27 no. 2 (2006): 323–48.
———. "Checks and Balances for Democratic Souls: Alexis de Tocqueville on Religion in Democratic Societies." *American Political Thought* 4 (2015): 100–19.
———. *Liberalism in Nineteenth Century Europe: The Political Culture of Limited Suffrage*. Hampshire: Palgrave MacMillan, 2003.
———. *Tocqueville, Democracy, and Religion: Checks and Balances for Democratic Souls*. Oxford: Oxford University Press, 2015.
———. "Tocqueville: Liberalism and Imperialism." In *French Liberalism from Montesquieu to the Present Day*, edited by R. Geenens and H. Rosenblatt, 152–66. Cambridge: Cambridge University Press, 2012.
Kaiser, John. *Commander of the Faithful: The Life and Times of Emir Abd El-Kader*. Rhinebeck, NY: Monkfish Book Publishing, 2008.
Kalivas, Andreas and Ira Katznelson. *Liberal Beginnings: Making a Republic for the Moderns*. Cambridge: Cambridge University Press, 2008.
Kasimis, Demetra. *The Perpetual Immigrant and the Limits of Athenian Democracy*. Cambridge: Cambridge University Press, 2018.
Kateb, George. *Patriotism and Other Mistakes*. New Haven, CT: Yale University Press, 2006.
Katznelson, Ira. "Flexible Capacity: The Military in Early American Statebuilding." In *Shaped by War and Trade: International Influences on American Political Development*, edited by Ira Katznelson and Martin Shefter, 82–110. Princeton, NJ: Princeton University Press, 2001.
———. "On Liberal Ambivalence." *Political Theory* 40, no. 6 (December, 2012): 779–88.
Keay, John. *India: A History*. London: Harper Press, 2010.
Kettunen Pauli. "The Concept of Nationalism in Discussions on a European Society." *Journal of Political Ideologies* 23, no. 3 (2018): 342–69.

Kielstra, Paul Michael. *The Politics of Slave Trade Suppression*. London: Palgrave Macmillan, 2000.
Kilberg, Andrew G. I. "We the People: The Original Meaning Of Popular Sovereignty." *Virginia Law Review* 100, no. 5 (September 2014): 1061–109.
Kirss, Alexander. "Does Grand Strategy Matter?." *Strategic Studies Quarterly* 12, no. 4 (2018): 116–32.
Kissam, Philip C. "Alexis de Tocqueville and American Constitutional Law: On Democracy, the Majority Will, Individual Rights, Federalism, Religion, Civic Associations, and Originalist Constitutional Theory." *Maine Law Review* 59 (2007): 54–56.
Knee, Philip. "Réligion et souveraineté du people: de Rousseau à Tocqueville." *Canadian Journal of Political Science* 23, no. 2 (1990): 211–32.
Kohn, Hans. *The Idea of Nationalism: A Study of Its Origins and Background*. London: Routledge, 2005.
Kohn, Margaret. "Empire's Law: Alexis de Tocqueville on Colonialism and the State of Exception." *Canadian Journal of Political Science* 41, no. 2 (2008): 255–78.
Kołakowski, Leszek. *Main Currents of Marxism*. New York: W. W. Norton, 2008.
Koritansky, John. *Alexis de Tocqueville and the New Science of Politics*. Durham, NC: Carolina Academic Press, 1986.
———. "Decentralization and Civic Virtue in Tocqueville's 'New Science of Politics'" *Publius* 5, no. 3 (1975): 63–81.
Kotkin, Stephen. "Russia's Perpetual Geopolitics: Putin Returns to the Historical Pattern." *Foreign Affairs* 95, no. 3 (2016): 2–9.
Krastev, Ivan. *After Europe*. Philadelphia: University of Pennsylvania Press, 2017.
———. "Sovereign Democracy, Russian-Style." *Insight Turkey* 8, no. 4 (2006): 113–17.
Krastev, Ivan, and Stephen Holmes. *The Light that Failed: A Reckoning*. Penguin, 2020.
———. "Explaining Eastern Europe: Imitation and Its Discontents," *Journal of Democracy* 29, no. 3 (July 2018): 117–28.
Kraynak, Robert. "Tocqueville's Constitutionalism." *American Political Science Review* 84, no. 4 (1987): 1175–95.
Lacam, Jean-Patrice. *Tocqueville et la République*. Paris: L'Harmattan, 2020.
Lambert, Frank. *The Barbary Wars: American Independence in the Atlantic World*. New York: Hill and Wang, 2007.
Lamberti, Jean-Claude. "La Liberté et Les Illusions Individualistes Selon Tocqueville." In *Tocqueville et l'esprit de La Démocratie*, edited by Laurence Guellec, 149–66. Paris: Presses de Sciences Po, 2005.
Lawler, Peter. "The Human Condition: Tocqueville's Debt to Rousseau and Pascal." In *Liberty, Equality, Democracy*, edited by Eduardo Nolla, 1–20. New York: New York University Press, 1992.

———. *The Restless Mind: Alexis de Tocqueville on the Origin and Perpetuation of Human Liberty*. Lanham, MD: Rowman & Littlefield, 1993.

Lawlor, Mary. *Alexis de Tocqueville in the Chamber of Deputies: His Views on Foreign and Colonial Policy*. Washington, DC: Catholic University of America Press, 1959.

Le Cour Grandmaison, Olivier. "Quand Tocqueville légitimait les boucheries." *Le Monde* diplomatique, June 2001. https://www.monde-diplomatique.fr/2001/06/LE_COUR_GRANDMAISON/1706.

Legutko, Ryszard. *The Demon in Democracy: Totalitarian Temptations in Free Societies*. New York: Encounter Books, 2018.

Lepore, Jill. *These Truths: A History of the United States*. New York: W. W. Norton, 2018.

Lerner, Ralph. *Revolutions Revisited: Two Faces of the Politics of the Enlightenment*. Chapel Hill: University of North Carolina Press, 1994.

———. *The Thinking Revolutionary*. Ithaca, NY: Cornell University Press, 1988.

Levitsky, Steven, and Daniel Ziblatt. *How Democracies Die: What History Reveals about Our Future*. London: Penguin Books, 2018.

Lincoln, Abraham, "First Inaugural Address," March 4, 1861, Washington DC, US. The Avalon Project, transcript, https://avalon.law.yale.edu/19th_century/lincoln1.asp.

———. "The Gettysburg Address," November 19, 1863, Gettysburg, Pennsylvania, US. Abraham Lincoln Online, transcript, http://www.abrahamlincolnonline.org/lincoln/speeches/gettysburg.htm.

———. "House Divided Speech," June 16, 1858, Springfield, Illinois, US. Abraham Lincoln Online, transcript, http://www.abrahamlincolnonline.org/lincoln/speeches/house.htm.

Locke, John. "Second Treatise of Government." In *Two Treatises of Government*, edited by Peter Laslett, 265–428. Cambridge: Cambridge University Press, 1996.

Loughlin, Martin, and Neil Walker. *The Paradox of Constitutionalism: Constituent Power and Constitutional Form*. Oxford: Oxford University Press, 2007.

Lupel, Adam. *Popular Sovereignty and Globalization*. London: Routledge, 2011.

Mair, Peter. *Ruling the Void: The Hollowing of Western Democracy*. London: Verso, 2013.

Maletz, Donald J. "Tocqueville on Mores and the Preservation of Republics." *American Journal of Political Science* 49, no. 1 (2005): 1–15.

Manent, Pierre. "Democracy without Nations?," *Journal of Democracy* 8, no. 2 (1997): 95.

———. "Guizot et Tocqueville devant l'ancien et le nouveau." In *François Guizot et La Culture Politique de Son Temps*, edited by Marina Valensise, 26–34. Paris: Gallimard, 1991.

———. *La raison des nations*. Paris: Gallimard, 2006.

---. *Tocqueville and the Nature of Democracy*. Translated by John Waggoner. Lanham, MD: Rowman & Littlefield, 1996.

---. "Tocqueville, Political Philosopher." In *The Cambridge Companion to Tocqueville*, edited by Cheryl B. Welch, 108–20. Cambridge: Cambridge University Press, 2006.

Mansfield, Harvey C. "On the Difference between Party and Faction." In *Philosophy, Politics, and the Conversation of Mankind*, edited by Todd Breyfogle, Paul Franco, and Eric Kos, 211–26. Colorado Springs: Colorado College, 2016.

---. "Providence and Democracy." *Claremont Review of Books* 11, nos. 1–2 (Winter-Spring, 2010–11). https://claremontreviewofbooks.com/providence-and-democracy/.

---. "Self-Interest Rightly Understood." *Political Theory* 23, no. 1 (1995): 48–66.

---. "Tocqueville and the Future of American Constitutionalism." In *The Normative Constitution: Essays for the Third Century*, edited by Charles W. Johnson, Kent E. Robson, and Richard Sherlock, 45–58. Lanham, MD: Rowman & Littlefield, 1995.

---. "Tocqueville on Religion and Liberty." In *The Spirit of Religion and the Spirit of Freedom: The Tocqueville Thesis Revisited*, edited by Michael Zuckert, 189–216. Chicago: University of Chicago Press, 2017.

Mansfield, Harvey C., and Delba Winthrop. "What Tocqueville Says to Liberals and Conservatives Today." In *Democracy and Its Friendly Critics*, edited by Peter Augustine Lawler, 1–6. Lanham, MD: Lexington Books, 2004.

---. "Tocqueville's New Political Science." In *The Cambridge Companion to Tocqueville*, edited by Cheryl Welch, 81–107. Cambridge: Cambridge University Press, 2006.

Mantena, Karuna. *Alibis of Empire*. Princeton, NJ: Princeton University Press, 2010.

---. "Mill and the Imperial Predicament." In *J. S. Mill's Political Thought: A Bicentennial Reassessment*, edited by Nadia Urbinati and Alex Zakaras, 298–318. Cambridge: Cambridge University Press, 2007.

---. "Popular Sovereignty and Anti-colonialism." In *Popular Sovereignty in Historical Perspective*, edited by Richard Bourke and Quentin Skinner, 297–319. Cambridge: Cambridge University Press, 2017.

Marx, Karl, and Friedrich Engels. "Manifesto of the Communist Party." In Marx and Engels, *Marx-Engels Reader*, 469–500.

---. *The Marx-Engels Reader*. Edited by Robert C. Tucker. New York: W. W. Norton, 1978.

Marx, Karl. "Economic and Philosophic Manuscripts of 1844," in Marx and Engels, *Marx-Engels Reader*, 66–125.

---. "The Eighteenth Brumaire of Louis Napoleon." In Marx and Engels, *Marx-Engels Reader*, 594–617.

———. "On the Jewish Question." In Marx and Engels, *Marx-Engels Reader*, 26–52.

Mason, Matthew. "Keeping up Appearances: The International Politics of Slave Trade Abolition in the Nineteenth-Century Atlantic World." *William and Mary Quarterly* 66, no. 4 (2009): 809–32.

McDougall, James. *A History of Algeria*. Cambridge: Cambridge University Press, 2017.

McLendon, Michael Locke. "Tocqueville, Jansenism, and the Psychology of Freedom." *American Journal of Political Science* 50, no. 3 (July 2006): 664–75.

Mearsheimer, John J. *The Great Delusion: Liberal Dreams and International Realities*. New Haven, CT: Yale University Press, 2018.

Mélonio, Françoise. "L'idée de nation et idée de démocratie chez Tocqueville." *Littérature et nation* 7 (1991): 5–24.

Meyer, Heinz-Dieter. "Tocqueville's Cultural Institutionalism: Reconciling Collective Culture and Methodological Individualism." *Journal of Classical Sociology* 3, no. 2 (2003): 197–220.

Mill, John Stuart. "Considerations on Representative Government." In *On Liberty, Utilitarianism and Other Essays*. edited by Mark Philp and Frederick Rosen, 388–407. Oxford: Oxford University Press, 2015.

———. *Collected Works of John Stuart Mill*. Vol. 30 of 33. Edited by John M. Robson. Toronto: University of Toronto Press, 1990.

Miller, Dale T. "The Norm of Self-Interest." *American Psychologist* 54, no. 12 (1999): 1053–60.

Miller, Joshua. "The Ghostly Body Politic: The Federalist Papers and Popular Sovereignty." *Political Theory* 16, no. 1 (1988): 99–119.

Miłosz, Czeslaw. *The Captive Mind*. Translated by Jane Zielonko. London: Penguin Modern Classics, 2001.

Mishra, Pankaj. *Age of Anger: A History of the Present*. Farrar, Straus and Giroux, 2017.

Mitchell, Harvey. *America after Tocqueville: Democracy Against Difference*. Cambridge: Cambridge University Press, 2004.

Mitchell, Joshua. *American Awakening: Identity Politics and Other Afflictions of Our Time*. New York: Encounter Books, 2020.

———. *The Fragility of Freedom: Tocqueville on Religion, Democracy, and the American Future*. Chicago: University of Chicago Press, 1999.

———. "Tocqueville's Puritans." In *Cambridge Companion to Democracy in America*, edited by Richard Boyd, 347–68. Cambridge: Cambridge University Press, 2022.

Montesquieu. *The Persian Letters*. Translated by C. J. Betts. London: Penguin Books, 1993.

———. *The Spirit of the Laws*. Translated by Anne M. Cohler, Basia C. Miller, and Harold S. Stone. Cambridge: Cambridge University Press, 1989.

Morgan, Edmund S. *Inventing the People: The Rise of Popular Sovereignty in England and America*. New York: W. W. Norton, 1988.
———. *The Puritan Dilemma: The Story of John Winthrop*. London: Pierson, 2006.
Mouffe, Chantal. *For a Left Populism*. London: Verso, 2018.
Mounk, Yascha. "America Is Not a Democracy." *Atlantic*, March 2018. https://www.theatlantic.com/magazine/archive/2018/03/america-is-not-a-democracy/550931/.
———. *The People vs. Democracy: Why Our Freedom Is in Danger and How to Save It*. Cambridge, MA: Harvard University Press, 2018.
Moyn, Samuel. *Not Enough: Human Rights in an Unequal World*. Cambridge, MA: Harvard University Press, 2019.
Müller, Jan-Werner. *Contesting Democracy: Political Ideas in Twentieth-Century Europe*. New Haven, CT: Yale University Press, 2013.
———. *Constitutional Patriotism*. Princeton, NJ: Princeton University Press, 2007.
———. "Is This Really How It Ends?: Democracy's Midlife Crisis." Review of *How Democracies Die*, by Steven Levitsky and Daniel Ziblatt and *How Democracy Ends*, by David Runciman, *Nation*, April 22, 2019. https://www.thenation.com/article/archive/how-democracies-dies-how-democracy-ends-book-review/.
———. "The Problem With 'Illiberal Democracy.'" *Project Syndicate*, January 21, 2016. https://www.project-syndicate.org/commentary/the-problem-with-illiberal-democracy-by-jan-werner-mueller-2016-01?barrier=accesspaylog.
———. *What Is Populism?*. London: Penguin, 2017.
Murray, Charles. *By the People: Rebuilding Liberty without Permission*. New York: Crown Forum, 2015.
———. *Coming Apart*. New York: Crown Forum, 2013.
Neem, Johann N. "Taking Modernity's Wager: Tocqueville, Social Capital, and the American Civil War." *Journal of Interdisciplinary History* 41, no. 4 (2011): 591–618.
———. "Who Are 'The People'?: Locating Popular Authority in Postrevolutionary America." *Reviews in American History* 39, no. 2 (June 2011): 267–73.
Nicholas, H. G. "Tocqueville and the Dissolution of the Union." *Revue Internationale de Philosophie* 13, no. 49 (3) (1949): 320–29.
Novak, William J. "The Myth of the Weak American State." *American Historical Review* 113, no. 3 (2008): 752–72.
Ober, Josiah. *Demopolis: Democracy Before Liberalism in Theory and Practice*. Cambridge: Cambridge University Press, 2017.
Orwin, Clifford. "Compassion and the Softening of Mores." *Journal of Democracy* 11, no. 1 (2000): 142–48.
Ossewaarde, Ringo. *Tocqueville's Moral and Political Thought: New Liberalism*. London: Routledge, 2004.
Pagden, Anthony. *Peoples and Empires*. New York: Modern Library, 2001.

Paine, Thomas. "Common Sense." In *Rights of Man, Common Sense and Other Political Writings*, edited by Mark Philp, 1–60. Oxford: Oxford University Press, 2009.

Pangle, Heather. "Liberalism and Nationalism." *National Affairs* (Fall 2019): 142–58.

Pangle Wilford, Heather, "Like a God on Earth: Popular Sovereignty in Tocqueville's *Democracy in America*." In *People Power: Popular Sovereignty from Machiavelli to Modernity*, edited by Robert G. Ingram and Christopher Barker, 160–181. Manchester: Manchester University Press, 2022.

Pascal, Blaise. *Pensées and Other Writings*. Oxford: Oxford Classics, 1995.

Pierson, George Wilson. *Tocqueville and Beaumont in America*. Baltimore, MD: Johns Hopkins University Press, 1996.

Pitts, Jennifer. *Boundaries of the International: Law and Empire*. Cambridge, MA: Harvard University Press, 2018.

———. "Empire and Democracy: Tocqueville and the Algeria Question." *Journal of Political Philosophy* 8, no. 3 (2002): 295–318.

———. Introduction to *Tocqueville on Empire and Slavery*, edited by Jennifer Pitts, ix–xxxviii. Baltimore, MD: Johns Hopkins University Press, 2001.

———. *A Turn to Empire*. Princeton, NJ: Princeton University Press, 2005.

Plato. *The Republic of Plato*. Translated by Allan Bloom. New York: Basic Books, 1991.

Plattner, Marc. "Illiberal Democracy and the Struggle on the Right." *Journal of Democracy* 30, no. 1 (January 2019): 5–19.

———. "Rousseau and the Origins of Nationalism." In *The Legacy of Rousseau*, edited by Clifford Orwin and Nathan Tarcov, 183–99. Chicago: University of Chicago Press, 1997.

Posner, Eric A. *The Twilight of Human Rights Law*. Oxford: Oxford University Press, 2014.

Putnam, Robert. *Bowling Alone: The Collapse and Revival of American Community*. New York: Simon & Schuster, 2020.

Qutb, Sayyid. "Milestones." In *Sayyid Qutb Reader: Selected Writings on Politics, Religion, and Society*, edited by Albert J. Bergesen, 35–42. London: Routledge, 2008.

Rahe, Paul. *Republics Ancient and Modern*. 3 vols. Chapel Hill: University of North Carolina Press, 1994.

———. *Soft Despotism, Democracy's Drift: Montesquieu, Rousseau, Tocqueville, and the Modern Prospect*. New Haven, CT: Yale University Press, 2010.

Rawls, John. *Political Liberalism*. New York: Columbia University Press, 2004.

Reséndez, Andrés. *The Other Slavery: The Uncovered Story of Indian Enslavement in America*. Boston: Houghton Mifflin Harcourt, 2016.

Richter, Melvin. "Tocqueville and Guizot on Democracy." *History of European Ideas* 30 (2004): 61–82.

———. "Tocqueville on Threats to Liberty in Democracy." In *The Cambridge Companion to Tocqueville*, edited by Cheryl Welch, 245–75. Cambridge: Cambridge University Press, 2006.

Roberts, Timothy Mason. "The Role of French Algeria in American Expansion During the Early Republic." *Journal of the Western Society for French History* 23 (2015): 153–64.

Rodrik, Dani. *The Globalization Paradox: Democracy and the Future of the World Economy*. New York: W. W. Norton, 2011.

Rosanvalon, Pierre. *Le moment Guizot*. Paris: Gallimard, 1985.

Rousseau, Jean-Jacques. "Considerations on the Government of Poland." In *Rousseau: The Social Contract and Other Later Political Writings*, edited and translated by Victor Gourevitch, 179–93. Cambridge: Cambridge University Press, 1997.

———. "Of the Social Contract." In *Rousseau: The Social Contract and Other Later Political Writings*, edited and translated by Victor Gourevitch, 177–260. Cambridge: Cambridge University Press, 1997.

Runciman, David. *The Confidence Trap: A History of Democracy in Crisis from World War I to the Present*. Princeton, NJ: Princeton University Press, 2015.

———. *How Democracy Ends*. New York: Basic Books, 2019.

Ryan, Alan. "Bureaucracy, Democracy, Liberty: Some Unanswered Questions in Mill's Politics." In *J. S. Mill's Political Thought, A Bicentennial Reassessment*, edited by Nadia Urbinati and Alex Zakaras, 147–65. Cambridge: Cambridge University Press, 2007.

———. "Utilitarianism and Bureaucracy, Democracy, Liberty: The Views of J.S. Mill." In *The Making of Modern Liberalism*, by Alan Ryan, 326–45. Princeton, NJ: Princeton University Press, 2012.

Sassen, Saskia. *Losing Control?: Sovereignty in the Age of Globalization*. New York: Columbia University Press, 2015.

Schacter, Rory. "Tocqueville's 'New Political Science' as a Correction of *The Federalist*." In *Exploring the Social and Political Economy of Alexis de Tocqueville*, edited by Peter Boettke and Adam Martin, 9–35. London: Palgrave Macmillan, 2020.

Scharpf, Fritz. *Governing in Europe: Effective or Democratic?*. Oxford: Oxford University Press, 1999.

Schleifer, James. *The Chicago Companion to Tocqueville's Democracy in America*. Chicago: University of Chicago Press, 2012.

———. *The Making of Tocqueville's Democracy in America*. Indianapolis, IN: Liberty Fund, 2000.

Schlosser, Joel Alden. "'Hope, Danger's Comforter': Thucydides, Hope, Politics." *Journal of Politics* 75, no. 1 (2012): 169–82.

Schmidt, Vivien A. "Democracy and Legitimacy in the European Union Revisited: Input, Output, and Throughput." *Political Studies* 61, no. 1 (2013): 2–22.

Schmitt, Carl. *The Crisis of Parliamentary Democracy*. Translated by Ellen Kennedy. Cambridge, MA: MIT Press, 1988.

Schmitter, P. C., and T. L. Karl. "What Democracy Is . . . and Is Not." *Journal of Democracy* 2, no. 3 (1991): 75–88.

Selby, David. *Tocqueville, Jansenism, and the Necessity of the Political in a Democratic Age*. Amsterdam: Amsterdam University Press, 2015.

———. "Towards a Political Theology of Republicanism: The Contours of a Natural Contrast between Carl Schmitt and Alexis de Tocqueville." *History of Political Thought* 39, no. 4 (Winter 2018): 749–74.

Selinger, William. "*Le grand mal de l'époque*: Tocqueville on French Political Corruption." *History of European Ideas* 42, no. 1 (2016): 73–94.

———. *Parliamentarism: From Burke to Weber*. Cambridge: Cambridge University Press, 2019.

Sessions, Jennifer E. *By Sword and by Plow: France and the Conquest of Algeria*. Ithaca, NY: Cornell University Press, 2011.

Shepard, Tod. *The Invention of Decolonization: The Algerian War and the Remaking of France*. Ithaca, NY: Cornell University Press, 2006.

Sides, John, Michael Tesler, and Lynn Vareck. *Identity Crisis: The 2016 Presidential Election Campaign and the Battle for the Meaning of America*. Princeton, N.J: Princeton University Press, 2018.

Sieyès, Emmanuel Joseph. "What Is the Third Estate?." In *Political Writings: Including the Debate between Sieyès and Tom Paine in 1781*, edited and translated by Michael Sonenscher, 92–162. Indianapolis, IN: Hackett Publishing Company, 2003.

Smith, Anthony. *Chosen Peoples: Sacred Sources of National Identity*. Oxford: Oxford University Press, 2004.

Smith, Jay M. *Nobility Reimagined: The Patriotic Nation in Eighteenth-Century France*. Ithaca, NY: Cornell University Press, 2005.

Smith, Rogers. "Beyond Tocqueville, Myrdal, and Harz: The Multiple Traditions in America." *American Political Science Review* 87, no. 3 (1993): 549–66.

———. *Political Peoplehood: The Roles of Values, Interests, and Identities*. Chicago: University of Chicago Press, 2015.

———. "Popular Sovereignty, Populism, and Stories of Peoplehood." In Atanassow, Bartscherer, and Bateman, *When the People Rule*, forthcoming.

———. *Stories of Peoplehood: The Politics and Morals of Political Membership*. Cambridge: Cambridge University Press, 2003.

———. *This Is Not Who We Are: Populism and Peoplehood*. New Haven, CT: Yale University Press, 2020.

Smith, Steven B. *Modernity and Its Discontents*. New Haven, CT: Yale University Press, 2016.

———. *Reclaiming Patriotism in an Age of Extremes*. New Haven, CT: Yale University Press, 2021.

Snyder, Timothy. *The Road to Unfreedom: Russia, Europe, America*. New York: Penguin, 2019.

Spector, Céline. "Commerce, Glory, and Empire: Montesquieu's Legacy." Translated by Patrick Camiller. In Atanassow and Boyd, *Tocqueville and the Frontiers of Democracy*, 202–20.

Spitzer, Alan B. "Tocqueville's Modern Nationalism." *French History* 19, no. 1 (March 2005): 48–66.

Stankov, Peter. *The Political Economy of Populism: An Introduction*. Abingdon: Routledge, 2020.

Stein, Janice. "Psychology and Foreign Policy." In *Oxford Bibliographies*, edited by Patrick James. Oxford: Oxford University Press, last reviewed September 2020. https://www.oxfordbibliographies.com/view/document/obo-9780199743292/obo-9780199743292-0252.xml.

Strong, Tracy B. "Seeing Differently and Seeing Further: Rousseau and Tocqueville." In *Friends and Citizens*, edited by Peter Denis Bathory and Nancy L. Schwartz, 104–5. Lanham, MD: Rowman & Littlefield, 2001.

Suh, Byong-Hoon. "Mill and Tocqueville: A Friendship Bruised." *History of Political Ideas* 42, no. 1 (2016): 55–72.

Sullivan, Vickie. *Montesquieu and the Despotic Ideas of Europe*. Chicago: University of Chicago Press, 2017.

Swedberg, Richard. *Tocqueville's Political Economy*. Princeton, NJ: Princeton University Press, 2009.

Tamir, Yael. "Not So Civic: Is There a Difference between Ethic and Civic Nationalism?." *Annual Review of Political Science* 22 (May 2019): 419–34.

———. *Why Nationalism*. Princeton, NJ: Princeton University Press, 2019.

Tate, Adam. "James Madison and State Sovereignty, 1780–1781." *American Political Thought* 2, no. 2 (Fall 2013): 174–97.

Taylor, A. J. P. *The Struggle for Mastery in Europe 1848–1918*. Oxford: Clarendon Press, 1954.

Taylor, Astra, dir. *What is Democracy?*. New York: Zeitgeist Films, 2018. DVD, 107 min.

Taylor, Quentin. "Radical Son: The Apprenticeship of John Stuart Mill." *Humanitas* 26, nos.1–2 (2013): 129–52.

Tessitore. Aristide, "Tocqueville's American Thesis and the New Science of Politics." In *The Spirit of Religion and the Spirit of Freedom: The Tocqueville Thesis Revisited*, edited by Michael Zuckert, 19–48. Chicago: University of Chicago Press, 2017.

Thomson, Ann. "Arguments for the Conquest of Algiers in the Late Eighteenth and Early Nineteenth Centuries." *Maghreb Review* 14, no. 1–2 (1989): 108–18.

———. *Barbary and Enlightenment: European Attitudes towards the Maghreb in the 18th Century*. Leiden: E. J. Brill, 1987.

Tillery Jr., Alvin Bernard. "Reading Tocqueville Behind the Veil: African American Receptions of *Democracy in America*, 1835–1900." *American Political Thought* 7, no. 1 (2018): 1–25.

———. "Tocqueville as Critical Race Theorist: Whiteness as Property, Interest Convergence, and the Limits of Jacksonian Democracy." *Political Research Quarterly* 62, no. 4 (2009): 639–52.

Tocqueville, Alexis de. *Democracy in America: Historical-Critical Edition of De la démocratie en Amérique*. Edited by Eduardo Nolla. Translated by James Schleifer. Edition. 4 vols. Indianapolis, IN: Liberty Fund, 2010.

———. *The European Revolution and Correspondence with Gobineau*. Translated and edited by John Lukacs. Garden City, NY: Doubleday, 1959.

———. "How Patriotism Is Justified in the Eyes of Reason and Appears to It Not Only a Great Virtue but the Most Important." In *The Tocqueville Reader: A Life in Letters and Politics*, edited by Alan S. Kahan and Olivier Zunz, 332–33. Oxford: Wiley-Blackwell, 2002.

———. *Journey to America*. Translated by George Lawrence. Edited by J. P. Mayer. New Haven, CT: Yale University Press, 1959.

———. *Lettres choisies: Souvenirs, 1814–1859*. Paris: Gallimard, 2003.

———. *Memoirs on Pauperism and Other Writings: Poverty, Public Welfare, and Inequality*. Edited and translated by Christine Dunn Henderson. Notre Dame, IN: University of Notre Dame Press, 2021.

———. *Œuvres Complètes*. Edited by Françoise Mélonio, 18 vols. Paris: Gallimard, 1989.

———. *The Old Regime and the Revolution*. 2 vols. Edited by Françoise Mélonio. Translated by Alan S. Kahan. Chicago: University of Chicago Press, 1998 and 2001.

———. *Recollections: The French Revolution of 1848*. Edited by J. P. Mayer and A. P. Kerr. Translated by George Lawrence. New Brunswick, NJ: Transaction Publishers, 1995.

———. *Selected Letters on Politics and Society*. Edited by Roger Boesche. Translated by James Toupin. Berkeley, CA: University of California Press, 1986.

———. *Writings on Empire and Slavery*. Edited and translated by Jennifer Pitts. Baltimore, MD: Johns Hopkins University Press, 2001.

Todorov, Tzvetan. *The Inner Enemies of Democracy*. Translated by Andrew Brown. Cambridge: Polity, 2014.

———. *On Human Diversity: Nationalism, Racism, and Exoticism in French Thought*. Translated by Catherine Porter. Cambridge: Cambridge, MA: Harvard University Press, 1998.

———. "Tocqueville's Nationalism." *History and Anthropology* 4 (1990): 357–71.

Toloudis, Nicholas. "Tocqueville's Guizot Moment." *French Politics, Culture & Society* 28, no.3 (Winter 2010): 1–22.

Torpey, John. "'The Problem of American Exceptionalism' Revisited." *Journal of Classical Sociology* 9, no. 1 (2009): 143–68.

Tuck, Richard. "Democratic Sovereignty and Democratic Government: The Sleeping Sovereign." In *Popular Sovereignty in Historical Perspective*, edited by Richard Bourke and Quentin Skinner. Cambridge: Cambridge University Press, 2017.

———. *The Sleeping Sovereign: The Invention of Modern Democracy.* Cambridge: Cambridge University Press, 2016.

Tugendhaft, Aaron. *The Idols of Isis.* Chicago: University of Chicago Press, 2020.

Urbinati, Nadia. *Democracy Disfigured: Opinion, Truth, and the People.* Cambridge, MA: Harvard University Press, 2014.

———. *Me, the People: How Populism Transforms Democracy.* Cambridge, MA: Harvard University Press, 2019.

Varouxakis, Georgios. *Liberty Abroad: J. S. Mill on International Relations.* Cambridge: Cambridge University Press, 2013.

———. *Mill on Nationality.* London: Routledge, 2002.

Villa, Dana. "Religion, Civic Education, and Conformity." In *The Spirit of Religion and the Spirit of Liberty*, edited by Michael Zuckert, 217–37. Chicago: University of Chicago Press, 2017.

———. *Teachers of the People: Political Education in Rousseau, Hegel, Tocqueville, and Mill.* Chicago: University of Chicago Press, 2017.

Viroli, Maurizio. *For Love of Country: An Essay on Patriotism and Nationalism.* Oxford: Clarendon Press, 1997.

Vlassopoulos, Kostas. "Free Spaces: Identity, Experience and Democracy in Classical Athens." *Classical Quarterly New Series* 57, no. 1 (May 2007): 33–52.

Vormann, Boris, and Michael Weinman, eds. *The Emergence of Illiberalism.* New York: Routledge, 2020.

Waltz, Kenneth. *Man, the State, and War: A Theoretical Analysis.* New York: Columbia University Press, 2001.

Walzer, Michael. *The Paradox of Liberation: Secular Revolutions and Religious Counterrevolutions.* New Haven, CT: Yale University Press, 2015.

———. "Political Action: The Problem of Dirty Hands." *Philosophy & Public Affairs* 2, no. 2 (1973): 160–80.

———. "Spheres of Affection." In *For Love of Country?: A New Democracy Forum on the Limits of Patriotism*, edited by Martha C. Nussbaum, 125–30. Boston, MA: Beacon Press, 2002.

Walvin, James. *The Slave Trade.* New York: W. W. Norton, 2012.

Watkins, Sharon. *Alexis de Tocqueville and the Second Republic.* Lanham, MD: University Press of America, 2003.

Weiss, Gillian. "Imagining Europe through Barbary Captivity." *Taiwan Journal of East Asian Studies* 4, no. 1 (2007): 49–67.

Welch, Cheryl B. "Colonial Violence and the Rhetoric of Evasion." *Political Theory* 31, no. 2 (2003): 247–56.

———. "Out of Africa: Tocqueville's Imperial Voyages." In *Tocqueville's Voyages*, edited by Christine Dunn Henderson, 304–34. Indianapolis, IN: Liberty Fund, 2014.

———. "Tocqueville on Democracy After Abolition." *Tocqueville Review / La Revue Tocqueville* 27, no. 2 (2006): 227–54.

———. "Tocqueville on Fraternity and Fratricide." In *The Cambridge Companion to Tocqueville*, edited by Cheryl B. Welch, 305–10. Cambridge: Cambridge University Press, 2006.

West, Thomas G. "Misunderstanding the American Founding." In *Interpreting Tocqueville's Democracy in America*, edited by Ken Masugi, 155–77. Lanham, MD: Rowman & Littlefield, 1991.

Whittington, Keith E. "The Political Constitution of Federalism in Antebellum America: The Nullification Debate as an Illustration of Informal Mechanisms of Constitutional Change." *Publius* 26, no. 2 (Spring 1996): 1–24.

———. "Revisiting Tocqueville's America," In *Beyond Tocqueville: Civil Society and Social Capital Debate in Comparative Perspective*, edited by Bob Edwards, Michael Folley, and Mario Diani, 21–31.Hanover, NH: University Press of New England, 2001.

Wilentz, Sean. "Many Democracies: On Tocqueville and Jacksonian America." In *Reconsidering Tocqueville's Democracy in America*, edited by Abraham S. Eisenstadt, 207–28. New Brunswick, NJ: Rutgers University Press, 1988.

———. *The Rise of American Democracy: Jefferson to Lincoln*. New York: W. W. Norton, 2005.

Wills, Garry. "Did Tocqueville 'Get' America?" *New York Review of Books* 1.1, no. 7 (April 29, 2004). https://www.nybooks.com/articles/2004/04/29/did-tocqueville-get-america/.

Winthrop, Delba. "Rights, Interests, and Honor." In *Tocqueville's Defense of Human Liberty*, edited by Peter A. Lawler and Joseph Alulis. New York: Garland Publishers, 1993.

———. "Tocqueville on Federalism." *Publius* 6, no. 3 (1976): 97.

———. "Writings on Empire and Slavery." *Society* 1 (2002): 110–13.

Wolloch, Nathaniel. "Barbarian Tribes, American Indians and Cultural Transmission: Changing Perspectives from the Enlightenment to Tocqueville." *History of Political Thought* 34, no. 3 (Autumn 2013): 507–23.

Yack, Bernard. *Nationalism and the Moral Psychology of Community*. Chicago: University of Chicago Press, 2012.

———. "Popular Sovereignty and Nationalism." *Political Theory* 29, no. 4 (2001): 517–36.

Zakaria, Fareed. *The Future of Freedom: Illiberal Democracy at Home and Abroad*. New York: W. W. Norton, 2003.

Zetterbaum, Marvin. *Tocqueville and the Problem of Democracy*. Stanford, CA: Stanford University Press, 1967.

Zuckert, Catherine. "The Saving Minimum?: Tocqueville on the Role of Religion in America—Then and Now." In *The Spirit of Religion and the Spirit of Liberty*, edited by Michael Zuckert, 241–66. Chicago: University of Chicago Press, 2017.

Zuckert, Michael. "James Madison." In Atanassow and Kahan, *Liberal Moments*, 43–50.

———. "On Social State." In *Tocqueville's Defense of Human Liberty*, edited by Joseph Alulis and Peter Lawler, 3–19. New York: Garland Publishers, 1993.

———, ed. *The Spirit of Religion and the Spirit of Liberty: The Tocqueville Thesis Revisited*. Chicago: University of Chicago Press, 2017.

Zunz, Olivier, and Alan S. Kahan, eds. *The Tocqueville Reader*. Oxford: Blackwell Publishing, 2002.

INDEX

Abd-el-Kader ibn Muḥyī al-Dīn, Emir of Mascara, 143–44, 147
abolitionism, 120–21, 123–24, 172
Africa, 127, 131–37, 143–44
African Americans, 85, 128, 130
Ageron, Charles-Robert, 138
Alexander the Great, 128
Algeria, 19, 106–7, 110, 114, 131–40, 143–44, 147
Allen, Danielle, 27
American Revolution, 26, 67, 155–56
Anglo-Americans, 23, 29, 40, 54, 128
aristocracy, 24, 65–66, 68–70, 72, 78, 83, 86, 87, 97; colonial rule likened to, 145; democracy contrasted with, 69–70, 72, 78, 86–87, 100; in England, 86; inequality of, 108; Tocqueville's broad definition of, 65–66, 68
Aristotle, 157
assimilation, 71, 139, 140, 146
association vs. *assimilation*, 140
Athens, 29, 65
Austria, 89

balance of power, 46, 117–22, 123, 125, 143, 169
Barbary states, 131
Berbers, 131
Biden, Joe, 162
Blacks, 43, 44, 128, 130
borders, 2, 9, 20, 110, 157

Bosteels, Bruno, 64
Bourbons, 131
Brown, Wendy, 1–2

Calhoun, John C., 45
capitalism, 1, 5, 6, 109, 110
Carrese, Paul, 114
case studies, 19, 42–58, 88–102, 126–41
centralization, 47, 79–80, 81, 136, 157–60, 162; administrative vs. political, 47
Chamber of Deputies, 89–90, 115
checks and balances, 4, 119, 150, 167–68
Cherokees, 129
China, 154
Christianity, 21, 117, 140
Cicero, Marcus Tullius, 113
Ciepley, David, 30
Circourt, Adolphe de, 141
civic associations, 77, 79, 104, 117, 159
civic virtue, 33, 44, 164
civilization, 54, 85, 105, 129, 134, 137, 139, 141, 145, 147–48; democratic, 18, 28, 106, 144; equal, 142, 170; homogeneity of, 44, 61; modern, 125, 146
civil rights movement, 160
Civil War, 160
Colombia, 154
colonization: aristocracy likened to, 145; by Britain, 41, 97, 109, 118, 121, 123, 127, 147; by France, 19, 106–7,

247

colonization (*continued*)
    110, 114, 131–40, 143–44, 147, 171–72;
    by Spain, 129–30; Tocqueville's
    defense of, 117–18, 127–37, 147
Communist Manifesto (Marx and
    Engels), 106, 109–10, 118, 130
Constant, Benjamin, 6, 35
constitutionalism, 24, 29–34, 60,
    150–51, 175
constitutional patriotism, 103, 165

decentralization, 47, 79, 162
Declaration of Independence (1776),
    27–28
democracy, defined, 7, 21, 69; direct
    democracy, 8, 30, 32; illiberal, 4–6,
    8, 11, 159
Democracy in America (Tocqueville),
    6–7, 11–12, 15; American practices
    detailed in, 29; American pride
    noted in, 84, 87; aristocracy and
    democracy contrasted in, 69–70, 78,
    86; Athenian democracy described
    in, 65, 107; civic involvement
    stressed in, 117; differing prospects
    for Union in, 56; federalist system
    detailed in, 43–44, 45–46; honor
    expounded in, 107–9, 141–42, 146;
    identity discussed in, 82–83, 101;
    popular participation stressed in,
    29–37; race relations discussed in,
    40–42, 85, 127–30; readers'
    reception of, 65
democratization, 7–8, 27, 77, 102,
    106–10, 115, 127, 142, 169
despotism, 8, 25, 34, 41, 116; church-
    state commingling linked to, 140;
    democratic, 22, 34, 47; regulatory
    state linked to, 22; territorial empire
    linked to, 128
diversity, 40, 44, 50, 53, 59, 81–82, 110,
    158, 162, 170; and equality, 160; and
    hierarchy, 70; human, 15, 128–30,
    144, 172; racial, 41; religious, 71

division of labor, 68, 108
domination, 5, 32, 121–22, 128, 141, 147,
    153, 172; Tocqueville on, 133, 135, 137,
    145

East India Company, 97, 98, 121
economy, 36, 41, 47, 66, 130, 158
egoism, 22, 122
Egypt, 89, 90
Engels, Friedrich, 106, 109–10, 118
equality: of conditions, 20–21, 28;
    convergence and differentiation
    linked to, 142, 173; differences
    eroded by, 100, 101, 105, 106, 112, 126;
    as dynamic force, 78, 118; in France,
    90, 124–25; illiberal exploitation of,
    4, 7–8; modernity linked to, 6, 7,
    145, 155, 173; obstacles to, 110;
    popular sovereignty and, 155–61,
    166; risks of, 2, 8, 87; self-
    determination and, 4, 9, 103; as
    universalizing principle, 9, 20, 110
"Essay on Algeria" (Tocqueville), 133,
    137
exceptionalism, 17, 54, 150, 164, 165
expansionism, 55, 109–11, 118, 123, 126,
    147–48, 171

factionalism, 24, 81, 161
Fanon, Franz, 2
federalism, 43–47, 56, 60, 74, 76, 80, 159
Federalist Papers, 18, 30, 31, 33, 45, 48, 81
feudalism, 12, 68, 145, 156
France, 16, 17; as Britain's natural
    enemy, 119; centralized government
    in, 47; as colonial power, 19, 106–7,
    110, 114, 131–40, 143–44, 147, 171–72;
    isolationism of, 115–16, 118; in Middle
    East crisis (1840), 89–92; patriotism
    in, 74, 75–76, 95–97; peoplehood in,
    66; post-Napoleonic decline of, 115;
    as regulatory state, 22; Tocqueville-
    Mill debate over, 96–99, 163–64;
    universal rights in, 156

Frank, Jason, 160
freedom: American federalism and, 44; decentralization linked to, 80, 101, 159; equality and, 8, 124, 145, 171; individual isolation vs., 36; individual vs. collective, 8, 22; popular sovereignty linked to, 23, 159; preconditions for, 14, 15, 20, 22, 23, 33, 99, 116–17, 119, 121, 125, 159, 161, 168; Rousseau's view of, 32; self-interest linked to, 78–79; threats to, 159, 163–64, 174, 176
French Revolution, 36, 124, 136, 156; American sympathy for, 112; French national pride rooted in, 100; as threat to European monarchies, 90; Tocqueville's family and, 6

Garrett, Stephen, 111
Garsten, Bryan, 31–32
globalization, 4, 6, 9, 12, 19, 126; differentiation and convergence aided by, 148; Marxist view of, 106, 109; national identity and, 10, 169–70; paradox of, 141–48; Tocqueville's view of, 3, 18, 101, 105, 106, 110, 170–73
glory, 76, 91, 97, 116, 124–25
Gobineau, Arthur, comte de, 17
grand strategy, 114, 121, 126–41
Great Britain, 17, 66; as colonial power, 41, 97, 109, 118, 121, 123, 127, 147; as France's natural enemy, 119; in Middle East crisis (1840), 89, 90; national pride in, 86–87, 164; as naval power, 119; right of search and, 120–21, 124; slavery abolished by, 120–21, 172
greatness, (grandeur), 49, 76, 123–26
Grimm, Dieter, 63
Guizot, François, 18, 92–93, 99

hierarchy, 26, 68, 70, 78
Hindus, 141, 147

homogeneity, 44, 53, 58, 59, 61, 157, 173
honor: defined, 107–9; French concern for, 90, 94, 124, 125, 139, 144, 164; inequality and, 108; Tocqueville's view of, 124–25, 141–42, 146
How Democracies Die (Levitsky and Ziblatt), 149–54, 160, 161, 177
Hungary, 154, 161

identity, 2, 18, 27, 42, 50, 58, 61, 97, 108, 146–47, 164–65, 167, 169; American, 23–24, 41, 160, 164; France's, 114; national, 6, 10, 38, 63, 82–88, 99, 102–5, 125, 163, 168
identity politics, 166
illiberal democracy, 7–8, 159
India, 98, 121, 127, 141, 147
Indian tribes, 42, 43, 128–30
individualism, 22, 36, 78–79, 93, 104, 115
inequality: aristocracy linked to, 108; of wealth, 5, 21
instinctive patriotism, 73–74, 76–77
interest: vs. instinct, 55–58, 74–82; material vs. immaterial, 52–53; national, 46, 49, 120, 122, 125
international relations, 130, 156; Tocqueville's views of, 16, 19, 88–92, 96–97, 99, 101, 104, 106, 111–26, 130, 156, 167, 168
Iran, 154
Islam, 137, 138–40, 143, 147
isolationism, 115–16, 118, 168–69

Jackson, Andrew, 19, 41, 42, 45, 95
Jardin, André, 89
Jews, 138
July revolution (1830), 92, 93
justice, 14, 46, 60, 103, 129, 130, 138–40, 147

Kabyle people, 132
Kahan, Alan S., 140, 167

Kateb, George, 166
King, Martin Luther, 14
Kohn, Margaret, 134
Koran, 140

La Bruyère, Jean de, 85
legitimacy, 9, 30, 99, 101, 122; belief in, 84; of borders, 2, 157; deficits, 161; democratic, 61, 154, 159, 163; vs. development, 135; fountain of, 24; partisan, 176; political, 5, 52, 94; popular, 25–26, 156, 162; religious, 131; standard of, 32
Lerner, Ralph, 55, 100
Letters on Algeria (Tocqueville), 127, 137, 147
Levitsky, Steven, 149–54, 160, 161, 177
liberalism vs. democracy, 4–9, 153–55
liberty. *See* freedom
"The Liberty of the Ancients Compared with that of the Moderns" (Constant), 35
Lincoln, Abraham, 33–34, 41, 162
Louis Napoléon, 126, 138
Louis-Philippe, king of the French, 90

Machiavelli, Niccolò, 143
Madison, James, 81, 167
majoritarianism, 8, 80, 164
Mansfield, Harvey, 38
markets, 8
Marshall, John, 46, 60
Marx, Karl, 18, 19, 118, 121, 130; Tocqueville contrasted with, 106, 109–10, 148
Mehmet Ali Pasha, governor of Egypt, 89
Middle East, 88–90
migration, 5, 42, 55
Mill, John Stuart, 18, 63, 85, 88, 91–92, 104, 113, 172; nationalism viewed by, 96–99, 163–64
mission civilisatrice, 171
mobility, 21, 55, 87

modernity, 12, 139, 154, 169–70, 176; cultural difference and, 143, 148, 173; Tocqueville vs. Marx on, 109
Mohammed, 140
monarchy, 73–76
Montesquieu, Charles de Secondat, baron de, 6, 43, 73, 83, 107, 128–29, 130
mores: culture equated with, 68; freedom and pluralism linked to, 81; popular sovereignty linked to, 23, 36–38, 39, 56–57; unequal development linked to, 53
Morgan, Edmund, 27
Mouffe, Chantal, 166, 167
Müller, Jan-Werner, 166
Muslims, 137, 138–40, 143, 147

Napoleon Bonaparte, emperor of the French, 89, 131
Napoleonic wars, 115
Napoleon III, emperor of the French, 126, 138
national bank, 42
nationalism, 3, 4, 10, 12, 18, 19, 62; dangers of, 163–64, 165, 167; equalization linked to, 109; liberal democracy dependent on, 161–62, 165–66; nationhood distinguished from, 68–72; populism distinguished from, 63, 64; resurgence of, 165
Native Americans, 42, 43, 128–30
New England: governance in, 47, 79, 84; migration from, 55
"new political science," 105, 144, 175
New World, 17, 23, 25, 65
Northern Africa, 127, 131–32, 137, 143, 144
North Korea, 154
nullification, 19, 42, 45, 51

Orbán, Viktor, 161
Ottoman Empire, 118, 131, 143

INDEX

party politics, 111, 150–52
Pascal, Blaise, 83
patriotism: in France, 74, 75–76, 95–97; reflective vs. instinctive, 73–74, 76–77; Tocqueville's view of, 72–76, 80, 84, 88, 96, 100–104
peoplehood, 15, 38–42, 56–58, 62–63, 66, 163, 166
people vs. nation, 63–68
piracy, 131
Pits, Jennifer, 42
Plato, 2, 174
pluralism, 15, 47, 58, 60–61, 69, 71, 139
polarization, 58, 62, 81, 110, 150, 160, 161
Poles, 102
political parties, 80–81
popular sovereignty, 3, 10, 151; constitutionalism and, 29–34; equality and, 155–61; mores linked to, 23, 36–38, 39, 56–57; populist claims to, 4; public opinion born of, 71; social equalization linked to, 26–27; strong sovereign power linked to, 42; Tocqueville's view of, 7, 9, 11–12, 19, 20, 23–37, 46–61, 69, 71, 78, 153–54
populism, 4, 16, 103, 166; nationalism distinguished from, 63, 64
pride: American, 53–54, 75, 84–87; aristocratic, 86; civic, 84, 101, 102; English, 85–87, 141, 164; excesses of, 104, 168; French, 94–100; identity rooted in, 83, 148; liberty rooted in, 14; patriotism linked to, 63, 76; Tocqueville-Mill debate over, 19, 63, 85, 88, 96–99, 163–64; Tocqueville's view of, 83–84, 87–89, 165, 167, 168, 170
Prussia, 89
public opinion, 34, 71, 90, 93–95, 99, 111, 113, 120, 134, 144
public spirit, 73–76. *See also* patriotism
Puritanism, 28, 38–39

race, 16, 40–42, 85, 127–30, 137–38, 159
Reeve, Henry, 140–41

reflective patriotism, 73–74
religion, 13–14, 59; diversity of, 71; fundamentalist, 18
Reports on Algeria (Tocqueville), 127, 135, 136, 138
representation, 8, 29, 30, 31, 35
Republic (Plato), 2, 174
republic: ancient vs. modern, 30–31, 65, 154; defined, 41; democratic, 8, 37, 39, 153; unitary vs. federal, 81
republicanism, 11, 23, 25, 28, 38, 132, 154
right of search, 120–21, 124
Roman Republic, 65, 112
Rousseau, Jean-Jacques, 18, 57, 58, 64, 73, 83, 102; representation critiqued by, 35; republican principle viewed by, 25; sovereignty vs. government viewed by, 31–32
rule of law, 4, 8, 33, 146
Russia, 8, 89, 118, 154

Saint-Simon Henri, comte de, 132, 144
Second Republic (1848–52), 114
self-government, 26, 47, 84, 165, 169, 173, 175
self-interest, 78–79, 170
Sepoy Mutiny (1857), 121, 141
slavery, 16, 17, 35, 41, 42, 54, 128, 130; in ancient Greece, 65, 66; Barbary states' sponsorship of, 131; British abolition of, 120–21, 172
Smith, Rogers, 166–67
Smith, Steven, 22
The Social Contract (Rousseau), 31–32
socialism, 17
social state, 7, 21–22, 37–39, 60, 61, 78, 87, 102
society: civil, 31, 60, 79–81, 161; colonial, 145–46; defined, 57–58; feudal, 12, 47, 145, 156; modern vs. pre-modern, 21, 35, 65–66
Socrates, 2, 174
solidarity, 9, 51, 79, 100, 103, 161, 163, 164

South Carolina, 45–46
sovereignty, 3–5, 19, 45–57, 59–61, 63, 99, 121–22, 125, 149, 156, 166–67, 168–70; and centralization, 12, 47, 158–59; divine, 60; Islamic, 143; and isolationism, 114–17; monarchical, 63; and peoplehood, 48–50, 56–57; popular, 7–12, 20–61, 62–63, 69, 71–73, 78, 104–5, 151, 153–66
Spain: as colonial power, 129–30; in war of succession, 114
Spanish *conquista*, 129
Spector, Céline, 107, 128–29
Sri Lanka, 154
suffrage, 27, 65, 67
Syria, 89

Tamir, Yael, 165
Taylor, Astra, 1–2
Thiers, Adolphe, 82, 90
Thomson, Ann, 131
Tocqueville, Alexis de: as abolitionist, 123–24; Algeria visited by, 127, 137; American exceptionalism viewed by, 17, 54, 84, 164; on American Revolution, 67; as anglophile, 120; church-state separation defended by, 140; civic passions viewed by, 93–96; colonial dilemma acknowledged by, 137–41, 145–46, 171; colonization defended by, 117–18, 127–37, 147; as deputy, 90–91, 100, 114; as foreign affairs minister, 114, 126; foreign policy views of, 16, 19, 88–92, 96–97, 99, 101, 104, 106, 111–26, 167, 168; Guizot's split with, 92–93; historical determinism opposed by, 13, 14; idealism and realism melded by, 14, 125–26, 127, 169; Jackson condemned by, 95; legislating viewed by, 175; man and nation juxtaposed by, 115–16; Marx contrasted with, 106, 109–10, 148; on Middle East crisis (1840), 90–92, 114; military rule viewed by, 134–35; North-South conflict presaged by, 17, 41–43, 54–56, 61, 82, 85; practice vs. theory stressed by, 29, 177; public schools backed by, 77; religious beliefs of, 13–14, 59; religious diversity celebrated by, 71; religious fundamentalism feared by, 18; Roman brutality viewed by, 112–13; Rousseau's influence on, 18, 25, 31–32, 35, 58, 64, 73, 83; as social scientist, 12; stability vs. dynamism viewed by, 60–61; suffrage viewed by, 67; trade and cultural annihilation linked by, 130; Washington praised by, 95, 112
Tocqueville, Hervé de, 65
Trump, Donald, 150
Tunisia, 154
Turkey, 154
tyranny of the majority, 81, 164

unity, 27–28, 52, 61, 71, 80–81, 158, 168–70
universal rights, 7, 54, 84, 156, 157
unwritten laws, 150, 153, 160, 161

Venezuela, 150, 154

Washington, George, 95, 112
wealth distribution, 5, 21
Welch, Cheryl, 124, 145
Westernization, 148
"We the People," 24, 30, 82, 159, 161, 163, 177; exclusions from, 164; questions surrounding, 61, 62, 103
What Is Democracy? (film), 1–3

Ziblatt, Daniel, 149–54, 160, 161, 177

A NOTE ON THE TYPE

This book has been composed in Arno, an Old-style serif typeface in the classic Venetian tradition, designed by Robert Slimbach at Adobe.